THE PUTTING PRESCRIPTION

The Putt Doctor's Proven Method
for a Better Stroke

DR. CRAIG L. FARNSWORTH

John Wiley & Sons, Inc.

Published by John Wiley & Sons, Inc., Hoboken, New Jersey
Published simultaneously in Canada

Photo Credits: All photos unless otherwise indicated are by Christopher Wogan, © Craig Farnsworth; pages 54, 55, 133, 153 bottom, 186, 220, 231, 235: © Craig Farnsworth; page 248: courtesy of Solid Golf; page 249: PeakVision Sports.com; page 153 top, 155: EyeLine Golf

For general information about our other products and services, please contact our Customer Care Department within the United States at (800) 762-2974, outside the United States at (317) 572-3993 or fax (317) 572-4002.

Wiley also publishes its books in a variety of electronic formats. Some content that appears in print may not be available in electronic books. For more information about Wiley products, visit our web site at www.wiley.com.

Library of Congress Cataloging-in-Publication Data:

Farnsworth, Craig L.
   The putting prescription : the putt doctor's proven method for a better stroke / Craig L. Farnsworth.
      p. cm.
   Includes index.
   ISBN 978-0-470-37101-5 (cloth)
 1. Putting (Golf) I. Title.
   GV979.P8F36   2009
   796.352'35—dc21

2008045531

Printed in the United States of America

10 9 8 7 6 5 4 3 2 1

To my lovely wife, Mary Ann, the best partner and friend imaginable. Thanks for twenty-six great years, always by each other's side as we salute all our friends and loved ones, past and present.

CONTENTS

ACKNOWLEDGMENTS

I would like to extend gratitude to my publisher, John Wiley & Sons, and particularly to Stephen Power for an outstanding job with this publication. My gratitude also goes to my literary agent, Byrd Leavell of Waxman Literary Agency, for believing in this project from the beginning. In addition, special thanks go to Bob Russo, not only for his friendship but for his literary and organizational talents that helped make the "prescriptions" a big part of this presentation. Bob and his lovely wife, Judi, are the models for this book, done at their great course, Denver Country Club.

I want to recognize my students for giving me feedback on what portions of my lessons impacted their games the most. I also want to express appreciation to fellow instructors who shared their knowledge as well as provided feedback on the Putt Doctor's system during our time together. Many thanks to Mark Rivard for his input in helping me complete my philosophy on putting.

INTRODUCTION

Congratulations on purchasing this book! If you need help on the green, these pages offer a number of techniques and drills to assist you. If you are an elite putter, this book will help you become an even better one.

How many times have you heard someone say, "I could have had a much better round if I had made a few more putts?" As you are aware, nothing levels the playing field in this great game more than sinking putts, hole after hole. Putting is an area that all golfers can improve upon, and for most it is the best way to quickly lower their handicap. Good players will tell you that it always comes down to who sinks the most putts.

Between 30 and 60 percent of your shots on the course are on the putting surface, and close to half of them are from 6 feet or closer. If you look back at your last few rounds of golf, I am sure you will need more than your two hands to count the number of putts you should have made, but missed instead.

Time and again, the best putter wins the weekend bets, triumphs at a golf tournament, becomes a state champion, or, for a rare few, goes on to earn a good living as a Tour professional.

Every one of us can improve our putting. We know our goal is to make most of the putts we should make. Even more rewarding for each round is rolling in a putt or two outside of 10 feet. As Bobby Jones Jr. said, "A putt either mars or finishes every hole." After reading and digesting the recommendations in this book, you will finish the hole with a good putt time after time.

This text is designed to allow you to better evaluate and perfect your putting skills. I suspect a number of these faults began when you were first getting started in the game and have afflicted you throughout your golfing career, even if you are a Tour professional. Some problem areas are fairly easy to erase, while others may be pesky and reoccur over time.

I promise that if you are willing to spend some time with this book—perhaps a considerable amount of time—you are going to make many more putts, lower your scoring average, and be more competitive in casual rounds or in tournament play.

This book was written after exhaustive computer analysis and instruction of Tour professionals, the nation's top collegiate golfers, and many accomplished to beginning amateurs. It is truly designed to aid all levels of golfers—from those of you new to the game to you experienced, talented amateurs or professionals—get to the next level.

The Putting Prescription follows my first book, *See It & Sink It*, which was gratifying on many levels. It was published in 1997, shortly after my innovative putting system helped Nick Faldo win the 1996 Masters. Obviously, I was pleased to share the detailed insight that helped one of my favorite and most talented Tour professionals win a major championship. Nonetheless, since that book's printing, I have acquired a broader focus to every aspect of putting, from both technical and physiological standpoints.

Because so many of my players have given me the affectionate moniker "the Putt Doctor," stemming from my lifelong practice as an optometrist and performance instructor, I have chosen to incorporate that title and its clinical significance into this book. In the pages that follow, the Putt Doctor is going to provide you with *clinical* advice to enhance the health of your golf game, focusing on the easiest area of golf to conquer, which in my opinion is also the most important aspect of golf: putting.

Each section introduction contains bulleted points that relate to the prescriptions in the section. Each prescription includes a "Putt Doctor Diagnostic Test" designed to help you quickly define your problem areas. Additionally, I have included drills and techniques to help you cement crucial improvements into your putting game forever.

Despite the numerous prescriptions in each section, avoid over-medicating yourself. Don't take the entire prescription bottle at once. Tackle a prescription or two and practice them at home. You will discover several key points in each section that can positively affect your putting skills

Remember to review from time to time the key points you find particularly helpful. This will help you stay on the right path and keep problems from reoccurring over time. Be aware that it is easy to slip back into old habits. That is why they are called habits!

While this book could be labeled technical at first glance, it is presented in a step-by-step, simplified approach that revolves around the components that can affect your putting. If you are a beginning golfer, it may be best to be assisted by an experienced teaching professional. Overall, it still comes down to what works for you. As my good friend Nick Faldo recommends to his stable of junior players, be your own coach. This text is directed toward self-coaching, designed to help you to own your own stroke.

Let me also suggest that you do a portion of your practice without a hole. This will help you concentrate on important physical, mental, and visual keys that are specific to the techniques or drills you are practicing rather than on whether you make every practice putt. During some practice sessions, practice your stroke without a golf ball. With other drills, it may be advisable to eliminate the putter itself and simply focus on a particular posture that enables you to improve upon your motor efficiency.

Be mindful of the techniques outlined in these pages, and your putting will improve over time. Finally, as your confidence builds, it will fuel even more growth in your game. Above all, be patient and have fun while you are working to improve your golf game. Golf takes a lifetime to master. Few players become legendary. All the rest of us just work at it.

So, enjoy the process. Make it your personal journey toward exceptional putting. If you do, I promise that the Putt Doctor is here to help you every step of the way.

WHERE DO I BEGIN?

I know you will find the recommendations in this book of immense help, as they focus on each of the key areas of putting: setup, mechanics, distance control, alignment, green reading, equipment, and the mental aspects. Every one of these areas is addressed in this book in great depth. I sincerely hope you will focus on not just one aspect and one aspect only but read to learn from all the sections.

Elite putters know what they do when they putt well, while streaky putters aren't sure most of the time. The others either tend toward constant changes or they have no clue.

Which category are you and where should you begin?

First of all, if you discover that indeed you can consistently start the ball on line 80 to 90 percent of the time, it is foolish to initially work on stroke mechanics no matter your skill or handicap level! The majority of players should include Section Nine's speed drills as a prime focus as well as a focus on the Setup section, which can do wonders for most players, especially streaky putters.

For all levels, alignment (Section Four) is right up there on my initial checklist. Before jumping into Section Three on stroke mechanics, no matter your skill level, I would greatly encourage first reading Section One on the setup and Section Two on the grip. This will give you a strong foundation in order to execute a consistent and efficient stroke.

Find your category below. I encourage your attentiveness to the recommendations for your handicap range. Yes, you could use the range below more for your *putting handicap* than your registered handicap. For instance, you may be a 12 handicap but a 20 handicap on the greens. If you are unsure, ask your PGA instructor which category he or she would place you in.

Beginner or an average of five three-putts a round

- Have your PGA instructor help you through this book. Focus initially on your aim, utilizing the recommended techniques of Section Four, with the logo line or the Aim Aid tool to assist and potentially reeducate your visual system as to the correct aim. Have him help you with a practice schedule—see Section Twelve.

- Also have your PGA instructor take a look at your equipment per the suggestions in Appendix A and follow his recommendations.

- Proper setup (Section One) is a must for you, as are the grip recommendations in Section Two.

- Next, do a diagnostic test of your speed control, as discussed in Section Nine, and follow the recommended drills for your skill level. Reducing the number of three-putts can do wonders for scores immediately.

- Review the above areas often. Depending upon what your PGA instructor recommends, you may next want to focus part of your practice on mechanics (see Section Three).

90s shooter or a handicap in the 15 to 25 range

- Do a diagnostic test of your aim and apply the recommendations from Section Four if the test reveals you need assistance.

- Have your PGA instructor take a look at your equipment per our recommendations in Appendix A.

- Proper setup in Section One and grip in Section Two are next. Consult your PGA instructor as to which areas in these sections apply.

- If you average three or more three-putts per round, then apply the recommended drills and techniques in Section Nine.

- If three-putting is not an issue, take a look at your mechanics in Section Three.

- Read Section Twelve for purposeful practice drills.

- Take a look at Section Eight, which deals with green-reading basics, accompanied by a playing lesson with your PGA instructor.

80s shooter or a handicap in the 6 to 14 range

- Test your skills with the first drill in Section Twelve. If necessary, review Sections Six and Seven on misses to the left or right and see if any tips apply to you.

- If you are inconsistent at getting the ball on line, check your alignment skills in Section Four and your setup in Section One.

- Practice the speed drills in Section Nine, such as "Three Speeds" and "Making More Putts."

- A review of stroke mechanics in Section Three and drills in Section Twelve gives you a chance for purposeful practice.

- Read Section Five for ideas to solidify your stroke.

- Be diligent with your green reading. Chart your putts, per the recommendations in Section Eight.

Below a 6 handicap but not Tour quality

- It behooves you to take a look at Section Ten (Attitude, Confidence, and the Routine). See what you can mentally apply that gets you more consistent. In other words, going to the next level may not entail a focus on the basics of the stroke or alignment but rather your ability to focus under pressure.

- You could reduce your scores immediately with enhanced green-reading ability in Section Eight, as this is the number-one reason you miss putts. Include "mapping" the greens. Work toward a 100 percent commitment to your reads.

- Fine-tune your speed control with advanced drills in Section Nine.

- Check on the consistency of your aim as much as possible and be diligent in your practice to rehearse the basics of your setup and alignment skills.

- Check with your PGA instructor on any areas that he or she feels could be elevated, including the reasons you miss in Sections Six and Seven.

Tour Player

- You do way too many things well to get stuck in mechanics.
- Focus on Section Ten (Attitude, Confidence, and the Routine). Always take notes during and after practice and include what you learned and improved upon. Most importantly, what is it that you do well that you can apply to what you do not do well? Improvement can be that simple!
- Are you spending enough time mentally replaying the putts going in today that did not go in the day before? Do you have a good picture of the ball's speed before you putt on each and every green? Take a look at the speed-control drills in Section Nine that apply to your skill level: "A" for advanced.
- Be diligent on your reads to the point that you are able to read correctly 90-plus percent of the time. If not, take a look at the mapping and charting recommendations in Section Eight.
- Do not assume that your aim is spot-on without checking it occasionally. Use the logo check and have your instructor verify your aim. If possible, use laser devices to check your aim for putts that are straight, left-to-right, and right-to-left.
- There may be a point or two that you can derive from Sections One and Three, so take a look at what may bolster your already Tour-quality setup and stroke.
- Do not let a day go by without learning. Challenge yourself through goal setting, role playing, and games in the drill section for each practice session. Pay particular attention to writing down your practice schedule. Review your tournament play for areas that you can mentally practice, seeing yourself perform to your capability.
- Take a day or two off each week and more time off when needed. Everyone needs to recharge their batteries.

SECTION ONE

SETUP FOR SUCCESS

There's nothing more important than a proper setup to improve putting performance. In fact, it's my number-one priority with all my students. An efficient setup is the engine that drives your putting stroke. Consider the fact that setup is dependent on the proper equipment, directly affects stroke mechanics, and makes or breaks accurate alignment. The Putt Doctor's prescriptions in this section address a number of key principles that I call "Setup for Success."

Before we begin, a couple of definitions may help. "Stance" concerns the alignment of your body in relation to the target line—the imaginary line from the ball to the hole or a point beside the hole. This includes your shoulders, lower body, feet, and eyes. "Posture" refers to the angle of your upper back, the bend of your hips, the amount of your knee flex, and the position of your arms in relation to your body.

Your stance and posture combine to form the "physiology of function" that allows you to efficiently direct the motor action of your stroke. An efficient setup provides a much better chance of using your muscles as a single unit. Proper posture can help you avoid lower-body sway that can destroy the timing of your stroke, causing off-center hits and resulting in loss of acceleration in the stroke itself.

In addition to helping you establish a solid setup, I am going to introduce drills, practice techniques, and equipment configuration to help get your putts started consistently on line. If you find it difficult to adapt to the setup recommendations, or to maintain them, look at Appendix A for equipment-fitting tips or consult a PGA instructor. Without a proper fit of equipment, an efficient setup is difficult to attain consistently or at all.

Establishing a setup for success can be literally worth millions. When I worked with Y. E. Yang of Korea, I made a number of changes to his setup. He adopted all the recommended changes quickly and directly improved his putting stroke. He went on to finish first in putting on the Japanese Tour, something he had never done.

Some typical faults I observe with players concerning their setup are: shoulders open to the target line; an incorrect putter length; improper head positioning and eyes off line, often angled too high; poor connection of the arms and shoulders with the body; bending at the waist and not at the hips; too little knee bend and poor balance.

There are ten major problem areas highlighted in this section. However, making wholesale changes to your setup by following all the prescriptions at once could overmedicate you. So take things slowly. Tackle one or two prescriptions at a time.

Don't expect to be perfect, but be diligent. When you reach the desired setup position without thinking, you are ready to take your new setup to the golf course. Before long you'll apply and adapt to all the necessary changes.

These recommendations are best suited for an arced stroke path. Even if you believe in the straight-back-and-straight-through putter path, there are many areas of this section that apply to all golfers. I would highly recommend you pay attention to the first few prescriptions of Section Three before signing on to the straight-back-and-through philosophy. You may well be surprised to find, as many of my students have discovered, that your stroke has more characteristics of an arced stroke path than you previously realized. Otherwise, you may best visit the recommendations for setup and equipment discussed in Section Five.

Ten Prescriptions for Setup Success

1. Know your dominant eye
2. Three big musts to see the target line

3. The dominant eye dictates your stance

4. Get connected

5. Shoulder alignment and front-arm dominance

6. Bend at the hips, not at the waist

7. Neutral wrists and hands

8. Be diligent with the ball position

9. Hands at or slightly in front of the ball

10. Good balance is imperative

Know Your Dominant Eye

I am amazed at the number of students who don't know which of their eyes is dominant, let alone how that affects their setup. Your dominant eye is the eye you must count on to help you master golf's biggest challenge—aiming your club correctly at the target.

There is no dispute among medical professionals, including visual training specialists, that your dominant eye is what your brain uses as your "aiming eye." This means your dominant eye can help you avoid misaligning your clubface and mis-hitting putts.

Your dominant eye points your brain and body to the target. However, if you fail to take advantage of your dominant eye, you might miss your target by a few inches or more, despite how clearly you see the target. In other words, where you aim and align is based on accurate visual perception as opposed to how vividly you see the target.

How well you perceive the target's true location is a strong indicator of how much you trust the aiming function of your eyes. So, how well do you think you aim? Before you do anything else, take the diagnostic test on page 12 to determine which one of your eyes is your dominant eye.

Now, pick a target across the room or out the window. It could be a corner of a picture frame or the base of a tree outside. Look at your target, then close your eyes and extend one arm toward the target, pointing your index finger where you perceive the target to be located.

Without moving your head, open your dominant eye only and see

where your finger is pointing. If you are accurate, you are pointing at the exact point you saw when your eyes were open. If not, your finger is pointing left of, right of, above, or below the target's actual location, or a combination of errors—like to the right and below it.

Even if you were accurate, try a few more targets. Out of five targets, how many did you see accurately? If you ace this test, you are in a small minority of players who can truly trust the accuracy of their eyes. If you do not consistently aim accurately, don't worry. I'm going to help you trust your eyes. Vision specialists, including sports vision optometrists, routinely prescribe drills to enhance their patients' visual skills.

If you play right-handed and you're right-eye dominant, or if you play left-handed and you're left-eye dominant, you are classified as "same-side dominant." This means that when you address the ball, your back eye—the dominant eye—is naturally positioned to see the back of the ball, right where the putter will impact it. This is an advantage for you.

Being same-side dominant is to be in the majority of the population, as well as of golfers. Nick Faldo and Brad Faxon are two well-known golfers who are same-side dominant. If you are same-side dominant, you have more of a range of ball positions in your stance, as optically you are able to position the ball anywhere from the instep of your forward foot to midway between your feet.

If you are a same-side dominant player, be aware that you may tend to position the ball too far back in your stance, which in turn optically moves alignment to the right. This fault may help explain why you may fight being aligned too far to the right.

If you play right-handed and you are left-eye dominant or if you play left-handed and you are right-eye dominant, then you are "cross-dominant." About 25 percent of golfers are cross-dominant. This includes such great players as Ben Hogan, Jack Nicklaus, and Tiger Woods.

If you are cross-dominant, an advantage is that your dominant eye is positioned to access the target with no or minimal movement of your head.

As a cross-dominant player, you tend to position the back of the ball at or near the instep of your front foot. This further aids your dominant eye's ability to look at the back of the ball from behind the ball. Be aware that as a cross-dominant player, you may tend to position the ball too far forward in your stance. If this happens, your shoulders become open to the target line. Additionally, your alignment can shift to the left of your actual target.

It is important, when things aren't going well, to think simple. Pay attention to your tendencies and to how your dominant eye can affect your aiming, ball position, and other setup factors, which you will soon read about in detail.

PRESCRIPTION NO. 2

Three Big Musts to See the Target Line

I constantly hear players complain that they don't perceive the target line as often or as well as they would like. Although the target line is imaginary, good putters see it more often than poor putters do for several reasons. Properly positioning the eyes is a must for a successful setup. Here are three key areas you need to pay strict attention to.

1. Squaring the Head and Eyes

Poor putters characteristically have an incorrect head tilt to the right or to the left at address. Good putters seldom have their head and eyes cocked off line to the left or right.

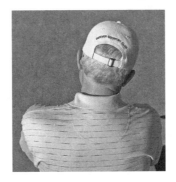
Head and eyes are tilted clockwise.

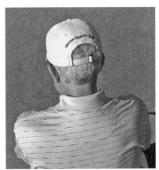
Head and eyes are tilted counterclockwise.

You can test your head and eye positioning at home with the help of a small mirror.

Place the mirror down on an imaginary target line with the top edge of the mirror on the line. Assume your address position with an imaginary ball on the mirror's top edge. Look into the mirror and check to see if your eyes are at an equal distance from the mirror's edge.

If one eye is farther from the mirror's top edge than the other, you do not have your eyes parallel to the target line. If your eyes are spaced equally, congratulations! Your eyes are properly aligned. You may skip the rest of this diagnostic test.

Another way to check your head and eye position is to lay a club down on the floor to represent the target line. With a pencil or pen in hand, assume your address position. Now hold the pencil horizontally across the bridge of your nose and parallel to your brow line. Look to see if the pencil is parallel to the target line.

If your eyes are misaligned, there's a simple solution I call "look up to square up." Stand erect and parallel to your target line—the mirror's edge. Look straight ahead with your head square in the middle of your body and square to the target line. Bend at the hips into your address position with your head angled down to look at an imaginary ball. Be careful to not

Squaring up eyes to body.

change your head's position. Now look at the mirror to check your eye position. Your eyes should be parallel to the target line. If this technique does not work, it is often because your shoulders are not square to the target line. Square them up in the mirror and try again.

Eventually, you'll begin to sense whether your eyes are out of alignment or are perfectly aligned with the target line. When you lose your target line, check your eye alignment first and foremost.

2. Head Position Can Accentuate Your Perception of the Correct Line

Good putters *rotate* their head down the line so their two eyes are always on line in relation to the target line. Less skilled players *swivel* their head. Which do you do?

How you use your eyes is predicated on your eye dominance and your head positioning. Look at the pictures below. Which matches your setup? If you are unsure of your head position, you can ask a friend to mimic your head position for you to evaluate.

Which one of these head positions is more proper for your eye dominance? Note the player on the left. He has his face more angled to the ground than in the right-side picture.

The Putt Doctor's

DIAGNOSTIC TEST Place a couple of clubs on the ground, handle to handle, so they represent a 5- to 6-foot target line. Place a mirror on the floor so the top edge is touching the shaft edge, near the clubface closest to you, where your putterhead and ball would be. Assume your address position, pretending to have a putter in hand. If you cannot see your head and eyes in the mirror, adjust your setup.

Now look at the far clubhead. Without moving your head, look back down with your eyes only to see where your head is positioned in the mirror.

If your head is level with the top of the mirror and your eyebrows are equidistant from the mirror's edge, you have properly *rotated* your head. If one eye is closer to the mirror's edge than the other, you have *swiveled* your head, which is undesirable.

When your head is angled, you are off-plane to the ground. If you are a same-side dominant player and your head is angled too far up, you are more prone to swivel your head to allow your back eye to see the target beyond your nose. This places your eyes off line, with your face possibly being turned 45 degrees away from the target.

If you are same-side dominant, you must get your face more level or parallel to the ground to allow your right eye to see the target line through the bridge of your nose. Otherwise, you will fight your shoulders being open to the target at address, as your shoulders tend to be pulled open by your dominant eye's need to see the target.

Be careful and use your neck to angle your head down, and not your back. If you use only your back, you'll end up hunched over. Another way to think of gaining a proper head position is to tuck your chin. Once you have your eyes parallel to the mirror when you are looking at the far target, close your non-dominant eye. If you can see the far target (the clubhead), then you are assured your chin is tucked correctly. If you cannot because your nose is blocking the target, tuck your chin further until you can see the far target through the bridge of your nose. This assures your head is positioned correctly at address.

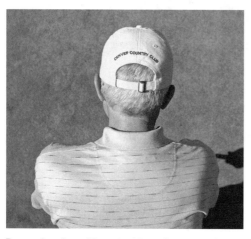

Proper head position at address for same-side dominant player.

If you are cross-dominant, your front eye is in position to see the target and target line with little or no movement of your eyes or head. On longer putts where you need to move your head more, you should let your front eye lead the rotation of your head. The eyes lead the body! Even so, most players rotate their heads better when they tuck their chins. Check it with the diagnostic test on page 15.

3. Position Your Eyes Correctly Over or Inside the Ball

Good putters, with few exceptions, position their eyes either directly over the target line or slightly inside the target line. By all means avoid the eyes being positioned outside the target line, as this can promote an out-to-in putter path.

In your address position, hold a ball in your back hand and place your putter on the target line with your front hand. You can place another club on the ground or use a string to define your target line. Hold the ball in front of your back eye socket. Drop the ball to the ground. Your eyes are positioned right above the spot where the ball hits the ground.

If the ball falls on the target line, your eyes are on the target line. If the ball falls inside the target line, near the putter's heel, your eyes are slightly inside the target line. If the ball falls outside the target line, your eyes are beyond the target line, which is most undesirable.

If needed, change your posture to get your eyes either directly over or inside the target line by adjusting the bend at your hips, angling your head more up or down, or altering the distance you are standing from the target line.

Then try the ball drop again. Ideally the ball will fall on or slightly inside the target line.

In Section Four, you will learn to fine-tune your eye position based on your aiming perception.

PRESCRIPTION NO. 3

The Dominant Eye Dictates Your Stance

A so-called truth about the setup is that you must have your entire body square to the target line. When I first started teaching putting, this concept made sense. As I worked with more and more elite putters, however, this truism turned into a myth at least for some players.

If you are cross-dominant, you will tend to prefer your body, from your feet to your head, to be square to the target line. But this has proven not to be the best setup for many same-side dominant putters. When aligning square to the target line, they often complain of difficulty perceiving the correct target line.

Which setup do you prefer? The answer is often in your dominant eye.

Find a left-to-right-breaking putt if you are right-handed, or the opposite if you are left-handed. It should be about 10 feet in length. Ideally the putt should break more than a hole's width. Place a ball on the ground and get into your setup as described in the previous prescription, with your feet squared up to the target line.

Now look at your perceived target line. Compare this to when you open, or flare, your lead foot. Which helps you better perceive the target line?

You may not see much difference except for mild to severe left-to-right slopes. However, in the long run if you are same-side dominant, you will prefer an open stance with your feet to better perceive the target line. You may only need to flare your lead foot outward instead of moving your foot backward off the line, as seen below. If you don't make this adjustment, sooner or later your shoulders will get open to the target line.

If you are cross-dominant, you will most often prefer a square setup, including the feet, as it does not interfere with your ability to see the target line. Still, all players should experiment with opening the lead foot to see if this helps you better perceive the target line, especially with left-to-right-breaking putts.

A reminder: Make sure your shoulders and eyes are parallel to the target line, with your head in the correct position to rotate your head down the target line.

Now find a similar putt that breaks right-to-left. If you are same-side dominant, you may prefer a square stance or a slightly open stance. If you are cross-dominant, you may like to close your stance slightly. That too is okay. In other words, you need your feet to support your ability to perceive the target line, not to hinder it.

Cross-dominant square feet setup.

Same-side dominant prefers to flare front foot in setup.

If you are a frustrated same-side dominant player who has problems seeing the line, feel free to open your feet as much as possible to determine if this helps you better perceive the line.

The key is to find a posture that improves your ability to perceive the correct target line. Seeing the target line translates into making more putts.

PRESCRIPTION NO. 4

Get Connected

When I watch players on the putting green stroke a few putts, it's easy to spot those who can consistently roll the ball on their target line with the proper speed. They're the ones whose stroke works as a single unit.

If you aren't a consistently good putter, you may have too many moving parts in your stroke. One significant problem is when your arms are disconnected from your body. When this occurs, your arms and even your hands can easily become a separate part of the action. This minimizes the use of your big muscles—your back and shoulders—which I consider the stabilizers of your putting motion.

A connected setup means the arms are as close together as possible without causing tension in the arms. This gives your arms, shoulders, chest, and back more of a chance to act together as a unit.

To help my students understand the importance of a connected setup, I always have them complete a simple diagnostic test (see page 20) to show where their arms are in their setup. Try this test yourself.

Specifically, I want your back elbow to be closer to your side while you place your front arm slightly in front of your chest instead of more on or near your front side. In other words, your front elbow joint is less angled or bent than your back elbow joint. Your arms are as close as possible to each other without creating tension. Your arms will be positioned inside your body lines. This

Player with arms disconnected at address—arms too far from body, often from a putter that is too long.

Stand erect with your putter held at waist height. Go ahead. Put the book down and give it a try.

Check your arm position in relation to your body. Now hold this position for several minutes—well, not quite.

Very quickly you may realize that you cannot maintain this position for long. You will instinctively bring your arms closer to your body and bend your elbows slightly at the same time to brace your arms against your trunk.

What does this tell you?

You need to keep your arms closer to your body. This prevents the problem of "overactive hands," which can easily occur when your hands are positioned outside your shoulder line.

If you adjust your setup correctly, your elbows will be positioned nearer to each other and your upper arms will be more connected to your body. This connection is essential to promote big-muscle control during your putting stroke.

is a most important part of a connected setup. If your putting goes awry, this is one of the key points to check in your setup.

Adopting a slight bend to the elbows helps make your arms softer and tension-free. Tension-free arms produce tension-free hands. If you find it difficult to get any bend in your elbows when in the address position, it may well signal that your putter length is too short. Check with your PGA professional and see Appendix A.

When your arms are too far apart at address, three undesirable things can occur in your putting stroke: (1) the arms can disconnect from the body during the stroke, (2) the hands can get too involved, and/or (3) the upper body can overturn in the stroke.

When you are connected, it becomes easier to use your big muscles to putt. Now everything—your arms, shoulders, back, chest, and hands—can work together as the power source for the stroke. Of note, this big-muscle focus has been an important step for those who have developed the yips (see Section Eleven) in putting and chipping.

Player with arms connected at address—arms are inside the body lines.

A great way to square up and get connected at the same time.

When you start with a connected setup, you have a lot better chance to stay connected during the stroke. Try this technique. Stand erect and parallel to the target line. Now bend from your hips to the ball. See how this provides a consistent positioning of your arms and body. Repeat this several times. Soon you can master this simple setup technique for each and every putt. Eventually, this will lead to an efficient and consistent putting stroke.

Once you get comfortable with your new setup position, don't be surprised if the ball starts to jump off your putterface. Putts you used to leave short may well end up in the cup or beyond it. Being connected is a lot more efficient and effective. In fact, I often ask my students to listen to the difference in the sound of impact. It sounds more solid because it is!

PRESCRIPTION NO. 5

Shoulder Alignment and Front-Arm Dominance

If you are a same-side dominant player, you no doubt fight a tendency toward open shoulders, caused by your body being pulled around by your back eye so it can better appreciate the target line. This brings us to another important part of the setup: the need for you to get both your shoulders and your forearms parallel to each other and parallel to the target line.

If your setup mimics example A on page 22, you will find it quite difficult to release the putter to the target. This setup promotes more of an out-to-in stroke, which follows the shoulder or forearm line and probably the eye line as well. This "cut" or "slice" stroke produces a tendency to open the putterface at impact, sending the ball off the intended line.

Position yourself in front of a full-length mirror. With the mirror on your back side, assume your address position with your putter. Now look back in the mirror and notice if your back forearm is in the position seen in example A below. This is where the back forearm is blocking or is higher than the front forearm. I call this "back-arm dominance."

I want you to see, at the very least, a little of the upper part of the front forearm when you look back into the mirror. I call this "front-arm dominance." This signals that your arms are parallel to each other, as your eyes will be looking from a position outside the forearms, yielding an off-angle perspective that will allow you to see the front forearm when the forearms are parallel to each other and the target line.

If your forearms are not parallel and the back forearm is blocking the front, you first need to square up your shoulders to the target line by looking at a mirror on the floor. If that does not help, position your back elbow closer to your side. This places the back forearm on a lower plane, as seen in example B.

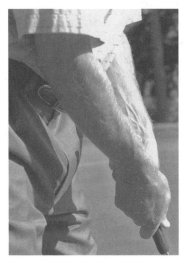

A. Back-arm dominance.

B. Front-arm dominance.

Again, I want your front arm slightly more on top of your chest, with your back elbow having more of an angle than your front elbow. This is especially helpful if you tend to pull your putts. If you experience an open putterface at impact, placing your front arm slightly more to your side at address allows you to release your back side better on the forward stroke. So there are options here, but either way, you still need to exhibit front-arm dominance in your setup.

An easy way to achieve front-arm dominance is to consider the cross-hand or front-hand-low grip. This automatically gets your front arm more on top of your chest while your back arm is more at your side. Tilting your back shoulder a little lower than the front side can also help promote the ideal front-arm dominance.

Also, to achieve front-arm dominance, you can place your back hand more under the putter grip than on top of it. This places your back hand in a stronger grip position. (See Section Two on the grip.) This positions your back elbow to point more vertically—up and down—instead of pointing down the target line.

If you pretend to roll a ball with your back hand down the target line from the address position, you will see that you instinctively adopt the back-elbow position seen in picture B on page 22. So why not go with the most athletic position?

You can obtain front-arm dominance when looking back in the mirror by closing your shoulders (that is, rotating your shoulders clockwise for a right-handed player) to the target line, but this is not ideal. Since the shoulders are the primary controller of the stroke, they need to be square at address and at impact in order to maximize your ability to square the putterface at impact.

PRESCRIPTION NO. 6

Bend at the Hips, Not at the Waist

Another common setup problem is bending to the ball at your waist and upper back. This places your hips under your body. Hunching your upper back promotes tension in your arms and shoulders and tends to disconnect your arms and hands. I want the bend to the ball to be done with your hip and knee joints.

I like the simple suggestion of "sticking your tail up and out." This places your hips out and not under your upper body. Start your address by standing erect, then bending from your hips to the ball. Now stick your tail out. You will also set up more consistently, having only one hinge to bend instead of the many hinges of the spine. As I say to my students, "Butt out! Nothing personal!"

Another means for you to get into the posture seen in the right-hand photo on page 24 is to start in an upright position. Hold your putter halfway between waist height and the ground. Now bend at your hips and slightly flex your knees to address the ball. The amount you bend

How is your setup position? Use a full-length mirror, positioned so you can view your backside. With putter in hand, get into your setup position. Compare your setup to those shown here.

Hopefully your setup position mimics the photo on the far right, which shows more bend or angle at the hips and less roundness to the upper back and shoulders than the other photo.

The posture on the far right is crucial for you to produce an efficient putting stroke.

This picture shows a posture that is too upright.

This picture shows has a good athletic posture. Note that the wrists and hands are not arched but are in line with the fore-arms.

is predicated primarily on the length and lie (angle) of your putter. The longer the putter, the less you need to bend.

The lie angle of your putter is the degree of bend of your putterhead away from the putter shaft. The minimum bend you are allowed under the rules of golf is 9 degrees away from vertical, or a lie angle of 81 degrees or less. The standard is 71–72 degrees. An upright lie angle—above 72 degrees—stands you taller, and the reverse is true of the flatter lie angles seen commonly on the Tour—69 degrees or less.

When bending at your hips into the address position, you may discover that your lie angle is off. If the lie angle is too upright, the putter's toe will be several degrees off the ground. You could be standing too far from the ball or the putter could also be too long. The latter would force your arms to your side as well. Choking down on the handle can help get the putter flat to the ground. You can also have your putter cut down in length instead of choking down on the handle. Most players prefer a 32–34-inch length.

While the toe-up problem can be minimized by choking down or by getting a shorter putter, both of which move you closer to the ball, I often recommend a flatter lie angle of less than 72 degrees (see Appendix A). A flatter lie angle often can promote a desired in-to-square-to-in stroke, as you tend to be farther from the ball.

If your putterhead heel is up in the air, it may be that your lie angle is too flat, your putter is too short, or you are standing too close to the ball. I want the lie angle to be such that if you extended the putter handle, it would intersect your body's center. This is just above the belly button and near the center of your back, as shown to the right. Also check to see if you are bending enough at your hips—get your butt up and out.

Another key point in the setup is that your knees should have a slight flex. The flex should be enough that your thigh angles match or nearly match the shaft angle of the putter in the address position. With too little bend, your weight is often shifted to your heels. Too much bend at your knees can shift your center forward onto your toes.

Player with shaft angle going through his center and his knee flex matching his shaft angle. When bending from the erect position, you will easily get your hands closer to your body.

PRESCRIPTION NO. 7

Neutral Wrists and Hands

So far I have focused on setup techniques that provide a better chance to use the big muscles of the shoulders and arms—acting as a unit—during the stroke. You may wonder what your hands and wrists do.

Your hands are your connection to the putter and provide valuable feedback. This feedback is mostly subconscious. When the putter is in motion, your hands give you a sense of the club's weight, its speed, its position. Your brain also receives feedback about the pressure of your fingers and palms on the putter handle.

First, let's take a look at your hands in your setup position.

Your hands should be below or even slightly inside of your shoulder line. In the picture above, if you drew a line from the middle of the shoulder straight down, it would bisect the two hands.

With putter in hand, get into your typical address position with a full-length mirror to your right (or left, if you are left-handed). Look back into the mirror to check if the bottom edge of your forearms and putter shaft form a straight line. Or is there an angle created by your hands and wrists that breaks the straight line of the bottom edge of the forearms and the putter shaft?

If the line is a straight one, you are in an efficient position to keep the putter "on-plane" during the stroke. If not, then you are adding a component that may introduce more hands into the stroke than desired. This makes it difficult to have the big muscles be the stroke's main engine.

Player with hands under his shoulders.

Your wrists allow your hands to angle up or down, as well as provide feedback about the amount of wrist angle you have.

If your hands and wrists are aligned properly, with no arch up or down, you are in a perfect neutral position. That is where your wrist and hand would be if you were to reach out and shake someone's hand. The wrists, forearms, and hands are all in a straight line. This minimizes tension on the wrists and hands. A neutral hands and wrists positioning is a must to allow your hands and wrists to best join the action of the big muscles instead of acting separately.

If your hands are too high, the wrist arch can force your putter open at impact. This problem can be magnified if you have too short a putter or too steep a lie angle.

If your hands are too low, you will see the toe portion of your putterface off the ground. This could also be caused by too long a putter or too flat a lie angle. This toe-up position can cause you to address the ball on the heel of the putter and, therefore, send your putts off line.

I often just extend my back hand out as if to shake hands, then place the putter in the hand in order to get my hand and wrist in a neutral position.

Practice a constant repetition of the correct connected setup, with your wrists and hands in a neutral position and your forearms, wrists, and hands in line with the putter shaft.

Although I ask many of my students to stand erect and then bend at

Hands too high. **Hands in neutral position.** **Hands too low—toe of putter is up.**

the hips to complete their address, many Tour players address the ball in a different manner. They grip the putter handle in their back hand so that the putter handle and shaft extend in a straight line with their forearm. They then reach to the ball by extending their back arm, as shown to the right.

I would strongly suggest that you use this technique if you are guilty of having your hands too low or too high at address. But be aware that this technique can cause you to be inconsistent in the distance you set up from the ball. To counter this, be sure to properly connect your right arm to your body and stay connected as you place the putter head behind the ball.

Note: If you find it difficult to get this straight line connection, consult Section Two, which recommends placing the putter handle more in the palms than in the fingers to assist your efficiency of setup. Otherwise, you have an incorrect lie angle and or length. Be sure to check your equipment characteristics with your PGA professional.

For a putter fitting, with no putter in hand, get into the

Player walking in with his back arm as an extension of his putter. Note that the bottom of the forearm, the wrist, and the hand are all in a straight line.

recommended setup position by bending at the hips, with your knees slightly flexed and your upper arms connected to your upper trunk with your hands and wrists in a neutral position. At this point, find the putter length and lie angle that allow you to maintain this setup position. (See Appendix A.)

PRESCRIPTION NO. 8

You Must Be Diligent with the Ball Position

Getting the ball on line consistently is partly dictated by the ball position in your stance.

Ball position requires two different measurements. First, you need to determine where the ball should be in relation to the center of your stance. The second important measurement is how far from your toe line the ball should be.

Ideally your ball position should be at or just in front of the bottom arc of your putter on the forward stroke. This gets the ball rolling faster and reduces the tendency for the ball to hop off the putter. What is your best ball position?

The nickel drill (see page 29) can help with this aspect. You need two nickels.

Ball is more near the middle of the stance for a same-side dominant player.

Ball is too far forward.

DIAGNOSTIC TEST There are various ways to determine where the ball should be positioned in your setup. One would be where your putterhead ticks the top nickel off the bottom nickel without altering your stroke.

Place one nickel on top of another nickel. Get into an address position and position the coins where the ball would typically be. Make a putting stroke. If the putter skips over the nickel, the coins are too far forward in your stance. If you hit both nickels, the ball is too far back in your stance.

When your putter can consistently hit the top nickel, the back of the ball should be positioned in your stance at the back edge of where the coins were placed.

It is important to note this distance in relation to your left instep (right instep if you are left-handed). Using the width of the ball as your measure, check how many ball widths from your instep the back of the ball is positioned, as shown in this picture.

The second measurement is your distance from the ball. Check to see approximately how far the near edge of the ball is from your toe line. Is it one, two, or more putterhead lengths away?

Spacing in relation to front foot.

As discussed previously, same-side dominant players have more flexibility to move the ball up or back in their stance due to the back eye's position in the setup. The cross-dominant player optically prefers the ball up in the stance. Still, the nickel drill and your alignment perception discussed in Section Four will yield a more exact indicator of the ball position.

Once you have determined the best position for the ball, somewhere between the middle of the stance and your front foot instep, you must get the ball into this position consistently.

If you are same-side dominant, you may have discovered that a ball's width in front of center is your best ball position. This is the best location to ensure a solid strike on the ball where the putter bottoms out during your forward stroke.

To obtain that position, address the ball by placing your front foot so that the instep is approximately one putterhead's length from the front of the ball. Place your back foot behind the back of the ball by the same amount as the front foot. This would put the ball at a position of one ball in front of the center of your stance. Of course, you could widen your stance from there.

A cross-dominant player will prefer the ball up in his stance so he can view the back of the ball with his dominant eye. You may prefer this position over the nickel drill position if there is a discrepancy, especially in your ability to perceive the correct target line.

If you are cross-dominant, place your front foot in a position where the back of the ball is even or near the instep of your front foot. Then position your back foot to provide a good base or balance, often a shoulder's width or more apart.

As a cross-dominant player, if you prefer the ball farther back in your stance, one recommendation is to slightly rotate your head away from the target. This puts your dominant eye in a better position to see the back of the ball.

To determine how much to rotate your head, close your "back eye" and notice if you can see the back apex of the ball. If not, rotate your head backward even more. Additionally, you could angle your upper body back to the right (for right-handed players) to better view the back of the ball.

The second important measurement is from the inside of the ball to your toe line. For a majority of Tour players, the typical distance is two putterheads. This equates to 9 to 11 inches. A distance farther than three putterheads almost always causes your hands to be outside your shoulder line. This distance would make you feel as if you were reaching for the ball and would tend to emphasize your hands as part of the stroke.

What is the best distance for you?

The best distance from the ball is predicated on several things, including your putter's lie angle and length. The best position feels comfortable and, most important, results in the ball being consistently contacted on the putter's center. In other words, if you are hitting the ball on the toe of the putter, the answer might be to use a longer putter or to get a little closer to the ball, and vice versa for those tending to impact the ball on the heel.

In your address position, if you look back into a mirror and your hands are under or inside your shoulders instead of outside your shoulder line, this ball position is often ideal for you. Once again, your lie angle could be a factor here.

I prefer a curved putter path to a straight-back-and-through path. An important check test for ball position is to place you on the Putting Template, which provides a desirable arc for you to measure your stroke path (see Appendix B). If your putter path is too straight back and not curved enough to be on the arc of the template, and you stay connected with your arms to your body during the stroke, you may well be too close to the ball at address.

If your putter path is too curved and goes inside too quickly, barely hitting the bottom of the arc on the template, you are too far from the ball. A problem here would be a putter with too flat a lie angle or too long a length, which may not allow you to be two or three putterheads from the ball. (See Appendix A and your PGA golf professional for putter fitting suggestions.) Another way to tell the correct distance from the ball is to see what distance gives you the most consistent ability to get the ball on line. Stroke putts using a chalk line or the string and needles discussed in Section Twelve. Which distance—often two, two and one-half, or three putterheads—gets the most balls to roll on the target line? Do ten putts for each distance.

Be diligent with your measurements. Check your ball positioning every day for a while. Make sure, for example, you are two putterheads away from the ball by measuring with your putter, as seen below. Be

Player measuring from inside the ball with her putterhead then measuring the second putterhead distance.

diligent so that your ball position is not too far forward or back in your stance. This should be an important part of your pre-putt setup checklist.

I ask my students to incorporate the distance check from the ball as part of their pre-putt routine, especially if they are inconsistent with their positioning. I have them measure the proper putterhead, move their feet to the proper distance from the ball, then place their putter behind the ball, look once again at the hole, and then back to the ball. It is a great way to maintain a consistently accurate ball position. Then they have mental permission to fire away!

Hands at or Slightly in Front of the Ball

The location of your hands in relation to the ball's position is another important fundamental of a good setup position.

Hands and ball too far back in the stance.

Hands in the proper position for cross-dominant player.

When I see a setup as shown to the far left, I know the player tends toward inconsistency with distance control. By putting his hands behind the ball at address, he is adding too much loft to the putterface. This sends the ball hopping off the putterface instead of skidding and rolling as it should.

One key to getting a consistent roll on the ball is to have your hands even with the ball so that the loft on your putterface is allowed to roll the ball the way it was intended.

Note the handle positions of the players here. In an ideal setup, the butt of your putter handle should be pointing more at or in front of the center of the zipper of your pants. Even if the handle is slightly in front of your center by an

Check to see where your putter shaft is positioned. Get into your address position with your putter and a ball so you can look face-on in a mirror.

If the shaft has "a reverse lean," the handle will be pointing back of your center with your putter shaft leaning toward your back side, away from the target. Your hands will be positioned slightly behind the ball. This not only adds unnecessary loft to the putterface at impact with the ball, but also promotes more hands in your stroke.

Additionally, check your ball position. Your ball may be positioned in back of the center of your stance, which would force your hands back as well. If the ball is positioned back of center, move it to the center of your stance, and this alone can properly position your hands.

If your hands are ahead of the ball, the shaft will lean forward— toward the target. Too much lean can cause you to flip your hands near impact. Otherwise you will drive the ball into the ground, as your putter will tend to impact the ball with too descending a blow.

Ideally, I want your hands to be at the ball or slightly in front of the ball at address. Make sure your ball position is at or in front of the middle of your stance. Check if your putter shaft is vertically aligned and your hands are positioned even with the ball by looking head-on into a mirror.

Hands too far in front of center.

inch or two, with the putter shaft vertical, the loft of your putter-face is typically more ideal to impart a good and consistent roll to the ball.

It is important not to get your putter shaft into a vertical position by rotating your shoulders open. Instead, shift your arms a couple of inches forward without moving your shoulders open.

Some players use a forward press, leaning their hands toward the target just prior to starting their backstroke as a trigger to initiate the stroke. Seldom do I see a player execute the forward press without opening his putterface to the target. The open face forces a necessary compensation during the stroke.

If you are using the forward press and you are a good putter, by all means stick with it. However, if you prefer to jump-start the stroke, a little tap of the putter on the ground can be a trigger to start the motion.

Good Balance Is Imperative

Golf is, in part, a game of balance. While it would seem that the balance required for putting is static and not dynamic, in fact, as soon as the putter starts moving, you are shifting balance.

Players with balance issues usually have one or more of the following tendencies:

- They place most of their weight on their heels (this is most common).

- They place more weight on their toes.

- They place too much weight on either their left or right foot while taking too narrow a stance.

The Putt Doctor's
DIAGNOSTIC TEST

You can do the balance test yourself. In your address position, try to rock forward toward your toes and backward toward your heels. If you lose balance quickly by rocking back on your heels, you probably have more weight placed there to start. Of course, the opposite is true if you have more weight centered on your toes.

If you find you are balanced comfortably on the balls of your feet, then you are in a good balance position.

I have students at my clinics get into their address position. I then tug backward, and then forward, on one of their shoulders. By using this simple technique, I can show the students where their weight tends to be placed. Ideally, your upper-body weight should be over your arches or under your shoelaces, and it should feel like it is over your thighs.

What are your tendencies?

Another indicator of having too much weight on your heels is a tendency to impact the ball nearer the putter's toe. Rocking backward slightly can cause you to impact the putter toward the toe. This can be confirmed by using impact tape.

If you have your weight on your toes, you tend to look as if you want to fall on the ball during the putting stroke. Often you are leaning on your putter or standing too far from the ball at address and have to reach for it. You may exhibit an outside loop to your forward stroke. Then, your hits are often toward the heel of your putter and, yes, your misses are often

34 THE PUTTING PRESCRIPTION

to the left. Part of any balance problem can lie in your putter length or lie angle, so check Appendix A for recommendations.

You can improve your balance by feeling you are sinking into the ground a little bit. This can be accomplished with an increase in your knee flex at address.

It is also imperative for you to avoid swaying sideways on the backstroke and forward stroke. If you do sway, it may signal too much weight on your front or back foot during your stroke. You could also be guilty of having too narrow a stance to offer proper stability.

Poor putters fight the entire body moving forward with the stroke, which may be from a tendency to peek, looking too quickly at the results of your putts. A focus on a contact point on the back of the ball during the stroke can help steady your eyes and head, which is another cause of swaying.

If you tend to sway, I recommend a wider stance. Also, keep the abs still. Allow the arms, shoulders, and back to do the work.

Another recommendation is to bump your hips toward the target to produce a weight distribution slightly toward the left side. This slight shift to the left serves to eliminate swaying and also helps minimize the forward stroke length, which is desirable. It differs from *leaning* to the left. This would tend to place too much weight on your left side and contribute to picking the putter up too quickly on the backstroke.

If you are prone to swaying with your lower body, you may try an old-time remedy—turn your feet inward at address. Or, bowing your knees outward can also steady your lower body.

THE GRIP

Your grip is an essential component of stroke mechanics. It can affect your ability to start the ball consistently on line. Your grip is the means by which your hands connect to the club. It also provides feedback in regards to grip pressure, weight of the putter, and the position of the putterhead in your stroke.

Grips come in all sizes and shapes, and may be as individual as any other part of the game. There are grips for those who are too handsy in the stroke, and different grips for those with the yips. If you pull or push the putt, cut across the ball, toe or heel hit, or are plagued with poor distance control, your grip may be part of the reason and part of the solution.

In this section I talk about grips that I call either conventional or unconventional and include a few variations of each. Also discussed are the more popular styles used today, as well as grip basics that are necessary for an efficient stroke.

Common grip faults include too tight a pressure, too much involvement of the first two digits of each hand, too much dominance of the back hand over the front hand in positioning, and poor positioning of the putter handle in the hands. Also, grips on the club often are placed on incorrectly or become twisted. This puts the hands in a position that can easily result in your putts starting off line. The new, softer grips have a propensity to twist easily. So be aware and check your grip often.

There are components of the grip that are important to make your stroke repeatable. I recommend also reading Sections Three and Five for more insights on the grip. Section Eleven will discuss various grips for the yips.

Prescriptions for Better Putting

1. The conventional grip
2. Soft hands and grip pressure
3. The unconventional grip
4. The split grip can work for you
5. "Hands-opposed" grip: it won for Mr. Runyan
6. Long-putter grip options

The Conventional Grip

In the conventional grip, you position your back hand below your front hand on the putter handle. The top of the heel pad of your front hand

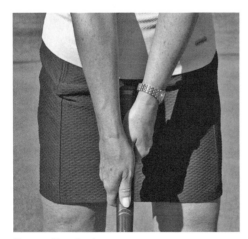

Conventional grip.

should be ½ to 1 inch below the top of the putter handle. Slide your back hand up the handle until your front-hand thumb slips into the lifeline on the palm of your back hand. This keeps your hands close together. Also, the palms face each other and are square to the target line.

In the conventional grip, the handle lies diagonally across the hands, going from the top of the palm near the index finger to just below the heel pad. The fingers are wrapped around the handle, which gives them control of the club. Both hands should have equal grip pressure on the handle, with most of the pressure in the last three fingers of both hands. I prefer the back hand's index finger separated from the middle finger, with minimal pressure on the handle by both thumbs and forefingers.

There are several variations of the conventional grip. A popular one among the good players is called the "reverse overlap" grip. This is where the index finger of the front hand is resting on top of the fingers of the back hand. This keeps the front-hand index finger from tightening on the handle during the stroke and interfering with the ability to square the putterface at impact.

Another variation is the ten-finger grip, where all the fingers are on the handle, with the hands either touching each other or separated from each other. Yet another variation has the back hand's last two fingers overlapping the front hand so only the back hand's middle finger, index finger, and thumb are touching the grip. I have seen players decrease the back hand's involvement by overlapping all the fingers over the front hand except the thumb and forefinger of the back hand, which rests lightly on the handle.

Many good putters hold the back hand's index finger with less bend at the joints, so it lies loosely around the handle, minimizing its ability to twist the putterface during the stroke.

Gripping with more pressure in the last three fingers reduces the tendency to twist the handle by the thumb and index fingers of both hands during the stroke.

I also prefer placing the handle in the lifeline of both hands. This would have the putter handle running more near the middle of the hands, with the handle pointing near the middle of the wrists. The handle is above instead of below the heel pads.

Placing the handle in both lifelines has two advantages for the setup. The first is that it positions the putter shaft, wrists, and forearms in a straight line. The second is that it prevents the back hand from getting too high on the putter handle, which could cause the forearms and shoulders to be open to the target line. This "lifeline

DIAGNOSTIC TEST

Take your customary grip on your putter. Close your eyes and use your tactile sensory system to feel where the pressure on the handle is focused in your fingers. If the pressure on the handle is equal in all fingers, or is more in the thumbs and index finger (first finger) of one or both hands, then I would recommend changing the focus of your pressure.

The lifeline grip can reduce the hands' effect on the putter during the stroke.

grip" can reduce the tendency of the back hand to overpower the stroke.

I also want the back hand to be turned slightly under in a stronger grip position. It accentuates the last three fingers of the front hand as the pressure points. Now, the back wrist is less likely to rotate closed and result in a pulled putt. With the stronger grip, the wrist is farther from the handle than is typical when the back hand is not turned under. This back-hand position has the palm facing more upward, nearly at a 45-degree angle, instead of pointing directly at the target. It also positions the back hand, wrist, and forearm in a straight line.

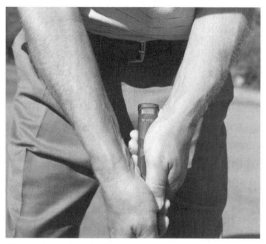
Strong back-hand grip.

In clinics I have students face each other and roll a golf ball back and forth to each other with their back hand. After a few rolls I ask them to hold their finish position. You do the same. Get your hand close to the ground and roll a ball a few feet. After rolling the ball, check your finish position. If you are like most people, your back forearm, wrist, and fingers all will be in line. This is an athletic position and should match your hand, wrist, and arm position at address.

A vast majority of clinic attendees and Tour players report how natural this stronger grip feels. It is a huge factor in being able to stroke the ball with more confidence. Another advantage of the strong grip is that it alters the positioning of the back side elbow so it is pointing more up and down. This minimizes the chance of it rotating during the stroke. I also like the front wrist to be angled (cupped) instead of straight. This helps prevent the back hand from overpowering the front hand during the stroke.

A great way to check if your back hand is properly positioned is the Ball-in-the-Wrist drill discussed fully in Section Six. If the golf ball can be easily held between your wrist and the side of the putter handle, your grip is correct. If you cannot hold the ball in place with your wrist, your back hand—and arm—are too high in your setup.

Another variation can be with the front hand turned to a stronger grip, as Tour professional Brad Faxon prefers.

PRESCRIPTION NO. 2

Soft Hands and Grip Pressure Points

Golfing great Jackie Burke Jr. is unmatched when it comes to providing unique and sage advice on the game of golf. He is brilliant and entertaining with his thoughts on this great game. This former Masters winner opened the Champions Golf Course in Houston in 1957 with the late Jimmy Demaret. It was there, as the guest of my brother Brooke, that I first had the pleasure of listening to Jackie's insight on the game of golf.

He and the late, great Paul Runyan were two people whom I have been around who looked like they'd been born with a putter in their hands. It was a thing of beauty to watch Mr. Runyan grab his putter and "roll the ball." Jackie also feasted on his fellow competitors on the Tour by making the putts others only wished they could have made.

It was when Jackie was the guest of Jim McLean's PGA West School that I heard his thoughts about putting. Jackie had few equals in his day on the greens and this was the primary reason he won the 1956 Masters. Right after being introduced, he asked the instructors what a player was trying to do when he putted.

He didn't wait for an answer. He stated, "It is simply to roll the ball, isn't it?" We watched him demonstrate rolling the ball along the floor with his hand. Jackie wanted us to experience the softness of the hands when the ball was rolled with the hands. "Are you using a soft or a tight grip when you roll the ball with your hands?" he asked.

Soft hands have become a major focus in my discussions on the grip.

Experiment with the grip pressure that allows you to maintain a constant pressure throughout the stroke. Softer pressure is better than too hard a pressure, but too soft can be a problem as well.

Also important is whether there is any change in your grip pressure during the stroke. Close your eyes

The Putt Doctor's

DIAGNOSTIC TEST

Close your eyes and grip your putter handle with a tight grip pressure—a ten on a ten-scale. Execute a number of strokes and slowly loosen your grip pressure with each one. The grip pressure that best allows you to feel the putterhead throughout the stroke is the pressure that I recommend for you. If the grip pressure is too tight, all you can feel is the putter handle.

Most good putters comment that their grip pressure is about a four on a ten-scale, and some will say it's a three or even a five. A six or above is common with the average handicapped player. What is your pressure rating when you best feel the putterhead?

and stroke a few putts, being aware of any change in grip pressure during your stroke. If you feel your grip tightening during the stroke, it may be because you have too loose a pressure to start. Good putters' grip pressure remains the same throughout the stroke.

One day I witnessed a Tour player missing a few makeable putts on the practice green. He felt his grip pressure was a three, and he then realized this made him regrip the handle during the stroke. After he tightened his grip a "notch or two," he made a number of putts in a row. With the five grip pressure, he did not regrip the club during the stroke.

Tiger Woods discussed in an article that his typical grip pressure is a five on a ten-scale, but at the U.S. Open he used a three, as the greens were quite fast and he needed to feel the clubhead more. I can say that not one elite putter has ever reported going above a five in grip pressure for the entire round.

If you start missing putts you have made before, take a look at your grip pressure. If anything, your grip pressure tends to be too high. By using softer hands, you should see more putts fall.

The Unconventional Grip

The most popular in the unconventional category, and becoming more common, is the front-hand low or cross-handed grip. It is the opposite of the conventional grip.

To implement this grip, take the handle with your back hand as you would normally, but place it near the top of the handle. Now place your front hand on the handle below the back hand, and slide your front hand up until your back hand's thumb slips into the lifeline of your front palm. It is best to get your back hand's index finger outside and overlapping the front hand, called the reverse-overlap grip.

The grip has a number of advantages, including better front hand control with less tendency for a breakdown of the wrists, getting your shoulders more level at address, and—my personal favorite—getting your back arm closer to your side and creating what I refer to as front-arm dominance (see Section One).

Both Arnold Palmer and Gary Player have been quoted as saying that if they could change one thing about their games, they would have putted cross-handed early in their career. The cross-handed grip places your front hand, wrist, and arm in a more dominating position for better control. The cross-handed grip can diminish your chances of pulling your putts. Pulls often are the result of your back hand overpowering your front hand and wrist, closing the putterface at impact and starting the ball off of the intended target line.

Reverse-overlap grip.

Another major plus for the cross-handed grip is that it positions your back arm closer to your side while it accentuates your front arm being closer to the chest, assuring that your front forearm is above your back forearm. This position helps free up the stroke.

Typically with the cross-handed grip, the back wrist angle is cupped while the front wrist angle has minimal if any bend. Some players prefer the front wrist to be straight, but I feel that a slight angling of the wrist will help it maintain the same angle throughout the stroke. If the front wrist is straight, it is more likely to bow forward and create a blocked stroke.

Cross-handed grip.

Initially, the cross-handed grip may feel awkward. I notice that those switching to a cross-handed grip tend to tighten their grip at first, contributing to the foreign or awkward feeling. Attempt to keep the same grip pressure as you had in your regular grip. Do not make it any more complicated.

I have introduced the cross-handed grip to a number of players, especially when it became a prime way for them to consistently get their shoulders and arms square to the target line at address. This alone made it a worthwhile switch for these players.

If this grip helps you make more of the shorter-distance putts than the conventional grip does, but you are more inconsistent with mid-length and longer-length putts, try the cross-handed grip for shorter putts and your traditional grip for longer putts.

 **The Putt Doctor's**
DIAGNOSTIC TEST

If you are having difficulty getting the ball on line consistently, give the cross-handed grip a try for a few putts. Try this inside a 10-foot distance. You may feel awkward initially, but soon you should find the grip more comfortable. You could alternate grips, trying three to five putts with the conventional grip and then three to five putts with the cross-handed grip. Repeat this for four or five cycles.

If you make more putts with your conventional grip, then by all means stick with it. If you make more putts with the cross-handed grip, then you may well adopt this grip. If you are still unsure, take a look at various adaptations discussed and then retry this test.

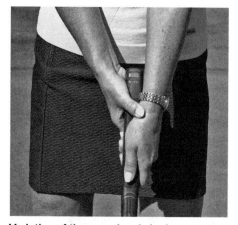

Variation of the cross-handed grip.

I have had some players, when the back hand became overpowering, leave the back hand's thumb and forefinger off the handle, placing it around the front hand's wrist as seen to the left. This becomes a different version of the cross-handed grip. Some prefer the handle to be pinned to their front forearm, but this tends to induce a blocked stroke.

If you like the front-arm dominance setup the cross-handed grip produces, but you do not like the feeling of this grip, consider starting the address with the cross-handed grip. Then carefully switch to the conventional grip but attempt to maintain as closely as possible the same relationship of your arms to your body that you had with the cross-handed grip. In particular, keep your front arm as close to your chest when you switch back to the conventional grip. If nothing else, this procedure helps keep your shoulders from opening to the target line—another plus to the cross-handed grip setup.

If you feel you need a little more assistance with putterhead control, position the putter handle along the lifeline of both hands. You may feel the front hand has more stability to resist any twisting of the putter. This is especially true if you tend to be wristy or handsy in your stroke.

The Split Grip Can Work for You

Several players at The Palms Golf Club, where I do my winter teaching, have experimented or switched to the split grip. We have 45 professionals as members, plus over 240 members with single-digit handicaps along with over 55 *plus* handicaps (this means they are below a 0 handicap), and a membership with an overall handicap average of 8! The Palms was recently ranked third in the country by *Golf Digest* in the lowest handicap index. So, there is no shortage of ideas coming out of these players.

J. D. Ebersberger, PGA professional and accomplished player, is the person most responsible for The Palms' elite membership. He came to the putting green wanting me to test him on my putting system. He showed markedly less manipulation of the putterface during his stroke with a split grip as opposed to a conventional grip. His hands were separated by a few inches with the front-hand thumb barely touching the pad of the back hand. I was mildly surprised at the results when I saw it on the computer readout, but J. D. was not. "I am making more putts this way," he said.

Since then I have recommended to several other players that they try the split grip. Some felt this was more beneficial than shifting the grip pressure from one hand to the other hand. If you feel the need to improve your ability to square the putterface at impact and get the ball on line more consistently, try the split grip.

The split grip is an option even with the belly putter. The belly putter has the handle of the putter anchored into, or most often slightly above, the player's belly. I have seen the connection of the putter handle to the body result in a more consistent arc of the stroke. This is partially because the top of the handle is fixed against the player's midsection.

Those feeling a need to switch from the standard-length putter often choose the belly putter over the long putter, believing the latter is too radical a change. Some feel that their setup with

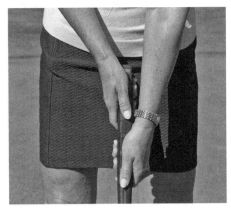

Conventional split grip.

One adaptation of the split grip and the mid-length putter approach.

the belly putter is closer to their setup with a regular putter, as the long putter forces them to stand too erect.

The belly putter is often 6 to 8 inches longer than the standard putter—usually 41 to 42 inches in length. The handle grip is extended so that the player can place his hands on the handle as if he were gripping a conventional putter; or the grip can be quite unconventional, as seen here.

One of the toughest challenges with the belly putter is to get the correct length, as well as to get a putterhead heavy enough. I would consult your PGA professional for a means to try several lengths to give the belly putter a fair trial.

An option is the mid-length putter, as seen to the left, where the handle of the putter is anchored to the body halfway between the belly and the sternum. This is a viable option for those who do not want to stand so erect, as they need to with the long putter. The split grip or the long-putter grip is an option here, but most use the long-putter grip.

The number-one complaint I hear from those using a belly, a mid-length, or a long putter is the inability to control longer putts. If you use the belly putter and suffer from a lack of distance control, you may try some of the following suggestions.

One member came to me before competing in The Palms Club Championship. Gary Hardin was not making anything from distances of 8 to 15 feet. I had him experiment with different hand positions on the putter handle.

The Putt Doctor's

DIAGNOSTIC TEST

With a belly putter, move your hands up and down the handle, depending upon the length of the putt. For shorter putts, grip down near the bottom of the handle. For longer putts, move your hands up the handle. This yields more usable length to the putter—think of a lever action in physics—which translates to more energy to the ball.

If you are still having control problems, try the split hands approach.

He found a position where his hands were a little higher on the grip than he previously had had them. This position allowed him to consistently square the putterface to the target line at impact. His speed consistency improved as well. Gary marked the putter handle for his back hand position and won his first Palms Club Championship.

"Hands-Opposed" Grip: It Won for Mr. Runyan

I was fortunate to have Paul Runyan, a golf Hall of Fame player and instructor, as a patient in my optometric practice. He became a friend as well as my instructor. Paul was about 125 pounds in his heyday. Obviously he was distance-challenged off the tee, often being outdriven by 50 or more yards by his Tour competitors.

But Paul could putt. He was known as "Little Poison" by his Tour colleagues. He shared his insights on putting with me often. He wanted to make sure I understood the grip he invented, which produced marvelous results. This was constantly demonstrated to me as he made putts with regularity from all over the greens when we played.

He called his grip "hands-opposed." Instead of the conventional grip of the palms of each hand facing each other, Paul's grip had both palms facing upward and away from his body. He accomplished this by rotating his back and front hands away from each other.

Paul felt that this grip helped immobilize his wrists and hands during the stroke. When you place your hands on the putter in this manner, it is easy to see how it diminishes the use of the wrists and hands as the power source. Paul felt that this assured he was not going to roll his wrists and create a problem getting the ball on line.

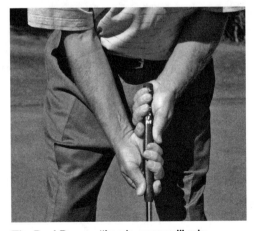

The Paul Runyan "hands-opposed" grip.

The Putt Doctor's
DIAGNOSTIC TEST

Give the hands-opposed grip a try. Putt to a target approximately 10 feet away. Try five putts with your traditional grip, using any means that will give you a consistent aim. How many did you start on line and how consistent was the speed?

Now do five more putts using the hands-opposed grip. Try to keep your grip pressure the same with both styles. How many did you start on line and how consistent was the speed with this grip?

Repeat this for a few more cycles and see if you gain an advantage with the hands-opposed grip. Practicing with this grip can be a useful drill to help you feel how quiet your hands can be in the stroke, even if you do not wish to use it during your on-course play.

If you are prone to being wristy or handsy, and fight too much pop in your stroke, you may find an immediate improvement in quieting your hands with the Runyan grip. The hands-opposed grip helps promote the bigger muscles of the shoulders and arms in the stroke.

Feel free to combine the Runyan grip with some of the suggestions in the following section on the Putt Doctor's Stroke. The hands-opposed grip is one of my favorites to minimize your hands in the stroke, and to square your putterface at impact. The Checkerballs training aid (see Appendix B) yields valuable feedback to check if your putterface is square at impact. It can be used even indoors on your carpet to see what grip or stroke gives you a consistently square putterface at impact.

There are other ways to minimize the involvement of the hands, including placing more weight on the handle end.

The large-grip putter helps reduce your grip pressure and likewise decrease the hands as part of the stroke. One is the Winn AVS grip and another is made by Super Stroke. You may have seen K. J. Choi use the large-grip putter handle and promptly win at his very next PGA Tour stop.

Larger putter handle.

Long-Putter Grip Options

The long putter has increased in popularity. For those with bad backs, the long putter allows for more practice with less back stress. For other players, they just make more putts!

A frequent comment I hear from players is that they prefer the long putter because it helps them better perceive the target line at address. It also takes away what I believe to be the primary problem for a lot of players—the difficulty of controlling the putter with both hands on the handle. "I feel I make more shorter-distance putts one-handed than I can with two hands, so this is an obvious advantage," one player commented on his switch to the long putter. After watching him putt with the conventional length and then switch to the long putter, I told him to never switch from the long putter. The difference in his ability to get the ball on line was amazing.

You may have thought about switching, or have given the long putter a brief try. There are numerous grip options that could help you improve your putting with the long putter. But there are too many to include all of them in this book. The grips I will discuss here are those with the front hand being the top hand. The front hand anchors the putter to the body. Certainly players have used the reverse, with the front hand below and the back hand on top, and the grip options with the bottom hand are numerous (see Section Eleven). The main grips to try are those with the front-hand thumb's position on the handle.

A most popular grip, seen in the first picture on page 50, has the handle locked onto the chest by the lead hand, which minimizes the putter swinging separately from the trunk. The putter is entirely controlled by the movement of the arms and shoulders. A variation of this grip is with the thumb placed on top of the handle, but the hand is still locked to the chest.

Having the thumb on top gives a better anchor than when using the entire hand as an anchor. PGA Tour veteran Scott McCarron likes the entire front hand to rest against his chest and to use his shoulders as the main action of the stroke. He says this gives a more solid feeling.

Another popular grip, seen in the second picture on page 50, has the front hand encircling the handle but with the grip primarily in the

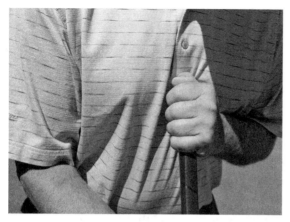

Thumb on top of the hand. **Grip around handle of a long putter.**

The Putt Doctor's

DIAGNOSTIC TEST

Set up a trial putting session with a long putter. Attempt five to ten putts with each grip. I would recommend two putting distances each time, one distance being 5 to 6 feet, and the other being approximately 10 to 12 feet. See if there is a clear difference with one grip over the others in your ability to get the ball started on line.

Repeat the test over a few days to see if a favorite grip can be established. If there is little or no difference with the grips in the two test differences, by all means go with the grip that feels the most comfortable and allows you to swing the putter the way that feels best.

first two or three fingers. The grip pressure is quite light on the putter handle. This allows more freedom for the back arm to swing the putter independently of the shoulders, or, as a number of players do, using some shoulder action but more arm motion. A variation of this is to have the thumb on top of the handle.

Be sure to check Section Five and Section Eleven for more grips that can contribute to a controlled putterface throughout your stroke.

SECTION THREE

THE PUTT DOCTOR'S STROKE

Let me introduce you to an innovative putting technique—the Putt Doctor's Stroke—that can help you become an exceptional putter.

I'm going to give you a detailed set of prescriptions to integrate this stroke into your putting method. The Putt Doctor's Stroke is different from what you are doing now or what you may have read about or been taught by other golf instructors. One of the fundamental differences is the stroke path the putter should follow, which naturally takes the shape of a mini-golf swing. My recommendations are based upon countless hours of instruction with golfers ranging from PGA Tour veterans to elite amateurs to beginning players. These recommendations also stem from my observations and interactions with great putters, as well as findings brought to light by my computer analysis of putting strokes.

The first five prescriptions examine the basics of the stroke. As you work with them, you will begin to feel more comfortable in your transition to the Putt Doctor's Stroke. Be sure to read these five prescriptions before taking your stroke to the practice green. They all work together to accomplish a simple yet important objective: getting the face of your putter to aim directly at your target at impact. The first three prescriptions are predicated on a correct setup. It is imperative to read and incorporate necessary changes in your equipment, posture and stance, as the correct setup is directly related to a majority of the Putt Doctor's Stroke mechanics.

Prescriptions six through nine are checkpoints to help you evaluate whether or not you are doing the first five prescriptions correctly. For example, prescriptions six and seven are important drills that give you feedback regarding the correct backstroke and forward stroke. The good news is that if you master the first five prescriptions, the other prescriptions will quickly fall into place. Nevertheless, these additional points are important to verify your understanding of the Putt Doctor's Stroke. Keep them in mind in your practice sessions.

Common faults that get in the way of an efficient stroke include a disconnected stroke, rocking the shoulders, the front side leading into impact, and the front side being overpowered instead of providing a brace for the back side.

Be sure to work on one prescription at a time. This will keep you from overthinking and will permit you to perfect one area before going on to another area. In this section, you will be introduced to my "extreme drills," which will help you gain a feeling for key techniques by "over-accenting" certain physical motions.

I am quite aware that one putting stroke does not fit all. If you believe your putter path has a straight-back-and-straight-through shape, you may wish to skip to Section Five and focus on the aspects of this stroke, including setup changes that vary from the ones presented in Section One.

However, I caution you that many of the players I have worked with realize after a demonstration or two, as seen in the first three prescriptions in this section, that they are not exercising a straight-back-and-through putter path. Most find that their putterface is open on the backstroke, so their path and putterface do not match up. Additionally, their path finishes inside the target line on the forward stroke, resembling a "cut" or "slice" stroke.

Remember, practice is just that, and play is not practice. On the course you must shift your mind-set to playing the game, not practicing mechanics. Even Tour players are guilty of applying the mechanics of the stroke instead of focusing on speed and a good picture of success before and during the putt. Your practice needs to be diligent so that you can stroke the putt on the course without thought.

Now let's get started!

Prescriptions for Better Putting

1. Embrace an in-to-square-to-in putting path
2. Staying connected
3. Big muscles turn rather than rock
4. The back side is your power source
5. The front side controls your stroke
6. Turning properly: A drill and a new concept
7. A feedback drill for streaky putters
8. Completing the turn and the transition
9. One lesson is seldom enough, and the proper finish

PRESCRIPTION NO. 1

Embrace an In-to-Square-to-In Putting Path

For years, golf instructors taught students to make a putting stroke in which the putter goes straight back and through and the putterface is kept square to the target line throughout the stroke. This has been called the "straight-back-and-straight-through" stroke as well as the "square-to-square" putting method.

You were told that the best way to keep the putter square to the target line was to rock your shoulders up and down like a teeter-totter. You were instructed to rock your front shoulder down and, simultaneously, rock your back shoulder up as you began your backstroke. Then you simply reversed that rocking motion as you began the forward stroke—front shoulder up and back shoulder down.

This technique actually requires a great deal of manipulation by the arms and hands. It also demands an unnatural rocking motion of the shoulders. Simply put, the player must hood, or close, the putter in the backstroke and open it on the forward stroke in an effort to keep the face square to the target line. The rocking motion also tends to induce too much neck and head motion during the stroke.

Furthermore, I have discovered through newly developed computer analysis that the vast majority of putters who believe they are using the straight-back-and-straight-through technique simply aren't doing it. The following computer analysis picture shows the putter at the end of the backstroke. The center line is the target line.

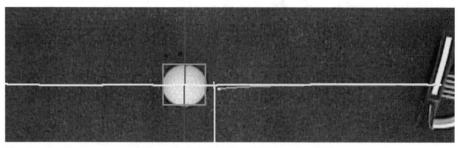

The face angle seen here at the end of the backstroke is typical of 90 percent of the players with a straight backstroke path.

Importantly, the putterface is not square to the path of the putter. It's wide open at the end of the backstroke. This means the putterface does not match the putter path.

Based upon my research and teaching of many PGA Tour players and elite amateurs, I am convinced that the ideal putting path is an "in-to-square-to-in" shape that mirrors, in a small way, the fundamental shape of a golf swing. In other words, the putter path is curved, not straight.

I call this a "natural stroke" because almost all of my students feel this path is a natural way for them to swing the putter. It should feel natural, if you think about the number of times you have swung at a golf ball with your irons and your woods. An important advantage to this method is that it enables the putter to swing without manipulation. In other words, the inside path occurs naturally. So it is much more likely to hold up under pressure.

On page 55 is a computer analysis picture showing the completed stroke of a Tour player where the stroke path moves inside the target line on the backstroke and finishes inside that line on the forward stroke. All the while the putterface remains square to the putter path.

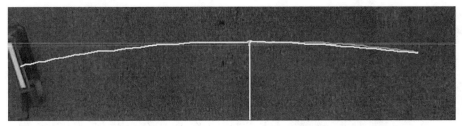

This dome-shaped stroke path of a PGA Tour player is typical of exceptional putters.

The importance of this path was reinforced during a lesson I once had with one of the greatest putters of all time—George Archer.

"George, what does straight back and through mean to you?" I asked. "Have you ever seen a door, Doc?" he said. I decided at that moment that George was a part-time comedian. "Yes, George, I've seen a door!" He then asked, "Well, what does a door do? It swings back and forth, doesn't it?" As he talked, his hand was swinging in an arc, much like the putter path seen above.

So let's conduct a quick test to determine your ideal putting path.

The Putt Doctor's
DIAGNOSTIC TEST

With your putter in hand, stand erect and in a connected address position, as discussed in Section One, with your putter at waist height with the putter shaft parallel to the ground. Position yourself so the putterhead is almost touching a wall. Imagine putting to a hole approximately 15 to 20 feet away. Simulate a backstroke to the target using your arms and shoulders. Go ahead.

Notice that your putterhead has moved a few inches away from the wall. Now slowly turn back to simulate a forward stroke. Note that the putterhead moves back toward the wall, then moves a few inches away from it as you complete your forward stroke.

In this quick test, you also will have noticed the putterface move from square to open on the backstroke, and then close to the target line on the finish of the forward stroke. Now repeat your backstroke. At the end of your backstroke, push the head of your putter out to near the wall and square the putterface to the target line. This demonstrates that your arms must lengthen or disconnect from your body if you are going keep the putter on the target line, as in the straight-back-and-straight-through method. You'll also see a turning of your hands and wrists to get the putterface square to the target line.

Repeat the above drill a couple of times, first with a turning of the arms, shoulders, and back, and then trying to do a square-to-square. Then choose which stroke feels more natural—straight-back or inside-to-inside curve.

I have the player hold her putter against my putter shaft, which represents the target line.

Note the putter arcs inside the target line on the backstroke . . .

and arcs again inside the target line on the forward stroke.

When your big muscles are used similar to your golf swing, you will notice that the putterhead stays on the target line for only 3 to 5 inches and then it curves inward. This means that any putt of more than 5 feet would produce a slightly curved stroke path on the backstroke and forward stroke. This motion should be quite natural when you think about your motion in the full swing.

For years, instructors advocated that if the putterface opened when the putter curved, the putterface would be off-plane. Furthermore, they said that the player would have to then anticipate the closing of the face to have it be square at impact. However, this is a myth. When a player makes a curved putting stroke—with no manipulation of the arms, wrists, or forearms—the putterface remains square to the path throughout the stroke. This is an on-plane stroke.

In reality, with a curved path and no hand manipulation of the putterhead, the putterface is always square to the path. So, it's not a timing issue to get the face square at impact. The only variable becomes the ball position in your stance. If your putts are pulled, move the ball back in your stance, and vice versa if you are pushing your putts.

With the straight-back method, unfortunately, the face is typically open to the target line, as is seen in the computer analysis on page 55, so the face doesn't match the path. That's what I refer to as an "off-plane" stroke that requires good timing at impact with your hands, which tend to break down under pressure. So keep the action in your big muscles, as this requires much less work in the long run. The big muscles include the upper arms, the shoulders, and the back muscles.

Staying Connected

Two key areas of focus in the Putt Doctor's Stroke are positioning the upper arms correctly in relation to each other and keeping the arms connected during the stroke.

First, in a connected setup, the upper arms are touching the upper trunk and the arms are positioned inside the body lines. While you want the arms to be close together, make sure they are not too close together, since this could cause tension. It is important for the arms and shoulders to remain relaxed throughout the stroke. Second and equally important is for the upper arms to stay connected to your upper body throughout the stroke. This makes for an efficient stroke. How well are you connected during your stroke? Here is a good test and drill.

The Putt Doctor's
DIAGNOSTIC TEST

To help determine if you stay connected during your stroke, wrap a towel around your chest and under your upper arms, or place a head cover under each armpit. Ideally, place the towel or head covers near the lowest point of connection of the arms to the body. This is similar to the drill that many players use for their short irons to perfect their path.

As seen here, you could place one head cover underneath your front armpit. That is because it is most common to see the front arm disconnect during the forward stroke.

Now make a stroke to a target approximately 15 feet away. If the head cover or the towel falls, you are not staying connected during the stroke. The goal here is to keep the

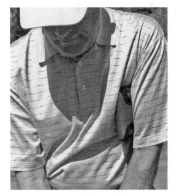

Staying Connected drill.

towel or the head cover in place throughout the stroke. Even though your arms tend to outrun your body to a small degree, you want to keep the upper arms connected so no gap is created between the upper arms and the upper trunk during the stroke.

Often a player who is not connected has his elbows positioned outside his shoulder line at address. During this setup, his upper arms do not have enough connection to his body. Be aware: if your upper arms are touching your sides down to your elbows, this position forces you to use too much trunk or hands in your stroke.

Can a player be connected and still have a gap between his arms and body at address? The answer is yes if he maintains the same gap throughout the stroke. But this proves to be a very difficult task for many players.

Picture the arms and shoulders forming a triangle at address. This triangle must be maintained throughout the putting stroke. A typical breakdown occurs when the back arm or hand "outraces" the front arm and hand, resulting in a pulled putt; or vice versa, with the front arm or hand outracing the back arm, resulting in a pushed putt.

Some instructors prefer all of the upper arms connected to the upper trunk, while others prefer just the higher part of the upper arms to touch the trunk. As discussed in the proper setup, I prefer the front arm to be positioned slightly closer to the front of the chest and the back arm closer to your back side. The front arm should feel as if it is riding across your chest during the stroke.

If the arms disconnect during the stroke, the power of the stroke becomes inefficient, making distance control more difficult to achieve. As can be seen in the far left picture, the player's front arm has disconnected from the body and the elbow is bowed toward the hole on the forward stroke. This common connection breakdown results in a blocked stroke motion and can result in a pushed putt.

Front arm disconnected on follow through.

Front arm now connected.

When your back arm stays connected on the backstroke and the front arm stays connected to the front side of your body in the forward stoke, it helps the arms, shoulders, back, and hands turn as a unit. However, if your arms disconnect in the stroke, I call this "splintering" the power source of the arms away from the back and shoulders.

When your front arm stays "home" and is anchored through the forward stroke, your back side is able to deliver more power to the ball. This is a key to the Putt Doctor's Stroke!

In the backstroke, turning the arms, shoulders, and back will force the back arm and elbow slightly more backward and more to the side from its address position, but the upper arm must stay connected to your upper trunk and not separate.

On the forward stroke, turning the back side will force the front arm to rotate slightly to the side from its address position. Similarly, the front arm keeps its same relationship to your body as long as possible throughout the forward stroke and does not gap from the upper trunk.

If your putting goes awry, there are three important areas to focus constant attention on. The first is to make sure the arms do not get too far apart at address, which causes a disconnected setup. The second is to ensure that the hands and wrists are in a neutral position at address. The third is to maintain the same degree of bend in both elbows throughout the stroke as they have at address. By attempting to maintain the angles of both elbows—as well as the wrist angles—you will diminish the chance of the putterface twisting in the stroke.

To help you achieve a connected feeling during the stroke, get someone to stand behind you and hold your arms just above the elbows. Have them gently keep your arms connected during the stroke by not allowing the arms to disconnect from your body. Stroke a few putts with your arms being held. You will see an immediate improved roll.

Those players who are typically short with putts often are amazed at the solid roll they are able to achieve when they stay connected. For most, this is a welcome change. Overall, staying connected on the back and forward stroke gives the balance you need in the path of the forward stroke. The radius of turn into and beyond impact becomes a continuous curve that is best done with the arms, back, and shoulders. Now let's take a closer look at the proper turn of the arms and shoulders.

Big Muscles Turn Rather Than Rock

The ideal putting stroke incorporates a connected setup and a turn of the shoulders, not a rock, where the shoulders remain relatively level throughout the stroke. Your arms pull your shoulders and back as they turn toward your back side, and then reverse their course and pull your shoulders and back through impact on the forward stroke.

It is important to attempt to turn around your spine, your body's axis. Your spine becomes the pivot point for the turn and helps prevent you from swaying back and forth.

The Putt Doctor's
DIAGNOSTIC TEST

How do you identify if you are rotating your arms and shoulders properly? One way is to check how much of your front forearm you can see at address when looking back into a mirror. Ideally, if your shoulders are parallel to the target line as I recommend, you should see at least a slight amount of your front forearm in the mirror. If not, then first you need to adopt the recommendations in Section One.

Now take a backstroke as if stroking a 10- to 15-foot putt. Check your forearm position in the mirror. You should see more of your front forearm than you saw at address as your shoulders and arms rotate on the backstroke as a single unit.

As you complete your putt, you should see less of your front forearm than was seen at address. This is accomplished with a proper arm and shoulder turn around your body's center and without turning the forearms separately from the shoulder turn. If you were not turning properly, the following drill will help you with the turn.

Setup position of forearms at address.

Backstroke position of forearms.

Follow-through position of forearms.

A valuable technique to perfect the proper turn is the Trunk Rotation drill. Stand erect and connected. Hold your putter at waist height, as shown to the right. Imagine putting to a hole approximately 15 to 20 feet away.

Now rotate your arms, shoulders, and back to simulate the backstroke and forward stroke. This will help you obtain the desired feeling that your shoulders remain somewhat level throughout the stroke. Your turn is initiated by your arms turning around your body's center. The arms pull and push your shoulders and back, as well as your upper chest, as they turn back and through. The arms do not turn independently due to your connected setup. Your head remains fixed during the stroke, and there should be no sway of the body backward or forward.

Trunk Rotation drill.

If your entire upper body, hips, and legs turn, it signals that this turning is foreign to you—or on the contrary, that you are so used to using the entire body for your golf swing that this turning is quite natural. It could also signal that your arms are positioned too much to your sides and they need to be more in front of your chest. Also, attempt to keep your chest as quiet as you possibly can, with the only movement being from the arms and shoulders pulling on the chest as they propel the stroke dynamics. You should make sure that when you stroke the ball, you always putt with a stable center, and this includes your head. I find that players get in trouble when they *try* to make the putter go inside with their head and body turning on the backstroke. This inside move should occur naturally with the turning of the arms around your center. The inside path occurs without trying to make it happen. Of course, this is done with the proper setup.

This drill, done at waist height, also accentuates the feeling of the large muscles of the arms, shoulders, and back controlling your stroke, not your hands and wrists. This feeling should be the same in the actual putting stroke. It is important to maintain the triangle that the arms, shoulders, and hands form at address throughout the entire putting stroke.

Some players feel awkward with the initial turn when they use both shoulders as their focus, often overturning the entire body, including their head. A major cause of this is if your front arm is positioned too much to your side at address. It can be helpful to focus on the back side—the back arm, back shoulder, and back—starting the turn instead of both shoulders.

Most players prefer to simply turn their arms around their spine. I like the upper arms to start the action and pull the back and shoulders in the turn. A focus on the upper arms frees up the stroke for many players. You still must stay connected throughout the stroke. Shorter putts, inside of 5 or 6 feet, require only a slight turn of the arms and shoulders.

If your putts are inconsistent in starting on the intended target line when turning your arms and shoulders, it may be from a rotation of your hands and forearms on the backstroke, resulting in opening and closing the putterface to the path during the stroke. Some players find that they minimize the face opening off-plane during the stroke by thinking of their wrists staying pointed to the target throughout the turn.

Hand rotation is also minimized by using a mind's-eye picture during the backstroke of the putter's heel moving at the same speed as the toe of the putter. In essence the putter's toe will open more because of the sheer nature of its position as the farthest point from the player. However, it should open only from the arm and shoulder turn, and not from your hands acting independently.

During the Trunk Rotation drill, it is important to keep the angles of your elbows as well as the wrists constant throughout the stroke. This can be an excellent focus for your practice putts of short to midrange length in order to better control your putterhead.

A good drill to see if you are turning properly is to place a tee approximately 6 inches in front and another tee 6 inches in back of the ball. The tees should be in line with each other and about a half an inch inside the putter's toe. Your backstroke and forward stroke will miss the tees if you are turning properly. If not, you are not staying connected and your arms and shoulders are not turning, as desired. Hitting the tees often relates to your hands pulling your arms away from your body, or at the least, pulling your arms into a straighter position by breaking the angle of the elbows you had at address.

What starts the motion of the putting stroke? A number of players prefer the forward press—where the hands are shoved toward the target a couple of inches. I believe this forces the putterface open. I prefer a slight tapping of the putter to the ground. After the tapping, the backstroke is started by arms pulling the shoulders. If your upper trunk turn is large, it is often because your arms are too much to your sides at address or your arms are not leading the stroke. The arms, shoulders, and back turn more than the chest, while the abdomen turns minimally if at all. For medium-length to longer putts, the pull of the back, shoulders, and arms will indeed move the upper chest and abdomen a few degrees.

In addition, if stopping your trunk and hips from overturning proves too difficult, then think of trying to keep your chest still and just have your arms and shoulders rotate around your chest and spine. Keeping your trunk still is an effective focus for all putts.

At the finish, the arms, shoulders and back turn only a few degrees beyond the address position. The turn is never an amount that has the chest facing the target at the stroke's completion. This would be a distinct overturn of the upper trunk. This overturn is often coupled with the wrists breaking down, resulting in a long forward stroke that forces you to come out of the putt.

Another important point to remember is that your hands should not swing beyond the outside the back leg at the end of the backstroke or outside the front leg on the forward stroke on any putts except long putts beyond 35 to 40 feet.

While the hands seldom travel outside the body's width, it should be made clear for all putts, the putterhead travels farther than the hands both on the backstroke and on the forward stroke. This is due to the physics of motion, with the farthest point—where the clubhead is—always traveling farther than where the handle is anchored, the hands. It may help you to picture the pendulum swinging on a grandfather clock.

I recommend that you incorporate this Trunk Rotation drill into your pre-putt routine for a few weeks, especially if you are a handsy putter. I want you to look at the target while doing these rotations. Make the rotation or stroke length match the length of your putt. Then bend at your hips and knees to the ball to finish your address, take a look or two at the target, and execute your stroke.

If you stay connected and turn around your center, you do not have to think of a curved path—it should happen naturally. Some students prefer to picture a curved path to help their turn, and that is certainly acceptable. When you think about it, with your regular swing your swing takes a natural shape of a semicircle. This is helped by your distance from the ball being farther than for putting.

When you execute the turn properly, the ball comes off the putter with a nice "click" instead of a tinny sound. The roll of the ball will be distinctively better. You will feel the difference as well as see the difference. *Vive la différence!*

PRESCRIPTION NO. 4

The Back Side Is Your Power Source

What is "releasing the putter?" Simply stated, releasing the putter applies to the putterface going from open to the target line on the backstroke, to square at impact, to closed to the target line beyond impact.

I have seen PGA Tour players as well as instructors describe the release as keeping the putter handle consistently pointing near the body's center throughout the stroke. Unfortunately, this can lead to problems. When attempting to finish with the handle pointing at the body's center, players tend to over-release the putter by breaking down their wrists or by rocking their shoulders. This causes the putterhead to arc up quickly, increasing the effective putterface loft. This results in the ball hopping in the air, rather than the desired skid and roll if the putt is struck correctly.

Importantly, the release is accomplished by turning the back-side arm and shoulder into the front side on the forward stroke.

Of all the prescriptions in this section, using the back side as the power source on the forward stroke appears to be the

The player's hands have over-released the putter because the handle is pointing back of center.

With a correct release, the handle is pointing in front of the player's center.

most significant for my students. In essence, the forward stroke is characterized by the back-side arm and shoulder being the focus of the turn. As the back side powers the turn as a unit, this helps the wrists and hands maintain consistent angles throughout the stroke.

During the backstroke, the arms, shoulders, and back turn around the body's center. The putterhead leads the hands, as it has traveled farther from its start position. For example, your putterhead is near the back foot while your hands and the putter handle are only a couple of inches back of your body's center. However, the move back to impact will require the most practice, as it encompasses the most change for the vast majority of my students.

Many students are used to the front side pulling, either from remnants of former instruction of the front side leading in putting, or from their full swing, when the club is above their body readying to move forward with the lead arm wrapped around their chest. This differs greatly from the club being a few inches from the ground and the upper body and arms only traveling a few inches or a few feet.

The move on the forward stroke should be with the entire back side turning into impact for putts of any length beyond a few feet. When the entire back side—the back arm, shoulder, and back—act as the power source, it greatly helps reduce or eliminate the hands in the stroke. The feeling should be of the back side on the forward stroke moving in a more level and circular direction. Some students prefer the feeling of the lower part of the back as the power source and others prefer the upper part of the back shoulder moving forward and down, as if they are "trapping" the ball.

If you are used to impetus for the forward stroke coming from the front arm pulling, from a rock of the shoulders, or from your hands flipping, you will have to work to get the trap feeling. This also holds true if you are used to a straight backstroke.

The Putt Doctor's

DIAGNOSTIC TEST

Let's check if you properly implement a correct turn with your back shoulder. Putt a ball to a target about 10 feet away. When you complete your stroke, hold your finish position. Ideally, for a putt of this length your hands should not finish beyond the center of your front leg. Also, be cognizant that this finish position does not entail a bowing of the front wrist near impact.

Check to see where the handle of your putter is pointing. If it is pointing somewhere in front of your pants' zipper, nearer your front side, you have released the putter properly. However, if it is pointing at your zipper, you have over-released it. Try this a few times and carefully note the position of your putter's handle at the completion of your stroke. This will give you some valuable feedback on your ability to release the putter properly.

The upper back and the scapula region.

During the forward stroke, some players prefer to feel as if the back scapula, or upper back alone, is the power source. If your finish position has your back forearm blocking your front forearm from your view when you look back into a mirror, you have released the putter by trapping the ball with your back shoulder. As discussed, when your mirror view has the front forearm covering the back forearm, it is caused by the turn of the back side into the impact area and beyond.

The back-side emphasis is especially helpful for players with a tendency to pull putts because their back hand is too active in the stroke. Similarly, it can help those who tend to disconnect or lead with their front side or hands into the impact area and push their putts.

If the ball is hopping off of your putterface, try turning your back shoulder around, instead of rocking. This should minimize any increased loft at impact by helping the handle of the putter to stay slightly ahead of the putter blade at impact. When you finish this stroke correctly, the handle of your putter should be pointing in front of your body's center, even for shorter-length putts. If the ball is still hopping, it could be from your ball position being too far forward or from too much loft on your putter.

Importantly, if you attempt the trapping motion and you tend to pull your putts; most often the pull is from using your hands as part of the stroke or your path is too straight back. Feel as if your back side or your arms are leading your hands into the hitting zone, instead of vice versa.

To accentuate the feeling of the back side as the power source as much as possible, putt several 30- to 40-foot putts to an empty part of the green. Accent the feeling of the back shoulder coming around and down more than under with a rocking motion.

I will sometimes push a player's upper back, between the shoulder and the back scapula. This can cause an overturn through impact, yet the player finds that it helps her feel that the shoulders are more in charge. Players can return to this exaggerated motion and drill any time they feel their hands getting too involved in the stroke.

Please be aware that the phrase "trapping the ball with your back shoulder" has more to do with painting a picture for you to use the big muscles of the arms, shoulders, and back to turn into the impact area. This is to counter the front arm leading as well as the hands leading. In actuality, the putter is rising slightly near and beyond impact due to the physiology of the stroke's natural arc upward on the backstroke and upward on the forward stroke.

You may have noticed when you accent the back shoulder as the power source that your putterhead finishes farther than you are used to on the forward stroke. This doesn't look Tour-like, you may be thinking! The next prescription will help you keep your finish in check.

I will help the player feel the back-side power source by pushing on her shoulder while restricting her hands in the stroke by holding the putter shaft as an extreme drill.

The Front Side Controls Your Stroke

As you build a solid golf swing, you learn how to turn into your front side. The front side is a brace or stabilizing force that permits the accomplished golfer to properly release the club down the target line. In your full swing, the front side helps you keep your golf swing on plane, and aids in rhythm and balance. It becomes the *control* side.

Many elite golfers think of "posting up on the front side" using the front leg as a fulcrum that stabilizes their turn toward a finish position. This posting allows for the centrifugal force of the shaft to gain speed into the hitting area that far outraces the speed of the arms—like cracking a whip or a towel! If you fail to brace the front side, your body moves ahead of the ball in a swaying motion that ruins the timing of the swing.

During a putting stroke, if you were to use solely your back side, your stroke could become imbalanced and might cause your putts to be pulled or pushed off line, resulting in a sliced, out-to-in stroke from an overturn of your shoulders and upper body. Your finish would be too high and your shoulders would be wide open at the finish.

Your front side must control, or *resist*, the back side as it delivers the energy to the ball from the end of the backstroke through impact. This control is from three areas. First, the front wrist is stable and maintains the same angle throughout the stroke it has at address. This keeps your back hand from overpowering the front hand.

Second, your abdomen and chest resist your upper body, preventing it from turning too far in the forward stroke. This core resistance still allows your arms to turn more than the shoulders, but it helps control your back side from overturning, which would result in your chest facing the target—acceptable for the full swing but not for the putt.

Third, on the forward stroke, the turn of your back side compresses the inner portion of your upper arm into your front side. Specifically, the resistance is felt when the turn of your back shoulder through impact pushes your front arm and shoulder to a position where the front arm is vertically aligned at your front side. This resistance appears to be more natural or instinctive when the front arm is pushed to a vertical position. It also comes by way of establishing and maintaining a connection of the front arm to the front side on the forward stroke. This last is a most important point. A means to assure this connection is by way of lightly pressing the front arm into the side or starting with the front arm closer to the chest as opposed to the side.

The front-side resistance keeps the wrists more stable, reduces the chance to overturn your upper body toward the target, and lessens the chance of your lead arm disconnecting during the forward stroke. It also promotes more of a shortened forward stroke (which will be discussed more in this and other sections). This also helps the player accelerate through impact. The front-side resistance is primarily felt in the triceps area and the front shoulder. The front-side resistance helps you "crack the towel."

As the front side braces, you will notice that your front shoulder rises up slightly. This is in part because of the resistance in the front upper arm and shoulder area. You want your shoulder rising from this move rather than from a rocking motion of your shoulders. Watch almost any PGA Tour player, and you will see the front shoulder rise slightly as the forward stroke nears and goes beyond impact. These elite putters are turning their shoulders and also staying connected, using resistance from the front side.

If the front side leads the action, the front arm tends to disconnect, resulting in a blocked stroke. Ideally, the front side is pushed by the back side on the forward stroke. The importance here is that your front side is the control side as the back side delivers the energy.

Note the front shoulder is higher at finish of stroke.

DIAGNOSTIC TEST This is an extreme drill to experience front-side resistance. Stand as seen here with your front foot out in front of your target line. Take your putter back a foot or so to simulate a backstroke. On the forward stroke, hit into your front foot with a mild momentum.

You should feel your front side's tricep and lats tighten slightly as you impact your foot. This is the resistance you should feel on your moderate-length to long putts. Of course, you will feel it less on shorter-length putts, but it will still occur, it just will be a lesser degree of tightening due to the decreased speed of the putter through impact.

Drill to experience front-side resistance.

It would be helpful to hit into your front foot a few times on the practice green to obtain the feeling of front-side resistance, then stroke a few putts duplicating this feeling.

The front side is used to counter an overturn of the trunk through impact that would occur for any length backstroke used for putts longer than 5 to 10 feet. This is contrary to the full swing, of course, as putting is more of a mini-swing, not a full swing.

Of note, the front-side resistance can be felt best by tightening your biceps-triceps area as the forward stroke pushes the front arm into your side, when the arm reaches its original address position. You may prefer tightening your biceps-triceps area a slight amount at address to help your awareness of resistance from the back side's forward motion.

I find this to be a useful tool to improve distance control efficiency. When players have trouble getting the ball to the hole, I will have them work on front-side resistance as an alternative to increasing their backstroke length.

It's important, with front-side resistance that the arms and shoulders not stop at impact. If your upper arms stop before impact, the hands will take over the stroke, causing your wrists to flip into the impact area.

As an extreme drill, I will push on the player's front side to help him feel the brace.

This is a common fault, especially with beginners. A focus on the ball as the target will tend to stop the putter or stop the arms at or near impact with the hands and wrists flipping through the impact area.

If pulling putts is a tendency, have someone stand next to you and place his hand on your front shoulder. Stroke a putt. During your forward stroke, have your friend push against your front shoulder near impact so your shoulder is not allowed to turn beyond the address position. This should keep the ball on the intended target line or might even cause a push of the putt instead of a pull. The exaggerated action helps promote the feeling of bracing against a firm front side and for a release of the putter without pulling the ball.

This technique will also allow you to evaluate whether or not your hands are overactive. If the putt is pulled, even with this technique, it is your hands that are most often too active. A key suggestion here is to practice the Trunk Rotation drill often as well as work to emphasize the arms pulling the putter into the impact area instead of the hands leading the arms into impact.

To summarize, think of the Putt Doctor's Stroke this way. The Putt Doctor's Stroke effectively uses both sides of your body. Your back side is your power source, and your front side provides resistance for stroke length and speed control. The arms start the stroke and pull and push on the shoulders.

So, now you have been through my five basic keys to the Putt Doctor's Stroke. I feel they are applicable to all forms of equipment, including the belly and long putter. Be mindful that change isn't supposed to be comfortable initially. To improve, you often have to get out of your comfort zone. Before long, you not only will get comfortable, you will be making a lot of putts.

PRESCRIPTION NO. 6

Turning Properly: A Drill and a New Concept

I have given you the five key components of the Putt Doctor's Stroke. Now, let's focus on what can be done to obtain feedback to determine if you are doing the stroke correctly.

To further their understanding and feeling of the shoulders turning, instead of rocking, into the front side, I have students implement a one-handed drill. Putting one-handed is a popular drill and is useful if performed correctly. It should be performed as a back-arm-only drill.

In my opinion, most players and many instructors execute the one-handed drill improperly, either by using the wrong arm or by not gaining feedback as to what they are doing. They often use just their arms and subsequently disconnect the arm from their body during the stroke. It becomes an arm-only stroke. The front-arm-only is not a good

Front-hand-only drill promotes a disconnected, chase stroke.

practice drill because it promotes the wrong side as the power source, and almost always results in the front arm disconnecting from the body.

One elite student complained that he was often leaving his putts short of falling in the hole. I had him putt to a hole approximately 15 feet away. The putt headed right at the center of the hole. Unfortunately, it stopped no more than a ball's length short of the hole. "That's my miss right there," he said.

"Look at your finish position," I said. At that point he could see that his putterhead was over a foot off the ground and it was extended more than a foot beyond his front foot. I call that a "chase stroke," where the putterhead appears to chase the ball to the hole.

I pointed out that he had disconnected his front arm from his side through impact. "That finish places the emphasis on the wrong side of the body for the power," I added. "Your chase and high finish are from disconnecting your front arm from your side, giving the front arm too much control."

The diagnostic test on page 73 is my recommended one-handed drill. It provides valuable feedback as to the proper turn and the proper release.

With the back- and front-side connection, and the trunk remaining still as well as the front side resisting the back side, your forward stroke will have the putter finishing shorter and subsequently lower to the ground than if the front side is the power source. This shortened forward stroke ideally is about 40 percent of the total stroke length, while your backstroke is approximately 60 percent of the total stroke length. You can best attain this ratio by not pushing your front arm beyond a vertical position to the front side for most putts of moderate length or shorter.

The front hand gives you feedback to the proper turn back and through.

With your back hand only, grip your putter as shown on the bottom of page 72. Place your front hand on the middle of your chest. Connect your back arm to your back side anywhere from the bicep to the entire upper arm down near the elbow.

The Backstroke: As you initiate the putting stroke, your front hand will give you feedback if the stroke is executed correctly. Through your hand, you should feel your chest being moved by the turn of the arms, shoulders, and back. The chest and the shoulders should stay level, in contrast to moving up and down, which would occur with a rocking of the shoulders.

If you don't feel any movement through your front hand, this signals that you are using only your arm. The larger muscles must power the stroke, and this is done best by you staying connected before and during the stroke. An arm-only stroke defeats the purpose of the drill.

The Forward Stroke: After a slight pause, as the stroke changes direction and starts to go forward, your front hand should feel the back side of your chest being pushed forward, toward the target. If the putt is mid-length or longer, the back-side chest feels as if it is expanding as it meets resistance from the front chest and side. (This feeling may not be realized on the shorter-length putts.) The abs and chest remain still. The main movement is the turn of the arms more than the shoulders.

The old technique used a short backstroke and a long forward stroke, which produced a fast, handsy transition. While the 60–40 ratio is not meant as a hard-and-fast rule, it helps players visualize the ideal stroke length with a backstroke that is longer than the forward stroke by approximately 20 percent.

This allows the backstroke to supply the energy more efficiently and effectively than can be done by extending the follow-through length. Paul Azinger, when discussing this concept, said to me, "We are talking inertia here, Doc."

To better appreciate this concept, I give my students a simple problem. "You have to stroke the ball to the edge of this green. It is approximately 50 feet away," I tell them. "You have two choices. You can take the putter back only a foot, but you can follow through as far as you desire. Or, you can take the putter back as far as you desire, but you can only finish the putter a foot beyond impact." It just takes one attempt to show them the benefit of the long-back, short-through stroke.

Practice the one-handed drill often to promote the use of your front and back side effectively. Stroke 10 to 15 putts a day with it.

A Feedback Drill for Streaky Putters

The Putt Doctor's

DIAGNOSTIC TEST

Place a club on the ground behind your putter with the top of the handle touching the back of the putterhead, as seen on page 75. Close your eyes and start your backstroke. What do you feel is the power source that starts the motion? Is it your hands, your arms, your shoulders? Repeat the stroke if you aren't sure.

The resistance of the club on the ground will help you feel if your hands are taking the club back. Starting the stroke properly is crucial. Streaky putters are especially guilty of starting the stroke with their hands. It is preferable for your arms to start the stroke —not your hands.

I have been using a favorite drill to point out those players who know they should keep their hands out of the stroke but are unaware if this problem applies to them. Of all the feedback drills, this may be the most important for streaky putters.

A Tour player came to me with his instructor. He had had a good year and retained his exempt status. His statistics showed that his ball-striking was excellent. His putting stats were the opposite. He started the following season with more of the same. "The cuts he missed were for one reason only—his putting," said his instructor.

The computer analysis revealed that his stroke rhythm was not matching Tour statistics.

The test and drill to the left helps uncover the handsy putter. Those who use their hands to draw the putter back at the start of the stroke usually finish the process with a handsy wrist-flip at or near impact. If I see the putter moving back too quickly or coming off the ground too fast on the backstroke, I look for two potential problems. The first is if they are leaning too far forward on their front side at address instead of having the desired slight hip bump toward the target.

The second, and by far the most common, problem is that the hands are starting the backstroke. If you are guilty of a handsy takeaway, this test will not only assess your tendencies, it also can provide immediate benefits for your putting stroke when used as a drill.

Repeat this drill ten to twenty times a day for two weeks, and then occasionally to check if you are guilty of starting the stroke with your hands. Your goal is to

Club Push drill.

move the club back with your large muscles without thinking about it.

If you tend to start the club back with your hands, it is often because your hands are too far from your body. A connected setup, with your upper arms closer to your body, allows for a better chance to start the stroke with your big muscles.

To initiate the stroke, I like the feeling of the arms pulling the shoulders. Some prefer a feeling of turning around the body's center as their focus. Either way, start the stroke with the big muscles.

When I placed a club down on the ground behind the Tour player discussed earlier, I asked him what he felt started his stroke.

"Hands—I expect that isn't what you wanted to hear."

"This doesn't surprise me," his instructor commented. "He tends to start his putter with a quick inside move and that has to be with his hands."

Another benefit you will derive from this test is with your stroke tempo. I often have heard one player suggest to another, "Slow down your backstroke!" I am not a big fan of that being the focus of the backstroke. It often results in the forward stroke going like a rocket trying to subconsciously make up for the slowed backstroke tempo.

When your big muscles are in charge of the action, they will take care of your stroke tempo by themselves. Let the arms, shoulders, and back perform as a unit. When this happens, the club will not be jerked back, but will be taken back with a smooth, controlled pace. The transition from the backstroke to the forward stroke will be smooth as well.

If you practice this drill, it will not be long until you can appreciate the feeling of the proper takeaway. Applying this feeling on the course will reap big benefits. Do not be afraid to go back to this drill often so

Forward-Stroke Resistance drill.

that you can verify you are starting the stroke properly. I like students to close their eyes on occasion while executing the trunk rotation to be aware if their hands are involved too much.

Completing the Turn and the Transition

This prescription contains two diagnostic tests that highlight common problems I observe in students. They may apply to you as well.

A number of players consistently stop their bodies, including their arms and shoulders, before impact, with their hands and wrists flipping through impact. They may have been doing this for a long time.

If your body, including your arms, tends to stop before impact with a subsequent flipping of your hands, practice the drill shown here at home. Initially, if you are prone to stopping your body turn and flipping your wrists and hands, you should not be concerned with over-turning your shoulders. It would also be of benefit to close your eyes when performing this drill in order to provide more feedback as to the turn of the shoulders beyond the impact area.

Eventually, you can focus on avoiding over-turning the back and shoulders, no matter the length of the putt. You should never finish with the upper body facing anywhere near the target. This is from over-turning of your shoulders because the front side has not offered resistance to the back side. If over-turning is hard to overcome, try to keep

Place a club under your arms, as seen in the photo to the right. Use a full-length mirror so you can check key positions. As you get into your setup, the club under the arms should be positioned so that the handle is pointing parallel to your imagined target line, as are your shoulders. With putter in hand, imagine putting to a target 15 feet away.

Now, complete your backstroke with a rotation of your arms, shoulders, and back. If the rotation was done properly, the handle of the club under the arms will now be pointing right of where it was pointing at address (if you are right-handed). If the shoulders rocked or you used only your hands and wrists, the club will be pointing left of the target line as it was in the address position.

Finish your stroke. The handle of the club should now be pointing to the left of its original position. If the handle is pointing at the same position at address, there is a good chance you

Club under armpits in address position.

are stopping your body too soon. This will force your wrists and hands to take over the stroke.

When the stroke is executed properly, your shoulders will close to the target line on the backstroke and then open to the target line at the finish. The amount of opening and closing is more predicated on the amount of the turn, with the longer putts requiring more of a turn back, and the finish will be slightly more open because of the momentum of your arms pulling your upper body through impact.

Backstroke position.

Finish position.

With putter in hand, get into your address position. Imagine hitting a putt of approximately 15 feet. Close your eyes and take your putter back to the top of your backstroke. Now, complete your stroke, paying attention to your grip pressure.

First of all, did you feel the putter going back smoothly? Second, did you feel any change in your grip pressure as you started your forward stroke, particularly in your back hand's thumb and index fingers? If you are not sure, repeat the drill with your focus on your grip pressure during the stroke.

your chest still during the stroke and just turn your arms and shoulders around your chest.

Now let's look at a vital aspect of the putting stroke. It is at the transition from the end of the backstroke and the start of the forward stroke, where too many players get the hands involved. Do you start your forward stroke with your hands, your arms, or your back side?

If your grip pressure did not change through impact, you may well have used your arms, shoulders, and back as a unit. If you noticed a slight increase in the grip pressure of the hands, and particularly the back hand, as the stroke started or at the start of the forward stroke, you might be using your hands during your stroke.

If necessary, part of your practice should focus on maintaining the same grip pressure during the start and during the transition from backward to forward stroke. If this is impossible during several trials, you may be gripping the putter handle too loosely. Ideally you should be somewhere between a three and a five grip pressure—with ten the highest.

PRESCRIPTION NO. 9

One Lesson Is Seldom Enough, and the Proper Finish

I am amazed at students who think one putting lesson is enough. They schedule umpteen lessons on the full swing—and maybe one or two on the short game, which includes putting. There are a number of checkpoints that need to be addressed with putting alone, including alignment, the setup, stroke mechanics, distance control, and green-reading skills. Should we add a consistent routine to the checklist as well? Of course they want all this to be checked in one hour!

Several sessions are usually required to address problems that can surface when a player begins to work on his putting technique. Also, what is observed of a player at one session can change 180 degrees by the next session. A case in point is a mini-tour player whose initial session included computer analysis. The primary fault we saw was a tendency to aim with an open putterface to the target and to close the putterface at impact to get the ball on line, which he did fairly consistently. He was not surprised by the computer analysis and believed he mainly needed to focus on his green-reading skills. We spent the remainder of the lesson on his green-reading, and he knew he must enhance this skill and, as importantly, trust and commit to his reads.

A second session a few weeks later began with a half-hour discussion on the difference between his seventeen birdies in his two practice rounds following our first session and the two lousy rounds of putting during the state open the following week, when he missed the cut with only four birdies total in the two rounds. "I still need to better commit to my reads," he said, "but what else is going on?"

I filmed his stroke again and it was clear that the action of his putter was not the same as it had been in the previous session. He was aiming better than previously and his putter was finishing to the inside of the target line as preferred. But the putterface was facing straight down the target line, what I call "holding on" to the finish. This meant he was manipulating his putterface open at impact. This was opposite of his first visit, as now he used his hands to arrive at a blocked position. This situation is not uncommon.

I repeatedly tell my students to "Hold your finish!" I want them to obtain feedback as to the path and the face of the putter. Where is your putter facing at the finish?

The "hold-on" finish where the putterface is pointing straight well beyond impact.

The correct finish with the putterface closed and inside.

Set up to stroke a putt to an imaginary target 10 or so feet from you. Use a club or yardstick to represent the target line. After mimicking a stroke—without a ball—hold your finish. Where is your putterface pointing? Is it at the target or is it closed to the target?

The toe of your putter should be inside the target line with the face closed to the target, but square to the path of your putter. If the putter is inside the target line but the face is pointing at the target, as seen in the top photo on page 79, you are holding on to your putter. This may be the result of previous instruction of attempting the straight-back, square-to-square stroke method or just overemphasizing the need for the putterface to be square at impact.

Another common myth is that the face of the putter should be pointing toward the target at the finish of the stroke. My mini-tour student accomplished this hold-on by rocking his front shoulder up through impact and rotating his wrists and forearms slightly clockwise. It was no wonder he reported that his putts were pushed off line.

So I had him take the putter back to the inside, as he was doing previously, but with a motion that was more a turning of the back and shoulders than a rock of the shoulders. "Now, trap the ball with your back shoulder," I told him. I helped him accomplish this movement by pushing on the upper part of his backside shoulder with my hand.

He saw that the ball was going straight, despite his putterface being closed to the target at the finish. His putterface was inside the target line and also a few degrees closed to the target line—but square to his putter path. He believed that when this had happened previously, it would cause him to pull his putts. I told him that any pulls would only be caused by his hands being too active or the ball being too far forward in his stance.

"Now the putterface is swinging without manipulation, from you using only your big muscles instead of your hands," I said. He was accomplishing this by turning his arms and shoulders through impact.

Rocking of the shoulders also precipitates the coming up and out of the putting stroke. This is in part because of the tendency for the head to rock forward on the backstroke and backward on the forward stroke. This is due to the neck vertebrae acting as if they are fused to the spine. Instead, turn the shoulders. Turning the arms and shoulders will produce a much steadier head during the putting stroke.

IT IS ALL IN YOUR PERCEPTION/TRUSTING YOUR EYES

As I start my clinics, so shall I start this section. You must start the putting process accurately and consistently. The most difficult challenge in the game of golf is that of aligning your club to the target. Think about it: you stand at various distances from the ball from one shot to another, attempting to align your clubface to a target often over 100 yards away. All this is done with you facing at a 90-degree angle to the target line. From alignment alone, it is easy to see that golf, like other sports, is highly visual in its demands. There is nothing more purely visual in golf than aligning to a target.

Note: Although I usually refer to "alignment" as the aiming of the club while in the address position and I refer to "aim" when the player is standing facing the target, in this section I will interchange both words as is typically presented to golfers.

Golf requires constant aiming, from the tee through the green. Unfortunately, you may be among the vast majority who constantly find aiming a difficult challenge. The main purpose of this section is for you to learn to trust your eyes. If your eyes cannot be trusted, you can be plagued by all kinds of psychological blocks. My background as an optometrist allows me to provide unique insight into the challenges of alignment. You will aim better after adapting the techniques discussed in this section.

Personal misperception is often the major culprit with putting faults. If you misperceive the location of the hole as left of where it really is, then you will find it extremely difficult to consistently get the ball on line to the hole. With the slightest of alterations to your setup, including ball, head, or body position, your perception of alignment can be significantly affected—for the good or for the bad.

One fact is irrefutable: over 90 percent of the players I have tested misaligned by aiming outside the hole at 10 feet. For a majority of players, aiming outside the hole starts much closer than 10 feet! Their misperception incorrectly starts the putting process.

Form follows function in this case. Stroke errors often start with an alignment error being the root factor. Yet stroke mechanics are incorrectly blamed. With poor alignment, the stroke must be reshaped to compensate. Correct alignment brings with it much less work regarding your putting stroke. After you read your putt, you must take dead aim.

In my research, I have found that golfers generally aim better when using the leading edge of their putter—what I refer to as the putterface—than when they use the line on the putter. Optically, in the address position, the ability to aim a perpendicular line to a target appears more accurate than aiming a straight line. But many players need more help than just aiming with their putterface.

Even when traditional techniques of alignment are instituted, you may say to your instructor, "This doesn't look right. I feel I am lined up way left. I can't even make a comfortable swing or stroke with this look." And you are correct.

If you perceive you are off line with your aim, the resultant stroke will be a subconscious attempt to "right the ship." For example, if you believe you have a closed putterface at address, you will more often than not block the putt. If you perceive you are aimed with an open putterface to the target, whether consciously or subconsciously, a closed putterface at impact will follow.

I have tested the aiming skills of a number of PGA and LPGA Tour players. When tested, these players, while not having the same degree of error as amateurs, still had problems aiming their putter in the address position. Some have adopted different-style putters to improve their aim.

Some Tour players have the motor skills and spend enough time practicing so that their stroke compensates for their miss-aim. Unfortunately, most amateurs do not have the time or skill to be able to develop a stroke that will compensate for their aiming problems on a consistent basis.

If your alignment problems are long-standing, correcting your alignment can result in your misses being the opposite of what is customary for you. This is because your stroke has had to make up for your poor aim. If you used to have to push your putts with an open putterface at impact to correct for your aim to the left of the target, with your new aim you will most likely miss to the right. Hopefully you will be patient enough to work through this in your practice. Rest assured, you soon will start getting the ball on line. When you don't have to compensate as much, you will find a much freer way to stroke the ball. And that is worth more than a putt or two less per round.

Initially, at least, if a player is used to blocking putts as a cause and effect from aiming to the left, I will recommend moving the ball up in the stance to help get the ball on line—and vice versa for those who pull putts from aiming to the right of the target.

Prescriptions for Better Putting

1. Golf is a cruel game of aiming and aligning

2. The enhanced logo line for accurate aiming

3. Getting your logo line aimed properly

4. Adjusting your perception if alignment looks weird

5. If you dislike lines of any kind, try a spot

6. Squaring your putterface

7. Visual Re-education: Seeing the line

PRESCRIPTION NO. 1

Golf Is a Cruel Game of Aiming and Aligning

How well do you trust your eyes to aim at your intended target? There are a number of ways to assess your aim, including by your friends who may have already asked, "Where are you aiming!?" Having a friend stand behind you and visually assess your aim is not easy, however, even when the putter has a line on it. This is just one reason that your playing buddies' eyes aren't always your best assessment tools.

Aligning occurs when the player is in the address position and aims his or her clubface toward the target. It is important to understand your tendencies. It is a part of self-coaching. For example, when you realize

The Putt Doctor's

DIAGNOSTIC TEST

In my first book, *See It & Sink It*, I discussed a unique test. Sitting at your desk or kitchen table, draw two dots on opposite corners of an 8.5 by 11 inch blank sheet of paper. Take your credit card and place it on the paper so the dot closer to you is at one of the card's long edges. Now aim the edge of the card at the far dot. Be sure to aim the card as if you were in your address position, looking down at the dot (instead of looking at the far dot from behind the card).

With a pencil or pen, draw a line through the dot and along the entire length of the card. Now take a ruler and continue the line until it is at, or even with, the far dot. If the line extends to the left of the far dot, it signifies your tendency to aim to the left of your target at address; and the opposite is true if you miss the dot to the right.

Another, more exact way to assess your tendencies is to place an aiming device on the face of your putter after you aim at a target. You can make your own aiming assessment device by constructing an isosceles (having two equal sides) triangle out of cardboard.

To check your aim with this device, place a ball on the floor to represent your target. Be sure that your carpet or floor does not have any lines that can assist your aim. Put another ball on the floor approximately 10 feet away and address that ball, aiming your putter at the far ball. (Do not use any aiming aids such as the logo line at this time; just aim the putter at the far ball.) Remove the ball from in front of the putter and place the base of the triangle against the putterface. Now, step behind the triangle and assess your aim, closing your nondominant eye and using only your dominant eye.

Ideally, you should repeat the test two or three times, having someone else assess your aim (while you close your eyes as he checks your aim). By having someone else assess the accuracy of your aim, you are not tempted to readjust your aim each time. Multiple tests also determine whether you are consistent or inconsistent with your aim.

your alignment is a prime reason for missing to the right, you will be less likely to blame your stroke and more likely to reflect upon improving your alignment.

A number of techniques will be discussed in this prescription and the others that follow to help with your ability to align. I encourage you to enlist the help of your PGA instructor. Many instructors have laser devices to assess your alignment.

When your putting goes awry, the first thing to check should be your aim. Don't be surprised if the results change from time to time. Your eyes are often engaged in visual duties that can stress them, such as working on the computer. These tasks can, in time, disrupt the eyes' ability to team efficiently.

If you know your tendencies, you are better prepared to meet them head-on. Awareness is the first step toward improving your aim and alignment skills. If your tests show that your aim is accurate, this section may not need to be your focus at this time. But be sure to retest your aim on occasion. It can change! A number of players, even those on the PGA Tour, have had to go with alternative methods of alignment at different times in their golfing careers. For example, if they aim left, they will move the ball back in their stance, and vice versa if they aim right.

PRESCRIPTION NO. 2

The Enhanced Logo Line for Accurate Aiming

A little-known fact concerning Tiger Woods's historic win at the 1996 U.S. Amateur—his third in a row—was a putting tip he picked up during practice rounds at Pumpkin Ridge from a student of mine, who was in the field. He had been a friend of Tiger's through junior and collegiate golf. Tiger noticed him putting well and wondered what he was doing.

"I am doing some eye drills, and my putting is much better," my student told him. Tiger wanted to know what he had learned, and was greeted with, "I'll give you the doctor's name I worked with."

As famed instructor Jim Hardy says, "Golf is a side-on game." Not only does golf require you to aim at a target from beside the ball, but you must aim at targets from a few feet to many yards away. To complicate things further, there are varied lengths of clubs in the bag, so this "side-on game" gets even more challenging as you are constantly aiming from different distances away from the target line.

Tiger watched my student closely during the practice rounds and then commented, "I see what you are doing. You're using a line you drew on your ball to aim at your target!" Tiger, never one to block out anything that could help, adopted the line for the first time—and the rest is history. I remember, as if it were yesterday, seeing his line on the ball rolling end over end into the hole when Tiger made those critical putts down the stretch. Tiger has drawn a line on every ball he has put in play since that time.

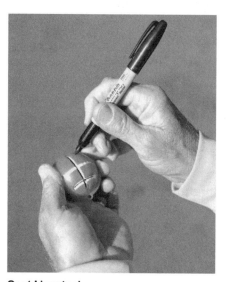

Spot Liner tool.

My studies show that few golfers are capable of correctly aiming their putter when in the address position. But take heart—there are numerous ways to make alignment easier. By far the best way I have found—logo alignment—was utilized by none other than the immortal Bobby Jones. If you already use logo alignment, the comments in this and other prescriptions in this section will enhance your skills with this technique.

Aiming the ball's logo is done standing directly behind the target line. By facing down the line, you are giving your eyes a better—and more natural—chance of aiming than when aligning your clubface to the target from the address position. It is a technique a number of Tour players have adopted, including Brad Faxon, Phil Mickelson, Vijay Singh, Rory Sabbatini, K. J. Choi, and Fred Couples.

My preferred marking—the enhanced logo line.

I would approximate the number of players on the PGA Tour that used the logo to align to the target as being barely a handful before my first book was published in 1997. A recent survey by a major golf publication showed that 91 percent of the Tour players now use the logo for aiming. Most of them use an "enhanced" (longer, bolder) logo line.

My research has shown that drawing at least a 2-inch-long, bold line will improve your aiming accuracy compared to using just the manufacturer's lettering already on the ball—for example, "Pro V1." Yes, drawing a line on the ball is within the rules of golf. If you prefer the enhanced logo line, you can draw it freehand, or use a ruler or the ring from the neck of a Gatorade bottle. A number of players, including Tiger Woods, draw a line freehand. Personally I use a device invented by N. F. Newcomb called the Spot Liner (see Appendix B). I place the long line of the Spot Liner device over the manufacturer's marking on the ball. I draw a line the entire length of the slot with a Sharpie. I also make a line perpendicular to that line with the device. This line is to help square the putterface to the target line.

For breaking putts, the logo line will be aimed at a point other than the hole to allow for the green's slope and grain. A large majority of putts will break. A putt breaking to the left, for example, would dictate aiming the logo line so it is pointing right of the hole by an amount equal to the break you guesstimate. Good putters, when faced with a moderate to severe break, will aim their logo line just above what they perceive to be the apex or high point of the putt's intended roll to the target. Aiming the logo line for breaking putts using the "gate" or "adjusted center" approach will be discussed further in Section Nine.

Some players use the logo line for relatively straight putts and use no line for putts with moderate or more break. Their reasoning is to focus on speed and not get tied up with the line during the stroke. I use the line for all my putts. I even use the enhanced logo line to aim at a target when on the tee. I have then taken care of alignment and can more freely swing without concern for my aim.

Even if you prefer to not use the logo when on the course, I strongly suggest you practice aiming with the logo when on the putting green every day for a few opening putts in order to fine-tune your alignment. This will give your visual system an *aiming check* to start the day. Remember, for some, aiming perception can shift from day to day.

The following prescriptions are different ways to help improve your aiming. Try each of them and give them a chance to work. You may choose to adopt several of them or even switch back and forth a few times for variety.

A couple of weeks after Tiger won the 2000 U.S. Open by a record fifteen shots, he was standing on the putting green at the Western Open. I went up to him and asked if it was true that he learned about the enhanced logo line for aiming from my student while at Pumpkin Ridge. Now, he could have answered this question with, "Oh, I have used this for years," or, "I read it somewhere." Tiger looked me straight in the eyes and responded, "Yes, sir, I remember it well." One more reason I admire Tiger Woods.

PRESCRIPTION NO. 3

Getting Your Logo Line Aimed Properly

Over time I have come across players having difficulty with the logo method of aiming. It has become apparent that there are classifications of alignment preferences. Certain players need to implement different techniques, including using one eye over two eyes.

Let's determine which is more accurate for alignment—both eyes, your dominant eye, or your non-dominant eye.

Practice your aim at home. Starting at a 3-foot distance, align the logo to a dime. Position the logo line on the top of the ball so it is not tilted left or right of center. Confirm your aim by moving three or four steps back from the ball.

A way to help you judge your aiming accuracy on the course is with the Zorro method discussed on page 90. Adjust the line if it is off. Note how little you have to move the ball to realign the logo. Often a dimple's worth of turn or less is enough. You may find it a chore to get it aimed properly if you have to realign the logo a few times. So practice the logo aim at home before going to the course. Golf rounds need to be sped up, not slowed down.

Practice the logo aim again and again until you are able to get the line aimed properly a majority of the time on your first attempt. Extend

There are four primary ways to align the logo line. See which gives you consistent accuracy.

You can either solicit the help of a trained eye such as your golf professional or you can assure the accuracy of aiming your logo using the string and needles recommended in Section Twelve.

On the putting green, position the needles in the ground so the string bisects the cup. Place your golf ball at a distance of no more than five feet from the hole and position the logo line so it is directly aligned with the string. Lower the string on the needles to help you assess if the logo is aimed properly. Now remove the string, step back a few paces, and assess the logo aim by positioning yourself using the following options to see which allows you to better appreciate the logo as aimed at the center of the cup:

1. You have both eyes open, which would have each eye at equal distance on each side of the target line; or

2. Your dominant eye only is open and is positioned directly in line with the logo and the target line; or

3. Your nondominant eye only is open and is directly in line with the logo; or

4. Both eyes are open and in the same position as "2."

You may not see much or any difference in your ability to perceive the logo as aimed correctly when you stepped back. If you are more accurate with the first position above, you are a binocular person who needs both eyes *triangulating* at the target. It is as if you have a third eye positioned above your nose, as aiming for you is best completed as a two-eyed task. Both eyes contribute.

If you prefer the second position, you are strongly dominant. Your dominant eye is so powerful in aiming, the other eye can only get in the way. When this occurs—which is most of the time in my research—it is imperative that you close the non-dominant eye when aiming.

If you prefer the third position, you are definitely in the minority. It often occurs when you aren't very dominant with one eye or you believe you switch dominance. The fourth position means you prefer both eyes open but benefit with the dominant eye in a better (aiming) position. By all means, go with what is most accurate. If the first technique is the most accurate, be sure to aim the ball initially with that technique.

the range when you start to improve your accuracy on the first attempt. Rest assured, after practicing this drill, your initial aim will become quite accurate over 80 percent of the time. Now, you are ready to apply it on the course.

It has been reported that Annika Sörenstam, shortly after learning this technique, spent two hours on the putting green solely practicing aiming the ball's logo. She did not hit one putt. She just worked on getting her aim correct initially so she would not have to re-aim the logo when on the course. Now, let's put the enhanced or the regular logo aim into action on the course. Here is how.

As an example, after reading the green, you determine it is a straight putt. Face the target and aim the logo line at the center of the hole, leaving your ball-marker on the green. Do this using the best method you found in the diagnostic test. Once it is aimed correctly, remove your marker and align your putter to the logo on the ball.

You Always Have a Straight-Line Connection

With many of today's putter designs, it's difficult for players to get their putter to hang straight up and down, which is a big reason that I prefer the Zorro method. This technique was named for its similarity to the fictional hero Zorro. It is a popular method for students. Years after I taught them, I see a number of players on the Tours still using the logo aim and the following method.

The Zorro method uses the shaft of your putter as a straight-line reference. Here is how. After you aim your logo:

The Zorro method.

1. Position yourself at least three paces directly behind your golf ball.

2. Make sure your dominant eye, the ball, and the hole are all in line.

3. Close your nondominant eye and position the edge of the shaft of your putter in line with the logo line, as shown to the left.

4. The ball will be near the bottom of the shaft and the hole will be near the top of the shaft, with both bisected by the shaft's edge.

5. If the hole (or distant target) is not bisected by the shaft line, the logo is not aimed properly.

6. Be sure your head is not tilted and the putter shaft is not tapered. (If the shaft decreases in diameter, then use a part of the shaft that is close to or is the same diameter to align the ball and hole with. This will entail the shaft being tilted more vertically.)

7. You could bisect the ball and the hole with the shaft, then move the shaft from one side of the logo to the other side to see if the logo line appears to be aligned properly (otherwise the ball will be covered by the shaft).

8. The Zorro technique could be used to find a spot in front of the ball to align to instead of using the logo line. Just remove the putter shaft and look for a spot on the ground where the shaft was aligned a moment before.

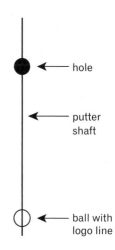

Diagram of the Zorro aim with ball, shaft, and hole.

Whether you use the line on the putter, the putterface, or another aiming method, it is often best to use only your dominant eye to assure an accurate aim. After all, it is your aiming eye.

Adjusting Your Perception If Alignment Looks Weird

A number of players who have tried the enhanced logo line aiming method have shelved it because once they got into the address position the logo line appeared to be off. Even though from behind the ball, the line appeared straight, at address, the line appeared to be pointing left or right of the target. This is an optical challenge of parallax. Is this a problem you have faced when you tried the logo line technique?

Those who perceive the logo line as off when in the address position often say, "I know I can trust the line and not look up to the hole and make more putts. But in my routine, I like to look back and forth to the hole."

When you believe that the line is miss-aimed, your brain tends to subconsciously signal your motor system to compensate. If the line appears to be pointed closed to the target, you are apt to block your putterface at impact. If the line appears to be pointed open to the target, your brain tells your motor system to pull your putt to get it on line. You must eliminate this optical parallax.

If the line appears off in the address position, the task becomes to make your perception match reality. This equates to perceiving the logo line as pointing straight at your target at address, just as you saw it when behind the ball.

If the logo line appears off at address, either pointing right or left of the target, you can change your perception to match reality in a number of ways. If you have a long-standing tendency to align with your putterface open to the target, your eyes will perceive the logo line as pointing closed to the target. Of course, the opposite will occur if you tend to align with a closed putterface. This misperception is often tied to an incorrect setup. When your setup position is off, the logo line will appear off. A correct setup position assists your ability to accurately perceive the target line.

To improve your perception, start at a 3-foot distance. If you are home, aim the logo at a dime. On the putting green, use a small target like a dime or a tee. This is because a smaller target yields more precise feedback when you are practicing alignment skills.

The general guidelines for matching your perception to reality are as follows for a right-handed player:

- At address, if you perceive the logo line as pointing to the right of the target, position your eyes over the ball. You may need to raise or lower your head. How much? Until the logo line appears to look on line to the target.

- Try squaring your feet to the target line.

- Position your head and eyes parallel to the target line. A technique that works almost all of the time is to look straight ahead and square your head to your body's center. Then lower your head back down to the desired position. As discussed in Section One, "Look up to square up!"

- If, after your eyes are square, all the above recommendations are not effective, you can position your head farther behind the ball by rotating your back eye higher or angling your upper body back, à la the Jack Nicklaus setup.

- You can align using only your dominant eye or you can move the ball forward in your stance.

- At address, if you perceive the logo line as pointing to the left of the target, position your eyes over the ball so they are parallel to the target line: "Look up to square up!" If this doesn't help, try the following.

  - Tuck your chin by angling your forehead closer to the ground so your face is parallel to the ground. This may place your eyes more to the inside of the target line than before, and this can move the perception of the logo to the right and on line with the hole.

  - Move your eyes so they are not as far behind the ball.

  - Align with your dominant eye only, or move the ball back slightly in your stance.

  - Change your stance. Angle the lead foot outward, or move the lead foot away from the target line. Keep your shoulders parallel to the target.

The key is to find the setup position that makes the logo line appear to be aimed at the target. Practice this at home and on the green until you find the right setup position that gives you an accurate perception. Soon it will look right on target every time.

At a great club in Florida called Marsh Landing, a student attended my clinic with one purpose in mind. He wanted a method to make the logo line appear correctly aimed when he was at address, instead of always appearing to be aimed to the left of the target. He was a right-handed, same-side-eye-dominant player. He knew the logo was his best aiming technique, but he couldn't trust his eyes at address.

I went through several ideas with him, but nothing helped his perception. Finally, I had him open his body to the target line—and I mean open! This immediately allowed him to perceive the logo as correct. He was able to get the ball on line more consistently with this setup than with a square-shoulder setup. Even though I prefer square shoulders to the target line, it was no surprise to me that this student got the ball started on line more consistently with a correct perception of the target line versus a square-shoulder setup.

If you are not an elite putter or a long-time player, and the logo line method has now corrected your alignment, you may still start putts off line due to your motor system's previous compensations for your inaccurate alignment. For example, if previously you typically had an open putterface at address, your tendency now, when using the logo line, would be to close the putterface at impact to get the ball started on line. This new tendency will result in pulled putts. Take heart, as other recommendations to follow will help you alleviate this problem. Often a little practice and patience are all it takes for your motor system to work through it.

For you right-handed golfers with a tendency to align to the left, I believe this is from the many practice strokes that are taken to the left of the ball's position. During your practice strokes, optically the eyes are fixating on the hole at a different angle than in the address position. When you move into the address position, your eyes are looking from the practice stroke position to a new position. Optically, this moves your eyes' perception of the hole to the left of its actual location.

Over time, this can be a contributing factor for the experienced player to misalign to the left of the target. You may try taking your practice strokes behind the ball facing the target. If you still desire to keep this position a part of your routine, then look at a point parallel to the hole during your practice strokes. Once you perceive the logo line as straight, you have determined your correct setup position with your head and eyes.

If you are optically challenged, the best way to start a practice session on the putting green is by aiming the logo line at a target 3 to 4 feet away. If needed, adjust your address position to visually confirm that the logo is aimed correctly. When you can match your perception to reality, you are ready to stroke the ball freely.

Over the years, I have changed a number of players from right-handed to left-handed putters. The reason was that they saw the logo line as straight while no other suggestion worked. Almost all of them were same-side dominant. I have had a number of people tell me their ability to better perceive the target line was the big reason they switched. Give it a try if nothing else has worked for you.

If You Dislike Lines of Any Kind, Try a Spot

You may well identify with those who share a dislike of lines on the ball as well as lines on the putter. You may find lines to be confusing at best. I have heard a number of players say they prefer to shape their putts, being "feel" players. Lines appear to disrupt these players' ability to visually shape the imagined path the ball must travel to go in the hole. They see the ball's roll being curved with no straight lines.

For those who prefer to shape their putts, there are a number of ways to align to the target. In recent years, a plethora of new putters has been developed and marketed. They have so many different features that it is hard to keep up. I have noticed two primary characteristics that can affect all skill levels of golfers.

The first is that the new (or some of the new) putters have such a better moment of inertia (MOI) that an off-center hit, compared to a center hit, will not negatively affect the distance the ball rolls.

Second, you have a variety of ways to aim different putters. If the putter has multiple lines on the top of the putterhead, you can aim all of them together, or just the top line, the center line, or the bottom line may be more accurate. You may discover that you aim better with the face of your putter. You can aim with longer lines or a longer putterface. You can try using a center-shafted putter, or aim with the back edge of the putter. You can aim with a putter design that has circles representing two or three golf balls. There are many options from which to choose.

Have your PGA professional help you find the best design for aiming, as well as for the proper length and lie. Checking your alignment should be done on the putting green at 10 feet using a straight putt. You should not conclude the results until you have done several aiming checks. He may suggest only a change in ball position.

While the logo line, in my research, is the best option for most golfers, spot alignment is a useful substitute. Aside from putter design, players are more accurate aligning to a closer target, such as a spot a few inches away, than to a target many yards away.

If you are barely off the green or in the fairway and cannot align your logo, spot alignment can be a very effective tool. This consists of locating a spot within a short distance—often a few inches in front of the ball—at which to aim your club.

If spot alignment hasn't worked for you previously, the fix could be as simple as changing your routine. You may have noticed when taking practice strokes *beside* the ball that you had difficulty finding your spot when moving to the address position. You can remedy this by taking your practice strokes from behind the ball, facing down the line. Locate your spot in this position and go right into your address, aiming at the spot. This allows you to keep your eyes and the spot in-line.

PGA Tour player Justin Leonard does it another way. After practicing his stroke beside the ball, he goes behind the ball to find an on-line spot. From behind the ball he goes directly into his address.

Another Tour player once told me he wasn't big on using the logo for alignment. He said it took too long and it made him feel like he had to be perfect. He preferred picking a small spot on the green in front of his ball and on line to his aim point. He would stand behind his ball and pick a spot on the grass a few inches to a foot in front of his ball. The distance of the spot could vary, as he would look for something distinctive such as a darker or lighter area of grass. The only problem came when there was nothing distinctive and he would have to self-generate—visualize—a spot.

But this player admitted that using his spot didn't result in the accuracy he desired and that he often got up over the ball and felt he was right or left of where he wanted to be. I recommended something that greatly improved his accuracy at the time and when I checked his accuracy several years later, he was still spot-on. Here is my recommendation, which you can follow yourself:

Like this Tour player did, use only your dominant eye to locate your spot. Now walk into the address position, aiming only with your dominant eye. I have found that one eye is better than two eyes for most players. If you spot aim or would like to give it a go, take the following test.

Choose a 3- to 6-foot straight putt. Zorro the ball and the hole, and with a Sharpie, mark a small spot on the green that is on the line to the middle of the hole. This can also be done using a yardstick (or the Aim Aid string and needles—see Appendix B) to accurately place the dot on the target line. The spot should be only a few inches in front of the ball.

Now stand or squat behind the ball at least two paces—3 to 6 feet. Close first one eye, then the other eye, and then keep both eyes open. See when you have the more accurate perception of the spot being on the target line. If you are not sure, get your dominant eye as close as possible to being directly on the target line.

Spot alignment with the dominant eye.

The Tour player was consistently accurate with his aim by keeping his non-dominant eye closed until after he finished aiming his putter to the spot. If you are better aiming with one eye, wait to open both eyes until after aiming your putter.

You may choose the Jack Nicklaus method. He used a spot behind and in front of the ball consistently in his career both for his putting and his full swing. If you have tried spot alignment and you still are not aiming as accurately as you desire, use two spots—one in front and one behind the ball—with both spots being on the target line. As you stand behind the ball on the target line, use the Zorro technique to pick a spot a foot or so behind the ball, and another spot a foot or so in front of the ball.

Now, move to beside the ball, keeping the spots in front of and behind the ball in your mind's eye. Stand so your body is squared to the two spots as you address the ball, and use the two spots to aim your putter at the target. I once recommended this technique to an LPGA instructor, Jamie Fischer. A few weeks later, she called excitedly to tell me the technique was responsible for her being able to trust her alignment and win a LPGA sectional tournament.

After you get into your address position, the same rules of perception apply as were mentioned when using the logo line. If the spot appears off at address, you may need to adjust your head or body position or even use your dominant eye only to look down the target line.

Squaring Your Putterface

If you are alignment-challenged, you may find that your aiming is more accurate when you use the leading edge of your putter. If you already aim your putterface and you want to be more accurate, the following drill will improve your aim.

You will need a T-square, a ruler, a string, and two knitting needles (for more detail on this, see Aim Aid in Section Twelve) as well as a Sharpie felt-tip pen. Use the diagram below to help you follow these directions.

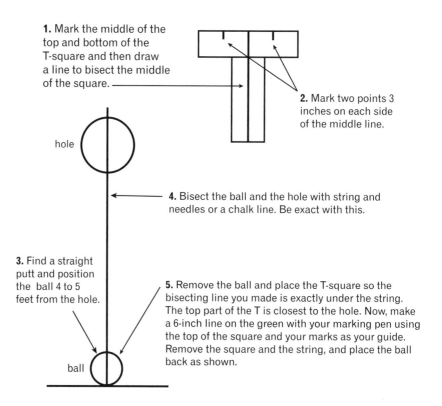

1. Mark the middle of the top and bottom of the T-square and then draw a line to bisect the middle of the square.

2. Mark two points 3 inches on each side of the middle line.

hole

4. Bisect the ball and the hole with string and needles or a chalk line. Be exact with this.

3. Find a straight putt and position the ball 4 to 5 feet from the hole.

5. Remove the ball and place the T-square so the bisecting line you made is exactly under the string. The top part of the T is closest to the hole. Now, make a 6-inch line on the green with your marking pen using the top of the square and your marks as your guide. Remove the square and the string, and place the ball back as shown.

ball

The key here is to find a straight putt of 4 to 6 feet in length. Stroke a couple of putts under the string to establish a straight putt. If it is a straight putt, the string attached to the needles will bisect the exact middle of the hole. Take great care to align the center line on the T-square with the string. An easy way to check this is to lower the string so it is almost touching the T-square.

When you remove the T-square, you should have a 6-inch line on the green that is perpendicular to the string. Also make a small mark in the middle of the line to show the ball's start position.

Remove the string and needles. Put a ball just in front of the line. Now place your putter down so the face is exactly parallel to the line drawn on the green and ever so slightly behind the line. Now, your putterface is square to the target.

If you need to correct your perception, implement the changes recommended in Prescription No. 4. Squaring your eyes to the target line may be all that is necessary for you to determine if the putterface is aimed correctly. You may need to tilt your head up or down until the putterface appears to be aimed at the target.

If the face still appears closed, move the ball back in your stance. Start with a half-ball change in position, and if you still perceive it as closed, move it a ball's-width back. If the face appears open, the opposite holds true: move the ball forward of your usual position.

One mini-tour player I tested was consistently misaligning beyond 8 feet when aiming with his putterface. He was incredibly accurate up to 20 feet using the back of his blade. Retesting a year later showed he was still accurate with the blade's back edge.

A number of players were more accurate when they aimed the back edge of the blade instead of the putterface. Additionally, I have found that using two points, whether it is the toe and heel or the back part of the putter blade, can yield accurate alignment.

A number of players visually perceive an accurate aim when they create a gap between the putter and the ball.

The Putt Doctor's
DIAGNOSTIC TEST

In your address position, where does the putterface appear to be aimed? If you perceive it to be aimed straight at the hole, your setup position is accurate and you see straight as straight. If the face appears to be closed, this means you typically align your putterface open to the target. Likewise, if the face looks open, you tend to close the face when aligning the putter to the target. If your perception is off, you need to alter your setup.

Creating a gap between the putterface and the ball.

One player perceived her putterface to be noticeably open to the target line yet in reality it was correctly aimed to the target. Nothing I did with her setup changed her perception as much as when a gap was created between the face and the ball. Then and only then was she able to perceive the face as square to the target.

You may find you can only perceive a square putterface by closing your nondominant eye. If this is the case, after the putter is squared, you can open both eyes. Remember, you are now done with aiming and it is time to focus on the speed of the putt. The aim is hard to ignore, but work through it. Fill your mind with pictures of the correct speed.

PRESCRIPTION NO. 7

Visual Re-Education: Seeing the Line

I received a call from a Tour player who was having no fun on the greens. He had just lost his Tour card the previous year because of poor putting. This was despite an average of 4 hours a day putting, either on the putting green or in his hotel room. Obviously he was *perfecting* the wrong thing in his practice. He scheduled a lesson to see if I could make some sense out of his putting. He aligned 6 inches outside the hole at a 10-foot distance. I used my optometric training to come up with a test and a drill to address these problems. Two weeks later I received a call from my optically challenged student, who said, "I am now seeing straight as straight." Later he called at the end of the Q-school finals to tell me he had regained his card and felt he could finally trust his eyes. He also had zero three-putts in six rounds.

Perhaps you, like this player, have not been able to trust your eyes for a long time. Aligning a foot right of the hole looks okay to you. No recommendations in this section have helped you so far. Understand that visual re-education will not happen overnight. It may take time for perception to match reality. But the test and drill I came up with for my student might help you as well (see page 101).

I have designed a training device, called the Scoring Line, that *Golf Magazine* labeled as "terrific" and "among the best aids we've seen," giving it four and a half stars out of a possible five (see Appendix B). It is great to use instead of a piece of tape. I have also found the Scoring

You will need a roll of white medical tape. The label should read "1 inch × 5 yards." Pat down an inch or two of one end of the tape on the floor and unroll the rest of the tape, stretching it out to make a straight line. Let the tape lie on the floor and avoid patting the rest of it down, as this will distort the tape. Look down the tape and see if it is straight. If not, pick up the loose end and realign it.

Assume your address position at one end of the tape with your putter facing down the tape. If you perceive the tape going straight, your misperceptions can be fixed quite easily. If you perceive the tape pointing right or left instead of straight, you have an embedded visual misperception. This signals that you have some work to do.

Line tape to be effective even for aligning irons and woods on the practice tee.

The above tape drill is designed to *connect space* from the putterface to the target. When my Tour student got into his address position, he commented, "The line looks like it is going way left. I know it is straight but it doesn't look straight." His eyes saw the tape as aligned to the left because of his long-standing habit of looking to the right of the actual hole.

If the tape doesn't look straight to you, it is because previously your eyes were looking off line. If you have an imbedded misperception of the target line, reread the portion of Section One on Setup that relates to the eyes being parallel to the target line. Based on your eye dominance, you may open or close your stance to see if this makes the tape appear straight. Don't be surprised if a change in your setup goes a long way toward reducing or eliminating your perception problems.

If none of the above suggestions totally eliminates your misperception, you will need to make visual re-education a part of your practice. It is best to use a less traveled place in your home or garage because walking on the tape will destroy its straight-line connection. Make sure there is enough room at one end of the tape to be able to get into your address position on the tape. Start the visual re-education with one eye, closing or covering the other eye. In the address position, visually track down the tape as if you were following a bug pacing down the tape. It should take approximately 40 seconds to track up and down the tape.

Then repeat the drill with the other eye. Next, repeat the entire drill with both eyes.

Do not be surprised if one eye perceives the tape as straighter than the other eye. The eye that perceives the tape as misaligned may well have astigmatism, a fairly common, benign condition. This can be corrected with glasses or contacts. When on the course, you may choose only the eye that perceives the tape as straight as the eye to look down the target line.

Work on this drill with one eye, then the other eye, and finally both eyes for one to two weeks. This should be enough time to eliminate your misperceptions. It may take a few sessions of five minutes a day and a few days, but eventually the tape will appear as straight.

Now you have another way to trust your eyes. What a good feeling.

ADDITIONAL TECHNIQUES TO IMPROVE YOUR STROKE

This section includes additional ideas to improve upon your putting expertise and to fine-tune the Putt Doctor's Stroke. They include options for the stroker and the hitter, and a couple of techniques inspired by Jack Nicklaus and Gary Player.

The drills in this section are designed to help counter the typical faults I see day after day. They include too long an overall stroke length, especially on shorter putts; too much of the hands involved in the stroke, which I call the "wristy" stroke; and too short a backstroke and too long a follow-through. A smooth transition from the end of the backstroke to the forward stroke may be as important as any other aspect of the stroke.

There also is a drill for off-center hits. Increasing the center contact on the putterface is a must, especially for the higher-handicap players, in order to get the ball started on line and with the correct speed. And if you are still convinced that your best stroke path is a straight-back, square-to-square method, and your PGA instructor concurs, you will read about the best setup and equipment to help you successfully execute the stroke you prefer.

Once you find a recommendation that works, write it down and stick with it.

Prescriptions for Better Putting

1. Tempo for the hitter and the stroker
2. A modern-day stroke
3. If you are missing short-range putts
4. A one-handed technique: reducing wristy strokes
5. Making more putts with center contact
6. Consider the Jack Nicklaus setup and stroke
7. Perfecting a straight-back stroke

Tempo for the Hitter and the Stroker

As in the full swing, the putting stroke tempo is of huge importance. There are some who believe that as your swing goes, so goes the tempo of your putting stroke. While this often rings true, you can change your putting tempo much more easily than your swing tempo.

For example, if you are rushing your transition in putting, just as you tend to do in your full swing, isn't it wise to practice in order to minimize or eliminate this fault? Especially in the putting stroke, I believe you can change a number of things with a little work, including your tempo.

There are a number of issues related to tempo. A smooth transition between the back and forward stroke is always desired while working on the following points. The focus here will be primarily on the speed and length of the overall back and forward stroke. Some notable changes have occurred in the last few years in regards to the putting stroke, maybe none as noticeable as the change in putting tempo and stroke length seen on the PGA Tour.

A study by golf expert Dr. Ralph Mann in the mid-1990s found that the Tour player's putting tempo, from the start of the backstroke to the finish, tended to range from 60 to 65 beats per minute (bpm.) This was and is a stroker's tempo. My own later measurements have shown that the present-day stroke tempo has gone through quite a change, as has the preferred overall stroke length. A majority of Tour players today register at 70 bpm or above. That is more of a hitter's tempo, and is directly related to the shorter stroke length becoming common.

Your tempo can correlate to your stroke length. If your stroke length tends to be long for most putts, it can point toward your tempo being more of a stroker's than a hitter's. Let's check your stroke length.

The Putt Doctor's

DIAGNOSTIC TEST   Choose a 20-foot putt. Place a marker next to the ball. Take a typical backstroke for this putt, but stop before starting the forward stroke. Check where the backstroke is, or have someone place a penny on the ground under the putterhead. Next, execute the forward stroke and hold your finish. Place a penny under where the putterface is at that point.

Stand to the side and take a look at the length of your backstroke in relation to the forward stroke. If your backstroke is 1½ feet long, and your back and forward stroke lengths are equal, you are more of a stroker. If your forward stroke is noticeably longer than your backstroke length, I deem you a chaser. If the reverse is the situation, and your back and forward stroke are a little more than a foot in length, then you have a hitter stroke tempo.

You can also use a metronome to see which category your stroke fits under. If you have a metronome, set it on 65 bpm. Address the ball and start the stroke on one beat and finish the stroke on the next beat. Realize that the putt's length is of no consequence, as the stroke tempo should be the same for all distances.

If the beat is too slow, you will have impacted the ball well ahead of the next beat. If the beat is too fast, you will find yourself rushing to impact in an attempt to match the beat. Adjust the beat until the start and finish of your stroke matches the two beats. You now have your typical stroke tempo. If you are a stroker, your tempo will be somewhere between 60 and 65 bpm. If you are a chaser or a hitter, your tempo will be near or above 70 bpm. I will address the chase stroke in detail in the following prescription.

Using the Eyeline metronome (see Appendix B), I have found that the modern-day player's tempo is about 70 beats per minute.

If you are having difficulty with your speed control or with getting the ball started on line consistently, try speeding up your tempo. With less time between the start and the finish, there is less time to do things incorrectly. When you speed up your stroke, your transition from the backstroke to the forward stroke must be smooth and not rushed.

A word of caution needs to be given for those who have a stroker's tempo. Several players I have tested on the PGA Tour have a long, slow stroke for a prime reason. They tend to mis-aim to their target, and need time to square the putterface to the target at impact. For instance, they start out aiming with a closed putterface to the target, but they open their putterface during the stroke. Unless their aim is improved, these players will be missing all day with a shorter stroke length and a faster tempo, because they don't have the time during the stroke to adjust the putterface in their customary manner.

If you use a lighter-weighted putterhead, you may already be somewhat of a hitter. A heavier putter, such as the Heavy Putter or a long putter, promotes a slower-tempo stroke. It is better in the hands of a stroker, but it can be a useful practice tool for those players who are fighting a too up-tempo stroke or who tend to be too handsy with their stroke. Players using the long putter will be more of a stroker based on the overall putter weight. But whether you are a hitter or a stroker, there are times when you need to be flexible.

A discussion of tempo always reminds me of a student who called me after a less than stellar putting performance at the Masters. His comment was, "I missed the cut because of my putting. I never could get the speed right. I seemed to always be a little fast with my speed." Now, this was a player who had played in the Masters a number of times!

I asked, "What did you do to adjust after a few holes?" His answer was that he had tried hitting the ball on the toe, mentally imagining the hole as closer—he knew this was one of my favorite recommendations—and just shortening his stroke. But that didn't help. Then, I asked him if he had tried changing his tempo. No, he hadn't thought of that.

I prefer the shorter hitter's stroke, especially for shorter-length strokes for most players. And I see more success with a majority of medium to higher handicappers when using a stroker's tempo for longer putts, especially beyond 30 to 40 feet. But there are times when you need to adjust for the conditions. Especially if you are a hitter, you may need to adjust to faster greens. If you are a stroker, you may need to adjust your tempo for slower greens.

I believe there is a reason for this adjustment. A hitter's tempo reduces chances for error with control of the path and face during the stroke on shorter putts, where getting the ball on line is imperative. For longer putts, center contact with the putter is imperative for distance control. I have seen more consistent center contact with the majority of players when they use a stroker's tempo and an overall longer stroke length.

A major problem for players with inconsistent distance control for longer-length putts is the lack of increased backstroke length. Instead, they rush their overall tempo as well as rush their transition. (See the next prescription and Section Nine for a detailed discussion of this point.)

If you are guilty of poor or inconsistent distance control, changing your tempo will require disciplined practice. Eventually, this will lead to improved results. Once again, make sure to check your aiming accuracy before you try to switch to a hitter's tempo. You will still use the larger muscles of the shoulders, arms, and trunk with the stroker's and the hitter's tempo. For the chasers, an equal back and forward stroke length is an acceptable change.

How long is too long a stroke length? A good check is the acceleration or lack of it into the ball. If the backstroke is too long, it can promote a deceleration into the ball. So remember, if you tend to decelerate, first check your backstroke length. Be sure to control the transition when attempting to quicken your stroke tempo to be like a hitter's tempo. This will occur naturally if the big muscles are the stroke's power source.

A Modern-Day Stroke

Not long ago, instructors used to advocate a short backstroke and an extended follow-through. It was as though the stroke was one part backstroke to three parts forward stroke. This was to promote acceleration through impact. With this stroke technique, the putterhead would end up above the knees and sometimes nearer the player's waist when putting to a target of over 30 feet. I call this the "chase stroke," as the putter appears to chase the ball to the hole.

Too often this stroke with its high finish leaves the player's putt well short of the hole. The reason is that the backstroke is too short to impart enough energy to the ball, so the hands are forced to be part of the forward stroke. When the hands get too involved in the stroke, the result is inconsistent distance control.

Many instructors now call for a technique of equal part backstroke to forward stroke length. This pendulum stroke appears to help consistently propel the ball closer to the hole, because the backstroke has enough length or load for the distance and this counters the need for the hands to be involved. As the greens have gotten faster, this technique has become more and more of a necessity. It lets the power for the stroke come from the big muscles of the body—the arms and shoulders. The equal back-to-forward stroke length is still the choice in many instructional circles.

A modern technique gaining popularity among some putting instructors is often referred to as the 60–40 stroke length. This technique emphasizes more of a hit to the stroke. In fact, there are more hitters than strokers on Tour. The long, flowing strokes of Stewart Cink and Loren Roberts are becoming less the norm, and the Tiger Woods–type short stroke length is becoming more typical. Compare the effects of the old and the modern-day strokes using the test to the left.

This test should help you appreciate that the loading of the stroke—the longer backstroke—is much more efficient. If you watch yourself on video, you will notice that the longer-back, shorter-through stroke looks a lot more efficient than the shorter-back, longer-through stroke. This is because the short-back, long-forward stroke tends to force you to be wristy and also tends to sway your entire body forward on the forward stroke.

If you are more like the player on the right in the

The Putt Doctor's
DIAGNOSTIC TEST

Try this experiment. Putt two balls from one end of the practice green to the other—at least a 50-foot length putt. With one putt, use a foot-long backstroke, and finish as far forward with your putterhead as you desire.

The second stroke will be the opposite of the first stroke. Use a longer backstroke—say, 2 or 3 feet. Your finish must be like the previous stroke's backstroke length—approximately a foot beyond impact. A good tip for the second stroke is to attempt to keep the putter as low as possible at the finish.

You will find that the second putting style—the longer backstroke—enables you to hit the ball much farther than the first style did, and with seemingly less effort.

photograph here, it should be obvious that you to have too long a forward stroke. She has over-rotated her body on the forward stroke and lost the spine angle she had at address. She is coming out of her stroke and is chasing the ball to the hole with her putterhead. The player on the left represents more current instruction preferences. He has maintained his spine angle throughout the stroke, with his hands still inside the body line at the finish.

The player on the right has a long follow-through. I recommend the follow-through of the player on the left, especially for distances inside 15 feet.

With the modern-day stroke, on a 40-foot putt your backstroke would be approximately 18 inches, and your forward stroke would be about 12 inches—the 60–40 ratio.

See if one style is generally more consistent for you. If your putts tend to come up short, and you are a chaser, you may want to work toward at least an equal-back-and-through stroke length.

If you pause slightly on the backstroke before going into the forward stroke, you may become aware that your hands are involved in the transition. The pause can give you a chance to start the forward stroke with the back side, diminishing the use of your hands and wrists. If you are inconsistent with speed control after applying the hitter's stroke for a while, you may be using your hands in your stroke. If so, apply the recommendations in Prescription No. 4.

PRESCRIPTION NO. 3

If You Are Missing Short-Range Putts

If the previous Putt Doctor Diagnostic Test revealed you to be more of a chaser and you want to change this, the following drill is effective in accomplishing the 60–40 stroke length ratio. It promotes a *tap* of the ball off the putterhead instead of the chase stroke's *push* of the ball. It is particularly effective for those of you missing short-range putts from 2 to 6 feet!

Gary Player won nine majors in his illustrious career. He did it with an all-wrist stroke. He would—okay, he still does—cock his wrists to the right on his backstroke, then flip the wrists back to the ball. This was commonplace in the older days when the greens were slow. And I mean real slow by today's standards.

Gary's forward stroke takes a descending angle into the ball. The putter pinches the ground, stopping abruptly just beyond the ball's resting position. It is what we today call a "pop" stroke with exaggeration. If you feel the ball is not coming off your putterface solidly, try the following technique.

I label this the "Gary Player extreme drill." I also refer to this technique as the tap stroke. My good friend and co-inventor of the Putting Template, Mark Rivard, introduced this terminology to me. The tap stroke should make a distinctive click at impact compared to a softer sound with the "push" stroke of a chaser. If done properly, the tap

The Putt Doctor's

DIAGNOSTIC TEST With your typical stroke, hit a few putts to a hole 4 to 6 feet away. Note the speed with which your putts hit the hole. Now attempt a modified Gary Player approach. Take the putter back with your arms and shoulders instead of with a wrist hinge and unhinge, as Gary Player does it. In the forward stroke, feel as if your putterhead is striking the ball with a slight descending blow. Your putter should be resting on the ground when it stops, and it should finish not more than a couple of inches beyond impact. In essence, that is the drill.

At address, it may help to bump your hips toward the target. This will place a little more weight on your front side, which helps accommodate a shorter finish. Also imagine the putter handle leaning forward at impact. This is to counter any tendency of your back wrist or hand to overpower the front hand, which would cause the wrists to lose the angles they had at address. Try this for a few putts.

You should experience more ball speed as it hits the hole compared to your usual speed. With this stroke there should be no putts that barely reach the hole. I like this drill, as I prefer increased speed for shorter putts, instead of the ball barely falling over the front edge (see Section Nine).

stroke should result in more ball speed off of the putterface.

This method is particularly effective up to approximately 10 feet. Farther distances often result in difficulty with efficiency.

The Gary Player tap stroke drill exaggerates a shorter, low finish of the forward stroke. I recommend this as opposed to the chase stroke's long follow-through. Keeping a mind's-eye picture of your putterhead finishing low is a good way to limit the forward stroke length. This drill produces a more consistent square face at impact, compared to a finish length that is exaggerated, such as the chase finish.

The purpose of this extreme drill is to exaggerate the use of front-side resistance. It may help you to place a putter cover under your front-side arm, near the elbow area, to make sure that your arm is connected. Of course, with a regular stroke, your putterhead will finish a few inches past the ball and off the ground, but the Gary Player tap drill is a good one to help you with the 60-40 ratio and help you achieve a consistent roll. Students often state that picturing the putter finishing close to the ground helps them better apply this technique.

Finally, as an important part of your pre-putt routine, be sure to always burn the image of the ball going into the cup at the speed you desire.

Stop the putter shortly after impact using front-side resistance.

PRESCRIPTION NO. 4

A One-Handed Technique: Reducing Wristy Strokes

There are times when we find ourselves so buried in technique—what I refer to as "how-to's"—that our ears are emitting smoke. Before you know it, when it is time to pull the trigger on the stroke, you are thinking instead of acting. Emphasis on technique is best saved for practice, often without a hole and initially without a ball. Keep it simple!

One player comes to mind who always plays the game with a minimum of thoughts. He tries to keep it simple during practice. Alex Coe often would say to me, "Just give me one thought to get the ball started on line and that is what I will go with."

Over time, Alex has listened to several key points and different drills. He eventually found one, and it was all he needed as his focus. The other points he filed away for when he might need them, as he put it.

Holding the back wrist with the front hand.

Alex prefers a focus on the back wrist staying square to the target line throughout the stroke. This is a simple picture to have in your mind during the stroke. A key to this concept is to have your back wrist square to the target line and square to your putterface at address.

Alex told me recently, "Even five years later, the picture of the back wrist being square to the target line at impact is what I go to when my putting is off." When I get too technical with him during a practice session, he reminds me that it will be a long time before he gives up his wrist stroke key.

Another way to simplify the putting process is to try to reduce the conflict that sometimes occurs when the two hands are acting together. I constantly hear players say that they feel they putt better with one hand instead of two, as they walk up and hit a 3-footer into the hole with one hand on the handle.

You may have seen PGA player Mike Hulbert putting one-handed during several Tour events. Like Mike, when it comes to shorter putts, you may believe you are better with one hand than with two. If this is the case, yet you do not feel comfortable using just one hand on the course, try the technique of holding the back wrist with the front hand to give your stroke more stability. It can provide better results than one hand alone. Try it, and if it shows promise, play a few rounds using this technique for putts of 10 feet or less.

The Putt Doctor's

DIAGNOSTIC TEST

Hold your back wrist with your front hand, as seen above. This lessens the tendency to rotate the wrist open or closed at impact. It can also be used to avoid being too "wristy"—a term used when your hands dominate the stroke and cause your wrists to flip during the stroke. Stroke a few putts with the front hand holding the back wrist. I recommend using a chalk line, the Aim Aid needles and string discussed in Section Twelve, or another device to assure correct alignment.

If you find that the ball starts on line more consistently, this is a useful technique to practice. On the course, a good focus is a mind's-eye picture of the back wrist being square to the target during impact. You may prefer the feeling derived with the back wrist staying firm and steady through impact.

Countering the Hands in a Wristy Stroke

If you are prone to using a lot of hands and wrists in your stroke, going to the belly putter at least as a practice tool is a prime suggestion. The belly putter anchors the handle into your belly and helps prevent excessive use of the hands, which causes the wrists to break down during the stroke.

If you choose to stick with your conventional short putter, here are a few suggestions I give my players:

- Reread and diligently work with Prescriptions 3 through 5 in Section Three, particularly the Trunk Rotation drill.
- Execute the Trunk Rotation drill with your eyes closed, so you can focus on the stroke starting with the arms and not the hands rotating the putterface open, then having to flip them to a closed position.
- Do other practice drills with your eyes closed to get good feedback on your attempts to maintain an even tempo with your putting stroke.
- Practice with the Club Push drill to provide feedback on what takes the putter back, preferably the shoulders and not the hands (see Section Three).
- Work on the Ball-in-the-Wrist drill described in Section Six.
- Try out the Brian Lackey training aid by Eyeline Golf.
- Wrap three to four ounces of lead tape around the handle.
- For your grip, place your back hand over the top of your front hand so the only back-hand fingers touching the handle are your thumb and index finger.
- Try the Paul Runyan hands-opposed grip discussed in Section Two.

- Try the claw grip discussed in Section Eleven, or the lifeline grip in both hands from Section Two.
- Try the split grip discussed in Section Two.
- Switch to a belly putter or a long putter.

If you are so ingrained with your wrist stroke, there may be no more important suggestion than to have you place both hands on the handle so the palms are vertical and facing the target line. This way, when your wrists do release, they will tend to release with the palms still facing the target line.

PRESCRIPTION NO. 5

Making More Putts with Center Contact

Consistently getting the ball started on line is often tied to hitting the ball with the center of the putterface, commonly called the "sweet spot." Impacting the ball near the putterface toe or heel minimizes your chance of getting the ball started on line. If the ball impacts the putterface near the toe, your putterface is automatically twisted open in relation to the target. Conversely, a ball impacting near the heel of the putter will tend to close your clubface in relation to the target. An off-center hit also can affect the amount of energy to the ball, yielding inconsistent speed or distance control.

You can experience the center and off-center hits for yourself by loosely holding the putter handle with the thumb and forefinger of your dominant hand. Tap the toe, then the heel, with a pencil eraser or your finger. The sweet spot is where there is no twisting of the putterface when it is tapped.

Making more 10-footers can be partly attributed to hitting the ball on the sweet spot. According to equipment designer Ralph Maltbie's statistics, on a 25-foot putt a Tour player tends to have a quarter-inch variance of distribution of contact points off the sweet spot of the putterface. A 0–5 handicap group has a variance of one half inch, while an 18-handicap player has a variance of one and a half inches. This much variance can reduce the energy to the ball by up to 40 percent, leaving a putt far short of its intended target.

Spray some water on your golf ball and your putterface. Next sprinkle some talcum powder or baking soda on one side of the ball, and that will be its area of impact by the putterface. You can use a wet-erase pen instead, but you must stroke the ball before the ink dries.

Putt the ball to a target approximately 25 feet away. After the putt, look at your putterface and note where the powder or ink is in relation to the putter's sweet spot. Putt four or five times, wiping the mark off the putter each time and applying more powder and water or ink to the ball as needed. If you are a half inch off of the sweet spot, on average, you are more like a scratch (0 handicap) player. If you are one inch off on average, you are more like a double-digit handicap player when it comes to off-center hits.

If it is difficult to consistently make center hits, then it would behoove you to work on the following suggestions as well as apply the recommendations in Appendix A.

First, see if you are addressing the ball off-center. Position yourself to check for this by looking back into a mirror. If you are off, position the ball's brand name at the line or dot on the putter, since that is most often the putter's sweet spot. Even though the ball is really on the center of the putterface, initially it may be appear to be on the putter's heel. But in time, your eyes and brain will adjust. Now, you can retest your impact position.

You could place a small dot near the ball's back apex and repeat the above drill. Look at the spot as a fine focus on the ball during the stroke. If it improves your center hits, focus on a spot on the ball or on the ball's marking during the stroke. An immediate help is the Tiger Woods tee drill in Section Twelve. This is a great drill for multiple reasons, especially gaining center contact on the putterface.

Also check your balance. Toe hits may be caused by your weight being more on your heels during the stroke. Heel hits can signal that your weight is too much on your toes at address and during the stroke. Toe hits can also be from a putter being too short for you. You could move a half a ball or so closer to the ball at address, if this does not interfere with the desired in-to-in path of your stroke. Conversely, heel hits can be minimized with a shorter putter or by moving farther from the ball at address.

Also, there are a number of putters designed for improving center impact, including the Momentus SOS Training Putter and the Cleveland Stubby putter. If you have a blade putter, you could place rubber bands surrounding the sweet spot to fine-tune your hit.

A smooth transition from the backstroke to the forward stroke is essential for center contact. Incorporate a slight pause at the transition to help you achieve more consistent center contact on the putterface.

Consider the Jack Nicklaus Setup and Stroke

When Jack Nicklaus was struggling with his putting early in his career, he sought out one of the greats with the flat stick, Jackie Burke Jr.

Jackie gave Nicklaus a setup to aid his ability to see the target line. This setup could also improve your ability to see the target line, as well as help you square your putter to the target line at impact. The following technique is based on an article Nicklaus wrote for *Golf Magazine*. He felt it gave him an effective way to get the ball started on line.

Nicklaus would open his stance considerably and lean his upper body noticeably behind the ball. He said he could better see the target line with this setup, compared to a conventional setup, because his dominant left eye was now in a better position to see down the line. His open stance got his feet out of the way, which is what I recommend for the same-side-dominant player.

He would get into a crouched position so his back forearm was as parallel to the ground as possible. He thought of his stroke as a simple movement of the back forearm going back and through in a pistonlike action.

Jack Nicklaus–like setup.

The Putt Doctor's DIAGNOSTIC TEST

The next time you practice, hit some 6- to 10-foot putts with your conventional setup. Repeat using the Nicklaus setup with your back forearm as the piston for the stroke. Your upper body stays still, and your back arm goes back and through along the front of your body. If you find this helps you get the ball on line, by all means stick with it.

PRESCRIPTION NO. 7

Perfecting a Straight-Back Stroke

As mentioned previously, there is more than one way to do anything. You may be firm in your belief in the straight-back, straight-through, square-to-square stroke technique.

I believe there are two primary ways to execute the straight-back stroke. The first and least seen, but possibly the most effective, is what I call the "arms roll" stroke. The second method is the most popular, purely a shoulder rock, with the back shoulder going up on the backstroke and the front shoulder rocking up on the forward stroke. This is a favored technique for the long putter among many elite players.

Note: It is helpful to get your upper back parallel to the ground. This will further help getting the putter to go more on a straight-back path. You may also try a putter with a more upright lie angle, perhaps 75 degrees or more. This will take your wrists and hands out of a neutral position and into what I call the Rosie Jones approach, with the hands and wrists arched down. This would place you closer to the ball at address, and you must be careful to not set up with your eyes outside the target line. Either tuck your chin or get your butt up and out at address.

The Putt Doctor's DIAGNOSTIC TEST

Are you a straight-back, straight-through stroker? There are several ways to determine if this matches your natural stroke, including placing the heel of your putter on a straight board or placing the toe of your putter next to a wall and executing your stroke. If the stroke feels natural with your putter against a surface, and the putterface stays square to the target line throughout, then you are more than likely a straight-back putter.

You could use a mirror and check the position of your forearms in your stroke. If the amount of the lead forearm visible in the mirror changes little to none at all during your stroke, you tend to be a straight-back, square-to-square player.

A flat upper back.

Additionally, the use of a face-balanced, shorter putter, even 30 inches or less, is also helpful. Just be sure to keep your desired swing weight by getting a heavier putter head or applying lead tape to the bottom of the putterhead. Your PGA professional can help you with this.

Arms Roll Stroke

I am familiar with this method, having seen it used by two quite good putters, one on Indiana University's golf team and one a member of the Arizona State University golf team. Each player's style is unusual compared to the rest of the team, yet it is very effective for him. Of note, both have used this technique since they were very young.

If you are a right-handed player, the "arms roll" backstroke features a *counterclockwise rotation* of your arms and to a smaller degree your shoulders, instead of the clockwise rotation of a conventional arced stroke. When your back arm and shoulder rock up and out, your back forearm is actually higher than the front forearm. As your back side comes up, you tilt your front shoulder down.

On the forward stroke, the action is reversed, with your front shoulder rocking up and out, bringing your front forearm now higher than your back forearm. A good way to check if you are executing this stroke properly is to use a full-length mirror positioned at your backside to see the forearm movements as described above. The counterclockwise movement (for a right-handed player) on the backstroke is meant to square the putter to the target line at the end of the backstroke. The clockwise movement on the forward stroke is also meant to square the clubface at impact. This becomes necessary because when the putterface is square at the end of the backstroke, you must rotate the putterface open to keep the putt from being pulled.

The upper arms can be connected to your trunk with this stroke, but most players free their upper arms so the back arm disconnects (moves away) from the back side on the backstroke. The upper part of the front arm then moves away from the body on the forward stroke.

This technique can be difficult to master, but is quite effective. Players using it usually start at a young age. If you observed Billy Mayfair

The player's forearms are in the same position for the address as they are for the backstroke.

putt before he went to the belly putter, his move was an exaggerated arms roll technique.

Rock—Don't Roll—the Shoulders

This is the most popular straight-back, straight-through method used today. It entails your shoulders rocking up and down. Players using long putters often adopt this technique.

To practice it, hold a putter across your chest by folding your arms in front of your chest. The butt end should be pointing out your front side. Your back hand holds the shaft on your front bicep region, and the front hand holds the shaft on the back bicep area. At address get your upper back nearly parallel to the ground. Now, point the butt end of the club at the edge of a full-length mirror or the edge of a wall opposite your lead side.

With your eyes fixed on the butt of the club, rock your shoulders so the handle goes down in a straight line as your front shoulder goes down and your back shoulder goes up. Now reverse the motion, with

The head tends to tilt with the spine angle.

The shoulder rock finish position has the front shoulder much higher than when the shoulders are turning. The head also tends to go back along the spine angle.

the club handle going back up the edge of the wall or mirror as your front shoulder rises and your back shoulder lowers.

You may be aware that your lower body is rocking as well, instead of staying steady as desired. If this is the case, it would be helpful to bump your hips toward the target line to steady your lower body.

Some players prefer pressing a thumb on the middle of their sternum to create a *pivot point* for the shoulders. They use that point as their focus when they actually putt.

I first encountered this drill while being an observer in the 1985 U.S. Open at Shinnecock Hills Golf Club. I came upon Payne Stewart standing at the green's edge and going through the shoulder rock drill. He was rocking his shoulders while pointing his club at a flagstick on the ground as his way of checking his rocking motion.

Another part of the stroke entails hooding the wrist to square the putterface to the target line on the backstroke. This motion is reversed on the forward stroke, with the wrists moving open to square the face to the target. I also recommend placing the handle in both lifelines to assist you in controlling the putterface during the stroke.

SECTION SIX

PULLING THE PUTT

Well, now is the time for you to learn everything you need to avoid the dreaded "pulls." For right-handed golfers, these putts veer to the left of the intended target line instead of directly on the target line. The opposite is true for left-handers. Just the thought of the pulls can become a nightmare for tournament golfers or anyone else who may be under pressure to make a lot of 5- to 10-footers.

I know from firsthand experience that Tour players hate pulling putts. In the locker room after a practice round at a Tour event, a player lamented to me, "I hate pulling putts so much, I do everything possible to keep my putterface open, so it doesn't get closed at impact." Other players who overheard this conversation immediately agreed.

Of course, pulling makeable putts frustrates any golfer. But whether you are a Tour veteran, a weekend tournament player, or just someone who is serious about scoring your best, you need to face the fact that pulled putts are caused by a breakdown in basic mechanics. Being aware of the typical reasons you pull putts off line to the left can give you a start toward remediation.

In all too many instances, golfers of all skill levels—including Tour veterans—don't understand why they are missing putts to the left. Often they attribute their failure to get their putts on line to inaccurate aiming of their clubface. While this can play a role in the pulls, especially if one is used to aligning right and pulling putts to get them on line, there are many other factors that come into play.

Incorrect aim or under-reading the break of your putts are among the reasons for missed putts, including those that travel left of the target. But aiming is usually not the principle reason for pulling putts off line. Here are the three common reasons putts are pulled off line:

1. Allowing the back hand to take over

2. Too long a backstroke, causing deceleration in the forward stroke

3. Taking the club back on a straight or outside path

Let's discuss these problems and give you some ways to coach yourself during practice or tournament play so that you can diagnose this affliction and effectively deal with it.

Prescriptions to Eliminate Pulled Putts

1. Keeping the big muscles (*not* your hands) in control

2. Control your stroke length and avoid stopping or decelerating the big muscles

3. Eliminate taking the club back on a straight or outside path

4. Try some other cures

PRESCRIPTION NO. 1

Keeping the Big Muscles (*Not* Your Hands) in Control

Overuse of the hands is by far the most common reason for pulling putts, regardless of your skill level. It seems to be inherent in all players, from neophyte to elite.

The hands should not outrace the arms in the stroke. So, before you do anything else, you must stop using your hands as your power source and start using your bigger muscles—your arms, shoulders, and back—

I can assure you that if you start your backstroke with your hands, you are going to start your forward stroke the same way. To discover if your hands are too involved, first close your eyes and focus on your grip pressure during your stroke. If you feel your grip tightening when you start the stroke, or when you start the forward stroke, it is an indicator that your hands are getting too much emphasis as the power source. Again, you want your hands to be pulled into impact by your arms and shoulders, not your hands pulling your arms into impact.

Now, with your eyes closed, pretend you are putting a 10-footer. After the putt, ask yourself, what did you feel was the power source that started the motion of your backstroke? Was it your left or right hand, your left or right arm, your shoulders? If you are not sure, repeat the test. Pay careful attention to the body parts that start your backstroke.

If it is one or both of your hands, the focus of your power is positioned too far below your shoulders, so your big muscles are not as involved as they should be in your backstroke. And if that is the case, then they are not going to be as involved as they should be in the rest of your stroke. Do this as a drill until you consciously feel that your backstroke starts with you turning your arms and shoulders, and not with your hands.

as your source of power. Using your big muscles to initiate your putting stroke cannot be overemphasized. Try this drill to decrease the involvement of your hands in your putting stroke.

During a putting lesson with a talented young amateur golfer, I positioned her arms and hands closer to her body and suggested that she stand a little taller at address. However, at her second lesson she told me, "I'm still fighting my hands in my stroke."

After watching her roll a few putts, I could see that she was still consistently pulling putts off her intended line. So, we worked on the above drill and the Club Push drill (in Section Five) for a while. Then, I asked her to stroke ten putts. During this test, she pulled only one of them. That's amazing progress!

As you become more aware of the important role of your arm and shoulder turn, at address, make sure your front arm is not resting on your side or away from your body. If it is, move it more in front of your body, nearer your chest than your back arm. This position helps you feel the front-side resistance during your forward stroke, while it also helps you avoid having your back side overpower your front side on the forward stroke. It will also reduce your back hand's influence in the stroke.

While it is difficult to decrease or eliminate the wrist component, it is not impossible. I constantly stress to my students to feel and picture their arms and shoulders pulling their hands into impact, instead of their hands pulling the arms and shoulders into impact. I also recommended the following drill, which I give to very wristy students.

Ball-in-the-Wrist Drill

The Ball-in-the-Wrist drill.

The Ball-in-the-Wrist drill is also a test and a useful tool to obtain feedback to see if your wrists are breaking down and, if they are, to help cure the problem.

After a few putts with the ball in the wrist, remove it and stroke a few more putts, focusing on reproducing this feeling of the wrist angle being kept the same throughout the stroke. You can place the ball in the wrist again if necessary. I have had students do this drill for most of their practice session.

The Putt Doctor's
DIAGNOSTIC TEST

Stroke a few putts to a target. Next, place a ball between your back wrist and the putter handle. As discussed in Section Two on the grip, it also helps you determine the correct straight-line positioning of the back forearm, wrist, hand, and putter handle. This can be a little awkward, so I recommend using your front hand to place the ball. Now stroke a few 3- to 6-foot putts, keeping the ball in its position between your wrist and the putter. If your putting stroke feels different, it may well signal that you are to handsy and your wrists are changing angles during your regular stroke.

If the putter handle is pointing at or near your belt buckle at the finish of your stroke it is an indicator that this drill can assist you in stopping your pulls. You can get more feedback regarding too much use of the hands and wrists by closing your eyes during these practice putts.

A top collegiate golfer got great feedback from this drill to correct his wrist flip. "I never would have believed I flipped my hands and wrists that much," he said. "I can feel the difference of pressure of my wrist on the ball at impact." He began to excel when he attempted to feel as if the putter handle was a little in front of the putterhead at impact, using his back side as the power source on the forward stroke. If his hands or arms, for example, felt tight or tense, he worked on reducing any tension.

When you see players on the Tour shaking their shoulder and arm with their free hand to get the tension out, it is usually the front side they are shaking. Hopefully, this translates to the back side as well. When you are relaxing your front shoulder, include the back one, too.

Decelerating: The Target Is Not the Ball

Hitting at the ball as if it is the target, rather than swinging your putter "through the ball" to a finish position, is a common problem for all golfers.

Stroking *at* the ball instead of *through* the ball results in a deceleration of the arms and shoulders, with the hands then flipping the putter. This is a perfect recipe for pulled putts.

Focus on Spot Beyond Ball

There are several drills designed to eliminate deceleration. Possibly none is more effective than getting your eyes to focus on a spot beyond the ball where you want the putter to stop. This technique is the number-one fix I hear from the Tour players when their putts are just not falling out on the course. The spot is often a few inches in front of the ball for short to mid-range putts. This drill incorporates using your eyes to get your arms and the putter through impact—the eyes lead the body! This can overcome the body's tendency to anticipate the hit and stop. Practice this technique initially without a hole.

I ask my students, "Where do you guesstimate your putter will finish for this putt of five feet? Show me by placing a coin on the ground. Now, while stroking the putt, look only at the coin. You can be aware of the ball more in your peripheral vision, but focus primarily on the finish point. Attempt to stop your putter at or slightly beyond that point— that is your only focus during the putt."

After a student putts, I often see his putterhead finishing beyond the point on the ground. I still praise the effort if he kept his arms moving through impact. The prime objective is to strike through the ball and not just at it.

Ignore Ball à la Johnny Miller

Another drill, one I call the "Johnny Miller technique," is to watch the putter handle or your hands while keeping your head still during the stroke. Johnny did this to help him win the 1973 U.S. Open. Ignoring the ball as a target helped him keep his mind free of negative thoughts and make sure his putter handle kept moving through impact.

PRESCRIPTION NO. 2

Control Your Stroke Length and Avoid Stopping or Decelerating the Big Muscles

A significant factor that can cause a breakdown at impact is too long a backstroke. When the putterhead swings too far on the backstroke, your brain can subconsciously trigger a thought process that, in effect, says, trouble is brewing. It relays that message to the motor system, which, in turn, tells your arms and hands to slow down as the putterhead nears impact.

This long backstroke often is a product of a handsy takeaway or a tight grip on the putter handle. When the hands start the stroke, you are less aware of the length of the backstroke, as is also the case when the grip is too tight. This is also the same case if your grip pressure is too tight.

The Super Stroke large-grip or the Winn AVS grip can be a useful tool for those who tend to have too tight a grip. Overall, if you are prone to a tight grip, this should be a focus during your setup.

As discussed in previous sections, a shorter overall stroke is desired on mid- to longer-range putts. Work to get the big muscles in control to shorten your backstroke length. (Also see Section Nine for techniques dealing with stroke length.)

On the flip side, how much is too short a backstroke length? If you have too short a backstroke, you might feel that you must get your hands involved to power the stroke through the ball. Since the back hand is the dominant hand for most players, it is easy to get that hand too active during the forward stroke. This kind of transition can become a major problem.

When the putter reaches the end of the backstroke and starts forward, you might rush the stroke as if in a hurry to get to impact. Obviously, you don't want to get into the habit of rushing your forward putting stroke. Having your shoulders in charge throughout the stroke greatly minimizes the possibility of a rushed transition—the moment you go from a backstroke to a forward stroke—or a rushed forward stroke.

If you felt the transition was smoother or your backstroke was longer than your typical stroke (you can have your golf professional assist you for this test), give yourself enough time in your practice sessions to devote ten minutes toward a concentrated effort of making a slight pause to begin your transition. This pause also tends to induce a desired longer backstroke. Your tendency for pulls can be greatly reduced with this technique.

Practice various backswing lengths so you can appreciate that your backswing is the horsepower that will determine how much energy is needed to get the ball to the target.

Eventually, you'll also discover another benefit of a paused transition: it will eliminate your anticipation of impact, which can result in your big muscles stopping and your hands taking over.

The Putt Doctor's DIAGNOSTIC TEST   How do you know if your backstroke is too short? As part of your practice, stop for a brief moment at the end of your backstroke. This brief pause can help your brain reorganize and be ready for the act of making a forward stroke. If you notice that this is a significant change in your transition tempo, it well may signal that your backstroke is too short and you then must use your hands for additional power.

Eliminate Taking the Club Back
on a Straight or Outside Path

The straight-back, straight-through putter path can produce a timing issue. Players who attempt this stroke path subconsciously know that their natural stroke is more of a curve, where the putterface moves on an inside path and is open at the end of the backstroke. So, when these players try to take the putter straight back, it produces a timing problem with the putterface having to close on the forward stroke. When the putter closes, the hands come in as part of the stroke, disengaging the big muscles as the main controller of the stroke.

The Putt Doctor's DIAGNOSTIC TEST

You may already be aware of these faults for yourself or if you aren't, it may behoove you to elicit the eye of your golf professional to check your stroke habits. You could also place a yardstick on the floor to represent the target line. Place your putter on the middle of the yardstick as you get into your address position. Close your eyes and take a backstroke that would mimic a 10-foot or longer putt. Now, open your eyes and check your path. Repeat this several times. If you find that your path is straight back or occasionally outside the target line, it is time to check a few items.

If these players mis-time their impact, the ball can be pulled because the putterface is closing too fast at impact. Of course, this kind of stroke can also cause a push if the player doesn't get the face closed quickly enough to have it square to the line at impact. I also see players with a tendency to take the putter back outside the target line on the backstroke. This out-to-in stroke path also spells trouble.

To avoid these path faults, first check your setup to make sure your eyes and your shoulders are square to the target line and your front arm is higher—or dominant—when you look into a mirror. Also, make sure you are two putterheads from the ball and that your arms are connected to your sides at address. Also take a look in Appendix A for putter-fitting suggestions.

Have a mental picture of a curved backstroke path. Remember, you don't want to take the putterhead outside the target line when you start away from the ball. It's actually better to be a little too curved, or inside and open, on your backstroke, especially if you are prone to pulling putts.

So, adopt the philosophy that you cannot go too inside on the backstroke if you are pulling putts. Just let the putter swing back—with a turn—with the big muscles controlling the action. If your putter is still going back straight, please review Section Three to make sure you are turning your shoulders rather than rocking them.

Try Some Other Cures

Additional cures for pulled putts include the following:

The Fault: Heel hits

The Fix: Address the ball on the center of the putter and not on the heel. Stand farther from the ball rather than too close to it. Try a shorter putter length versus one that is too long. Try a more upright lie angle. Try a face-balanced putter or a center-shafted putter. Your balance may be off, so lower your center of gravity.

The Fault: An in-to-out stroke path that results in heel hits or a stroke path that loops from in to out at the end of the backstroke

The Fix: Let the putter continue to swing on its arc past impact. Make sure the big muscles are used and the arms do not disconnect from the body. Try a shorter putter.

The Fault: When you close your eyes you notice during your stroke that your back-hand grip is tighter on the handle with the index finger and thumb.

The Fix: Adjust your grip pressure so that it is more in the middle fingers of the back hand and in the palm of the front hand.

The Fault: A closed putterface at impact

The Fix: Move the ball back in your stance, as the ball may be too far forward in your stance—a tendency especially if you are cross-dominant. If the ball is too far forward in your stance, this can also result in the putterface closing before impact. Check with your golf professional on your ball position. Try a heel-shafted or toe-hang putter, as it can slow down the closing of the putterface through impact.

The Fault: You are still pulling putts, especially under pressure.

The Fix: Change to a claw grip. Also, your shoulders are too rounded or your front side does not resist the back side. Get your chest expanded, and get your front arm more in front of your body. All too frequently, I see players exhibit too long a backstroke and forward stroke. So, work to shorten your overall stroke length, especially on putts inside of 7 feet.

SECTION SEVEN

PUSHING THE PUTT

If a pulled putt goes to the left of the cup (for a right-handed golfer), it stands to reason that a pushed putt goes to the right of the target. Either way, it's a missed opportunity to lower your score on the golf course.

Missing putts to the right is often the result of incorrect aim or misreading the green. But these are not pushed putts.

The most common reasons players push putts off line are:

- Coming out of the stroke caused by peeking at the results too soon.

- A chase stroke or a blocked stroke with the front side leading and also "holding on" to keep the putterface square well beyond impact.

- Opening the putterface on the backstroke and a back-side-dominant setup, resulting in an out-to-in stroke path.

Pushing putts is a common problem for beginner or higher-handicap golfers. Because they are so concerned with the outcome of the putt that they cannot wait to look at the ball rolling along its intended line toward the hole, these players tend to lift up their head and upper body too quickly. Golfers call this "peeking." Unfortunately, peeking usually forces the putterface open at impact, and sad to say, the ball rolls to the right of the target. If you just stood and observed players on the putting green you would be aware of how often peeking afflicts a majority of golfers.

As you work on remediating pushed putts, be aware that if one remedy doesn't work, move on to another one. Be careful not to overdo it. Fixing the problem may require your experimentation on several fronts. For instance, you may find that you are chasing your putts on your forward stroke. Addressing this problem may reduce the amount of push, but then you realize that your ball is still not starting down the target line. This leads to another discovery: you are also opening the face on the backstroke. So, you focus on the big muscles to start the stroke, coupled with reducing your follow-through, which helps get the ball consistently on line. Usually just a few alterations to your putting stroke will do the trick.

Prescriptions for Better Putting

1. Stay down through impact and avoid coming out of your stroke
2. Avoid a chased or blocked stroke
3. Avoid opening the putterface on the backstroke and an out-to-in path
4. Try some other cures

PRESCRIPTION NO. 1

Stay Down Through Impact and Avoid Coming Out of the Stroke

Day in and day out, the most common cause of pushing your putts is lifting your eyes, head, and body to peek into the future—to see the result of the stroke.

Spend a few minutes watching amateur golfers—beginners or intermediate players—on the practice putting green. It won't take you long to see that one after another appears to have his head attached to his putterhead by some invisible chain. As the putterhead nears impact, the player's head appears to be moving at nearly the same speed. Often, it can outrace the putterhead to impact as the player steals a glance

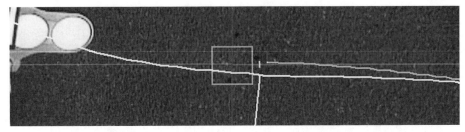

This computer-generated image of a player's stroke path at the end of his stroke shows him coming up and out of the stroke right after impact. (The square depicts the ball's position in the stroke.)

toward the hole. He is engrossed in the result of his putt rather than in attempting to make a proper stroke.

If your head moves forward, it can bring your body with it. When this occurs, you will have difficulty getting the clubface square at impact, often resulting in a blocked stroke that sends the ball off line to the right.

To build awareness, I have players watch their shadow during the putting stroke or watch a video of their head movement. A usual comment I hear afterward is, "You have got to be kidding me. I move my head that much?!" Try the following test to measure your head movement.

This test can really help you appreciate the importance of keeping your head still during your putts. Holding your head in its starting position will help ensure that you get the putterhead square at impact.

The Putt Doctor's
DIAGNOSTIC TEST

Place a tee in the ground. Get into your setup position with the sun behind you so the tee is at the left side of the shadow of your head.

Stroke a putt to a hole, preferably a 10- to 15-foot distance. Hold your finish position and look to see if your head is at the same spot as it was in your address position. If it is, then you are able to stroke the putt without moving your head forward. If your head did move, then advance to the second portion of this test.

Get into the same position with the shadow of your head at the tee. Close your eyes and stroke a putt. Now open your eyes. If your head did not move this time, you may well have experienced the freedom of stroking a putt without concern for the outcome.

Remember, your head, eyes, and body must be kept in their starting position throughout your putting stroke. No turning or peeking until the ball is well along its intended line. If you tend to move your head more with your eyes open than with your eyes closed, work on the drill below for a while to see if it helps eliminate your pushed putts.

Stroke a few putts with your eyes closed and feel the freedom of your stroke by keeping your head still. After a few putts, then stroke several more putts with your eyes open. Try to capture the same focus and mental freedom you experienced with your eyes closed. Remember, you are stroking these putts with a focus on holding your head still, not on results.

With my students, I ingrain this concept by using a tablet-size piece of paper. I ask the student to line up her putt and get into her setup position so her putterface is aligned at the target. Then, I hold the piece of paper next to her front eye so it obstructs the view of the target line and the hole. I give the student permission to stroke the putt. She quickly realizes that trying to peek is useless, as the paper blocks her vision. Try this drill with a friend to promote a steady head position. You'll soon see the ball rolling more consistently down the intended line.

Other means to help you stay steady during your stroke include the following:

- Fixating on a spot on the back of the ball, which can help anchor your eyes and in turn anchor your head and body.
- Fixating on a spot in front of the ball, rather than on the ball itself, during your stroke.
- Watching the grass spring back into view from underneath the ball after impact.
- Silently counting to yourself after impact, "One thousand and one," before looking at the ball or the hole.

Another helpful idea is to convince yourself that your real job in putting the golf ball is simply to attempt to roll the ball down the intended line at the speed you believe is necessary to make the putt. The key word here is "attempt." That's all you have control over. Period! Your job is never to make the putt.

My good friend and longtime student Nick Faldo has always kept his head down long after his putterface contacted the ball. On shorter putts, he listens for the rattle of the ball as it falls into the cup.

So, the next time you are over the ball, say to yourself, "Okay, my job here is to attempt to stroke this putt the way I believe is necessary." After you finish your putt, ask yourself the following question: "Did I do my job?" And if you did, I bet you stayed down throughout your stroke.

Avoid a Chase or a Blocked Stroke

Another reason you push putts is because you chase or block your stroke.

A chase stroke is when you extend your forward stroke length well beyond the impact position. A blocked stroke is when you hold onto the putterhead beyond impact—trying to keep the putterhead square to the target line for as long as possible—instead of allowing it to close properly after impact.

Many golfers I have observed have chase strokes that are two, three, or four times longer than their backstroke length. Their putter tends to finish near waist height, especially on mid- to-long-range putts. Players with chase strokes are often the product of what is now considered an old-style putting technique: a short backstroke and an extended follow-through, to accelerate through the ball.

The biggest problem with the chase stroke is that it forces you to come out of the stroke with your upper body, resulting in an open putter-face at impact. The chase stroke comes with additional problems. It can cause you to disconnect your front arm from your body during your forward stroke. Also, your hands can get too involved, especially on longer putts, because your brain subconsciously realizes that the clubhead cannot deliver enough energy to the ball with a short backstroke to get the ball to the hole without your hands helping power your stroke.

Here is another test to help you better understand these putting problems.

The player on the right is chasing the club to the target while the player on the left exhibits the proper follow-through length.

The Putt Doctor's DIAGNOSTIC TEST

Ask a friend to watch you attempt a 30-foot putt. Ask him to tell you which is longer, your backstroke or your forward stroke. After you stroke the putt, hold your finish. Now, ask your observer to give you feedback. Were your backstroke and forward strokes about the same length?

You are a chase putter if the forward stroke length is nearly two times, or longer, than your backstroke length, or if the finish position of your putterhead is more than a foot off of the ground.

What the better players commonly say is to "let the putter swing." This refers, in part, to having enough length on the backstroke to let the putter "drop on the ball." While this description is a little extreme, it does point to the desire to have enough length on the backstroke so you don't have to force the putter toward the ball with your hands.

If you want to measure it specifically, I prefer the total stroke length to be 60 percent backstroke and 40 percent follow-through. If you are a chase putter, try at first for a stroke that is 50 percent backstroke and 50 percent follow-through. You can measure this by placing tees on the putting green to represent your back and through length. Eventually work toward the 60/40 stroke length.

Keep in mind, if a shortened follow-through doesn't get the ball to the hole, you need to either increase your backstroke length or speed up your tempo.

A common problem associated with a blocked or chase stroke is when your front arm disconnects from your front side on the forward stroke. If this occurs the big muscles of your upper arms and shoulders can play only a support role during the forward stroke. The front arm becomes the power source, which is undesirable, and this can alter the face near impact.

Leading the forward stroke with the front arm is often a counter-measure for the player's back hand being too active. It is an attempt at correcting the symptom but not the cause. Another reason the front arm leads is from the belief that it should lead the forward stroke. But that is just not an efficient stroke.

If you try to keep your putterface square to the target line after impact, it can result in a blocked stroke. This is caused by a discon-nected left arm, a bowing forward of the left wrist, or a rotation of the hands opening the face. The front-arm disconnect tends to take the path of the putter more down the target line—a blocked stroke—instead of continuing the curve that started with the putter's position at the end of the backstroke; the putter path becomes a straight line, and this often carries with it an open putterface at impact.

The wrists should not change angles from the address position through impact. When you use the big muscles in the putting stroke the finish should find the putterface slightly closed on a shorter putt, and pointing nearly 45 degrees closed on a longer putt. When you allow your back side to release into your front side, you will have the putter swing on a continuous curve. Think of the stroke as a mini-golf swing—a curved path.

Also, make sure your grip and especially your forearms are soft and free of tension. Tense arms, especially the forearms, are often the cause of a blocked stroke. Here are four keys that can help you avoid the pitfalls of the first two prescriptions:

1. Focus on the chest staying still during the stroke.

2. Picture the Gary Player "tap" stroke.

3. Stay connected with the left side on the forward stroke.

4. Find a spot in front of the ball for your visual fixation focus.

Avoid Opening the Putterface on the Backstroke and an Out-to-In Stroke Path

It is common to see the putterface being open to the path during the backstroke. Use the Trunk Rotation drill (see Section Three) in your pre-putt routine or practice the Ball-in-the-Wrist drill (see Section Six) to emphasize the big muscles and not the hands in the stroke. Also, use the Putting Template (see Appendix B) to keep the face perpendicular to the path on the backstroke, with the path arcing to the inside.

An out-to-in stroke path is often from your shoulders being open at address. This is often a same-side-dominant affliction. Your shoulders are open because your back eye desires a better view of the target line and your head pulls your body open. This situation can also be from your feet being square to the target or from your face being angled and not square to the ground. Opening your stance and having your face positioned parallel to the ground can help alleviate this problem.

If you have your shoulders open, your stroke path tends to follow the shoulder line. This position hinders the proper release of the putterhead. This out-to-in stroke path signals your subconscious mind to open the putterface or the putt will be pulled. It would mimic the

Check your address position in a mirror. Even though you are familiar with the points in the Setup section, it will pay dividends to frequently check your setup position.
Can you see your back forearm when you look back into the mirror? If not, there is a good chance your shoulders are open. Place a mirror on the floor to check your shoulder line. It is important to get your shoulders as square as possible. Compare what your shoulders look like now to what is recommended in the following drill.

opening of the clubface if you took an out-to-in swing, like when you are trying to hit a high flop shot with the intention of swinging the club well inside on the finish.

If your shoulders are a little off line, stand erect and attempt to square your body to the target line with your putter held near waist height. This should promote squaring the body to the target line. Now, bend from your hips toward the mirror on the floor. Do your shoulders now look square? If so, then I would recommend using this as part of your pre-putt routine.

When looking back into a mirror, if your front forearm is not higher than your back forearm, square your shoulders and if necessary, tuck your back elbow closer to your body and place your back hand in a stronger grip. The back shoulder should be lower than the front shoulder with the standard grip.

If your shoulders still have a propensity to be open at address, you may need to position the ball farther back in your stance, or it may be time to attempt a cross-handed grip. There have been a number of players whose stroke shape has taken on a much more ideal path when they adopted a cross-handed setup.

If changing your grip in such a major way is too uncomfortable, at least adopt it for your setup. Then, carefully slide your hands into a regular grip, being mindful to not change your shoulder position. PGA Tour veteran Bob Estes has successfully used this technique.

In addition, your eyes may perceive the target line better if you open or flare your front foot to the left. This is helpful if you are same-side-dominant. Another way to help get your front side in the proper place is to tilt your back side lower at address.

Importantly, the proper setup gives you a much better chance to achieve the in-to-square-to-in stroke path that the elite putters implement as their natural stroke path.

If you finish with your putter well inside the target line on a mid- to-short-range putt, it may be caused by having your shoulders open at address, or it can also be the result of the front shoulder not resisting the back shoulder, causing your chest to be facing the target at the finish.

This overturn can also produce an opening of the putterface much like a cut shot out of a bunker. Use your front side to resist the overturn so your shoulders are only slightly open at the finish, even on the longer putts.

Some putters are marked to help the player get the ball centered with the sweet spot of the putter.

For those of you with problems making short putts in general, make sure your stroke is short and compact. Avoid too long a stroke for putts inside of 4 feet. Overall, your backstroke length should not be any longer than the length of your putterhead—about 4 to 5 inches. The same applies to your forward stroke.

One student, an LPGA Tour player, on her initial visit, made six straight putts from 7 feet during a practice session. Her stroke looked quite efficient. I asked her what was her primary reason for coming to see me, because it didn't appear that she was having trouble inside 10 feet. She said, "I have my problems with breaking putts inside three to four feet."

So I set her up to hit a short, breaking putt. She missed three straight putts. I could tell she was frustrated that she tended to miss short putts while she was able to make longer ones. I filmed her strokes and proceeded to show her that her stroke length was as long for the short putts as it was for the 7-footers. This was especially true for her finish position.

I asked her to shorten her stroke length on the back and forward strokes to no more than 4 to 5 inches. She then made the next six putts. I told her the excessive length had resulted in several problems, including deceleration, too long a time for the stroke to be completed, which increased the likelihood that something would go wrong—including thinking too much—and a tendency to block with her chase finish.

I suggested that during practice and when on the course, she picture keeping her putterhead as low as possible at the finish of her stroke. This helped her visualize the proper release position, rather than having the putter shaft pointing at the hole.

Try Some Other Cures

The Fault: Toe hits

The Fix: Address the ball on the center of the putter and not on the toe. Maintain better balance at address to avoid falling back on your heels on the forward stroke. Stand closer to the ball rather than too far from it. Try a longer putter. Try a flatter lie angle (68 degrees is Tour average) instead of one too upright (72 degrees is standard).

Ball on toe at address can promote pushed putts.

The Fault: An out-to-in stroke path or loop to the backstroke as well as attempting to get the putterface to finish square to the target for too long after impact

The Fix: Let the putter swing on its natural arc as it goes back with a body rotation—not a rock—with your big muscles and avoid your arms disconnecting from your body. Aside from the equipment recommendations in the first fix, check your setup position or try a face-balanced or heel-shafted putter.

The Fault: Still pushing putts?

The Fix: Make sure the ball isn't too far back in your stance—a tendency if you are same-side-eye-dominant—which does not allow you to get the face square but remains open at impact. Additionally, changing to a face-balanced putter can minimize the putterface from opening on the backstroke.

KNOWING WHERE TO LOOK, WHAT TO LOOK FOR, AND HOW TO LOOK

For the first time in Ryder Cup history, the European team captured three matches in a row: 2002, 2004, and 2006. There is no shortage of opinions on the reasons for their dominance over the U.S. team, winning five of the last six times. Reasons given include their camaraderie, their wish to prove they're every bit as good as the Americans, and their better team play. But I believe there is no reason more significant than their preparation.

I am referring primarily to how they go about dissecting the slopes and the grain on the greens—the Europeans' ability to better commit to their reads than the Americans. Christy O'Conner Jr., when interviewed during the thirty-sixth Ryder Cup at the K Club outside of Dublin, Ireland, in 2006, hit the nail on the head when he stated why he felt the Europeans were ahead during day two: "They know the course better."

Christy went on to prove his point, saying that "everyone in Ireland knows that the eighteenth green is the fastest green in Ireland and that was why the J. J. Henry and Stewart Cink team three-putted." Their match ended in a draw instead of a win. In short, the locals knew the green, but the Americans did not. U.S. captain Tom Lehman called the Europeans' play around the greens "magical."

Yes, they had played the K Club, which is a host course on the European Tour. But why did the Europeans out-putt us at Oakland Hills, outside of Detroit, in 2004? I believe they were more prepared, by getting to know the greens through information sharing, than the Americans. They had many fewer misreads than the U.S. side during the matches, and the same was true in Ireland! That was the "magic" that the European team displayed—nothing more, nothing less.

By far the number-one reason good players miss putts is misreads. Almost every putt has some break in it. In addition, there is no single factor more important than committing to your reads. To fully commit, you must be able to trust your reads. Often, those who do not commit are not as good green readers as those who commit more often to their reads. The exception is the "thinker" who tends to overthink his reads among other things and doesn't go with what he sees as often as he should. So how do you get to that point? Let us take a look at how to be better prepared to play the round, and better prepared to stroke the putt. It all comes down to knowing where to look, what to look for, and how to look.

Prescriptions for Better Putting

1. People need people: ask the right questions
2. Making it simple with the 90 percent rule
3. Where to look: a matter of perspective
4. Tunnel vision and knowing how to look
5. Knowing where to look and what to look for
6. The scientific approach: mapping your territory
7. Charting your putts
8. Your most important piece of equipment
9. Plumb-bobbing is not a scientific method
10. A basic guide and review

People Need People: Ask the Right Questions

If I were to ask you about the greens on your course, could you detail each green's characteristics? Could you say how many greens slope back to front, for example?

Years of experience have shown me that few sports participants use their visual system to an advantage. Golf perfectly proves this point. Too often golfers go "blind" out on the course. By that I mean they are looking without seeing. How many rounds does it take for you to appreciate the nuances of the golf course? For the average player, the answer is more like never. They just do not see enough.

The Tour elite often have improved scores on the weekend. I believe they have a better idea of the greens' slopes. Well, I should say most greens. Not even the Tour players see all the course nuances in the week of play. So, here is my question for them and for you: Could you learn more by asking questions of those in the know? This means asking the most knowledgeable, the head golf professional. It could be worth a few strokes if you were told, for example, to pay attention to where the clubhouse is, as most everything on the greens breaks away from it.

At The Palms in La Quinta, California, players had better know where the nearby Salton Sea is. The Salton Sea is some 200-plus feet below sea level. Putts tend to break in its direction with few exceptions.

Additionally, when a putt is heading toward the Salton Sea, it tends to be faster than you would expect, as the slope is more downhill than it appears. The ninth hole is a good example of this. The eighteenth green illustrates the reverse, as it slopes away from the sea, so a downhill putt will be slower than you might expect. There are always exceptions, with greens that break the other way or portions of the greens that are exceptions. Another exception at The Palms is that the far side of most greens—the farthest green portion away from the sea—tends to break toward the closest edge. That is a typical design for drainage.

The Putt Doctor's

DIAGNOSTIC TEST

What hints could you give someone playing your course for the first time?

Could you make up a "Green or Course Guidebook" for all the greens on the course where you usually play? If not, it may be time to reassess what you are seeing and perceiving when you get on the course. At the very least, arrange for a playing lesson with your PGA professional and learn from his or her eyes as a start to your green-reading book.

Here are points to know about the greens at your course that you might include in your guidebook (see the test above):

- Know the type of grass, meaning, is there grain (Bermuda) or minimal grain (bent)?

- If the grass is of a Bermuda-type grain, look around the hole's edges for wear areas (showing where the ball wants to go), or to see grain growing into or away from the hole.

- If your greens are Poa annua, they will tend to be slower in the afternoon than in the morning.

- Most greens break more toward the front. When the hole is near the edge, the break is often toward that edge.

- Pay attention to the high points near the greens, as many architects slope the greens away from the high point.

- Know what holes tend to break toward the fairway and what holes break from front to back. Ask the golf professional!

- Are the greens soft or hard? This can affect your targeting the landing area for your chips and pitches.

There can be no better shortcut than local knowledge. As an example, you ask at the clubhouse and are told that you will be playing on Bermuda-strain greens, and that they will "break toward the reservoir, the lowest point in the area." Even if you are told the reservoir is on the far north side of the course, once on the course it can be difficult to find a reference point. Many courses do not have nearby mountains or easily seen high points. Have the local professional draw an arrow on the card to show where the terrain slopes. If possible, use a scorecard map.

If local knowledge says you must factor grain, such as the Bermuda greens, in warmer climates in the South, the grain will grow toward the drainage area of the green. If the slope is mild, the grain tends to grow toward the setting sun. Increase your visual awareness. I recommend that during rounds on your home course you act as if you had previously never stepped on the green. Survey with your eyes as if you are going to make a map—which you should do! At least, make mental or written notes, such as after you putt, if the green appears faster or slower than it looks.

Making It Simple with the 90 Percent Rule

I run into a number of students I call *visually challenged*, for whom the act of green reading is almost futile. They just cannot appreciate the subtle to mild slopes. The slope would have to be significant—make that severe—for these players to see it, and even then they do not come close to borrowing enough break for the putt.

If you are visually challenged, what can you do to improve your performance on the green? Having a good caddie who reads putts for you never hurts. Of course, making a map of the greens could be of immense help, but you may think this is a lot of trouble. Maybe the 90 Percent Rule applies?

I used to make clinic attendees wait to hear the entire lecture on green reading before I talked about the 90 Percent Rule. After getting a number of blank stares for most of the lecture, I realized that I needed to cut to the chase for these visually challenged players.

What is the 90 Percent Rule? Ninety percent of greens slope toward the fairway. This means that a majority of your putts will eventually turn toward the green's front as the ball slows in speed. This is true of many of the old-style courses. These courses were

> ### The Putt Doctor's
> ### DIAGNOSTIC TEST
>
> Take a moment to recall the greens on the course you play the most. How many greens on your course slope toward the fairway? How many slope away? How many slope predominantly to the left or right? This should prompt you to make notes—on paper and not in your head—on the prevailing slopes. Refer to your notes when on the course in order to make your job on the greens a bit easier.

built to better receive the shots into the greens. At The Palms, built in 1999, all of the greens but one slope from back to front. The designer, Freddie Couples, is a traditionalist.

I was a guest instructor of head golf professional Rick Vershure at Quaker Ridge Country Club in the New York City metropolitan area. I asked his students if the 90 Percent Rule applied to their course. After some reflection the clinic attendees eventually realized that seventeen greens fit the bill. One green sloped mostly from right to left. For several in the audience, the light went on. Now, they had a way to figure out which way to play the break, possibly for the first time since playing the course.

Where to Look: A Matter of Perspective

The player is reading the break by looking at the green's slope from well beyond the hole—a very effective technique.

You no doubt have seen a difference between your reads from behind the ball and from behind the hole. This has to do with the eyes of the beholder better appreciating differences from one position than from another. Some of this difference can be attributed to areas of *visual interference* that can be found between the ball and the hole. Swales or dips that catch your eyes, but are not necessarily in the immediate vicinity, can also incorrectly influence your perspective. Overall, most players will get it correct from one position rather than the other. For me, it is behind the hole. For others, it is behind the ball.

It is important to isolate the last few feet in front of the hole when reading the green. This is where the ball's speed is decelerating and the slope will have the most influence. This relates to what is called the 75–25 Rule. That is, 75 percent of the break will occur during the last 25 percent of the ball's roll.

I call the last few feet near the hole the "critical zone." The main exception to the 75–25 Rule can be a moderate or steep downhill putt where you must pay attention to most of the slope, since the ball will not be struck hard enough to counter the slope near the ball.

Which side do you read the best from—behind the ball or behind the hole? Do you see it better standing or squatting? Closer or farther from the ball or hole? Perhaps you have discovered that you read downhill putts better from behind the hole, but you read all the rest better from behind the ball.

The most important point becomes: which is the terrain's high side that will tilt the ball toward the low side? You may discover that looking from behind the ball helps you better perceive the slope a few feet in front of the hole. You may see the slope near the ball best from behind the hole, which would be important for downhill putts. Yes, it takes time and patience to discover your best read position!

The Putt Doctor's
DIAGNOSTIC TEST

Read the slope on several putts from behind the ball, and then from behind the hole. Write down your best guesstimate of what you see from each position—how much does it break, and which way does it break? Your notes should include your reads when standing *and* squatting at each position.

What do you see from the sides, somewhere between the ball and the hole? This is not the place to assess anything except to see if the putt is uphill, level, or downhill. There will be more on this perspective later in this section.

Next, putt the ball. If you were not sure you got the ball on line or your speed was off, stroke another putt or so. You could use a green-reading level (discussed in later prescriptions and in Appendix B) to obtain a scientific reading of the slope in front of the hole. In short, use the ball's roll or the level to show you the slope.

Look at your results. Did you read more putts accurately from behind the hole or behind the ball? Do you read better standing or squatting? How far back gives you better reads? Be mindful that you will never read all putts well, let alone all putts from one position. Do not be discouraged if some putts are just darn hard to see.

Remember that people differ in optical perspectives when looking for slopes that can affect the ball's roll. Be diligent as you work to discover your eyes' perceptual tendencies. Here is how I recommend determining your best read position.

There are three choices from each spot—standing, squatting, or getting down on your hands and knees with your eyes very close to the ground. Television first made the ground level a popular viewing spot.

Standing or squatting—which yields the best perspective for you?

Camilo Villegas gets close to the ground in his Spider-Man crouch.

Initially, do your reads on the practice green from both behind the ball and behind the hole. Do this within three or four steps of the hole and ball, then from six, seven, or more steps back. Visually challenged players tend to better appreciate the slopes from farther back, and this may include being off the green. How do you know what works the best for you? Stroke or roll a ball to the hole and note the break as well as which position gave you the best read.

I discovered over a period of time that I read a large majority of my putts better from behind the hole, and squatting instead of standing. I found that I see that putt better behind the ball only if faced with a moderate to steep uphill putt, as the low side was the ball's position. You too may tend to read more accurately from the low side, whether from behind the ball or behind the hole. With all other putts, including level putts, I read the putt better from behind the hole. Dave Stockton prefers reading only from behind the ball, while Nick Faldo reads best from behind the hole. Brad Faxon uses a read in the address position as his final read. Who is correct? All of them!

You can save a lot of time out on the course when you settle on your best read positions instead of looking from all angles. It also saves you one heck of a lot less confusion. Obviously, this takes time before arriving at your best position. I say "best," as no one I know reads *all* putts correctly.

Tunnel Vision and Knowing How to Look

Television can be a great learning tool. More swings, setups, and mannerisms are copied from this visual medium than one could imagine. Watching situations unfold when viewing only a part of the action can fool us. An example would be when viewers watch a player squatting behind the ball with his hands against the sides of his face acting as blinders. When the viewers see this posture, they may conclude that this is the best way pros read their putts. What the viewers often do not see is the player as he walks up to the green and checks his yardage book for notes made during practice rounds. They often don't see him viewing from off the green and as he reads from his best positions on the green.

Player viewing the green with his hands acting as blinders.

The player is already armed with all that prior information by the time he places his hands on the sides of his face. He is now narrowing his focus to the immediate section—the target line only. He is using tunnel vision to block out any peripheral distractions that he feels are a nonfactor. Often, he is just visualizing the ball's roll over the terrain and into the hole.

This discussion brings us to a key point in green reading. There is a way to take in the correct amount of space near the target line—you don't want to be too narrow in your look, but you don't want to take in too much. It is all about *how to look*.

The Putt Doctor's

DIAGNOSTIC TEST

How far does your vision expand when you are reading the green? Think about it. When you look at the hole, how far do you see on both sides of the hole? Is it a couple of feet on either side of the hole, close to the entire green, or somewhere in between?

If you say that it is often somewhat a narrow focus, seeing mostly just the cup and barely a foot on either side of the hole, you are in the majority. And in this case, that is not a good thing.

Open up and expand your view at least 3 to 6 feet on each side of the hole at a minimum.

The best green readers do not narrow their focus. The best readers actually look with a "soft" visual look, as we optometrists call it. This means the player opens up his field of view. To understand what I mean, consider what your eyes are taking in at this moment. You are reading, so you see words. Stop reading for a moment. Note how much of your peripheral vision you can now be aware of while looking at the period at the end of this sentence.

You will notice that this soft, expanded peripheral view takes in a large area to the left and right as well as above and below the book. You have gone from a fine focus to a *soft focus.*

When a certain Tour player came for a lesson, he told me that his ability to read greens was okay. Since I never leave that area alone with this caliber of player, I had him read nine putts. He misread six of nine! I asked him how much of an area he took in as he looked down the target line. "Mostly I look at the cup," he responded. That prompted a discussion of what I felt was the proper way to look.

When you expand your vision to take in more of the terrain, you are more capable of seeing *relative* slopes that yield a better perspective than with a narrow focus. This soft focus is what you are using when you see the terrain better from farther away, sometimes off the green. When this Tour player expanded his vision, he was able to see more of the terrain's perspective, including an area that he had deemed to be right-to-left but now saw correctly as left-to-right!

If you are a poor to medium-level green reader, try reading from off the green before ever stepping foot on it. See if this wide view is helpful to see the actual slope. Get directly behind and in line with the ball and the hole. Open up and soften your visual look. After you use your soft focus to note what could be influencing the slope your putt will travel down, you can then put up your blinders to picture the ball's intended path.

Knowing Where to Look and What to Look For

To better your green-reading skills, you must pay attention to a few basics. Knowing where to look and what to look for are as important as how to look. I observe too many players looking from points on the green that only confuse them. This confusion is because their visual perspective results in what I call *optical delusion*. Optical delusion is created when you are positioned in the wrong place to assess the slope. Are you guilty of this? Also, do you tend to read from just one place?

Too many players either ignore the read from a position between the ball and the hole, or use it for all the wrong reasons. Many golfers are not sure what to do from the side position and often misuse this position, using it to help determine how much the putt is breaking to the left or to the right. The better putters are in tune with this position, and they spend time wisely here.

"I go here to make sure the putt is breaking to the right," was the comment from one Tour player who went below the hole. This position was off line between the ball and the hole—the low side is in the direction where he believed the putt was to break. This was after already reading it from behind the hole. I disagree with that perspective.

A look from the side cannot tell you which way the ball is breaking. It only produces the optical delusion I just mentioned. By looking at the hole from the side, the player will always be fooled into believing the hole tilts toward him.

You can check this out for yourself. Look from the side of your target line on almost any putt—the hole appears to slope toward you. When you go to the opposite side, the hole appears to again slope toward you. Optical delusion is at work. This is parallel to looking out at an ocean

The Putt Doctor's

DIAGNOSTIC TEST

Take a moment to recall your last few putts. When you read the putts, were you more concerned with the left-to-right break and spent little time if any looking at the uphill or downhill factor from a different point of view? Is this typical for you? All putts of any distance should encompass two read positions instead of one.

Your next question: When you stand in a position to appraise the slope from the ball to the hole—from the side between the ball and the hole—do you also use this to note if the slope agrees with what you saw from behind the ball or behind the hole? In other words, are you confirming from the side view if the putt broke left or right? If so, you could be fooled by optical delusion.

Viewing the slope from the ball to the hole.

or large body of water. The water nearest the horizon always appears higher.

In the situation pictured here, the player is in position for two observations. The first entails making a decision about the uphill, downhill, or level slope from the ball to the hole. In short, is the area the ball rests on higher than the hole, or vice versa?

The second observation, which is derived from the first observation, is to form a mind's-eye picture of the ball's roll. Visualization of the ball's speed as it goes over the terrain to the hole is a valuable tool for the all-important speed of the putt. I believe this is the best position for you to visualize the speed necessary for the putt. (See Section Nine for more on this subject.) After all, isn't this where you see the ball roll for other players' putts? When you stroke putts, your head and eyes should be anchored until well after the ball leaves your putterface, so you do not see the ball's entire roll.

I prefer you to be positioned halfway between the ball and the hole to best appreciate the terrain. Do you see the terrain better by standing, squatting, or getting your eyes very close to the ground? I also recommend you move farther away from the ball and the hole for a softer look if you are challenged in judging the slope.

The low side is percentage-wise the most popular place for the majority to read the uphill or downhill slope. If a putt is deemed to be breaking left to right, the low side would be on the right side—where the terrain is going to take the putt. Use this side for visualizing as well. How do you know which is correct? Either ask a player whose eyes you trust, or place a green-reading level on the surface, as discussed in the following prescriptions. I also encourage you to walk next to the path from ball to hole and try to feel the slope with your feet. This can aid the visually challenged.

PRESCRIPTION NO. 6

The Scientific Approach: Mapping Your Territory

When conducting private lessons, I spend a lot of time on green reading, including going on the course. Many players are untrained in the skill of *visual discrimination*, so I describe how to detail the greens like the Tour players. How do you develop your visual discrimination skills? You can improve upon this skill with some simple drills.

Using a scientific approach.

The Putt Doctor's DIAGNOSTIC TEST

Do you have a detailed map of your greens? Have you plotted the areas of greens that are difficult to read and recorded the information for future reference? Probably not!

How would you go about it? Take the first green at a course you often play. Pretend you have never stepped foot on the property and you are about to play the course. What would you place on the green map that could give you some local knowledge?

Is there anything you can put on the map of the second green that isn't readily seen, such as local knowledge that this green slopes subtly from the front to the back, as opposed to the other greens on the course? If so, place an arrow on the map to point where the local knowledge influence will take putts. These points should assist you when making your map.

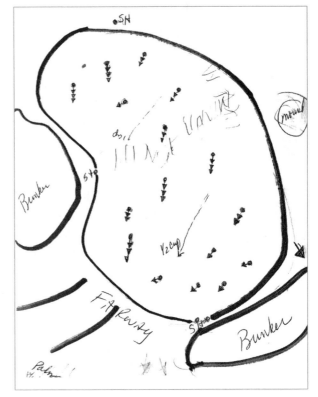

You can map the greens.

If your map omits the particulars near the green, it can be difficult to orient yourself to the arrows and where they and you are positioned on the green.

Approach the green as if you were a course architect. Start by drawing the outline of its overall shape. Add details around the green such as sprinkler heads, bunkers, and the like. When I am at a tournament mapping for players, I do this on day one of practice. The next day, I place a green-reading level down in several spots and draw arrows on the map corresponding to the location of the level on the green.

In the previous example, an arrow pointing toward the front of the green would mean the bubble in the green-reading level representing the high point of that spot would be oriented toward the back of the green. The center of the level would be between the bubble and the front of the green. The position the arrow would point is by running a line from the bubble's center toward the middle circle of the level. This would represent the high point to the low point.

When putting to a cup in that area, I know the ball will eventually roll toward the low side—away from the back of the green and toward the front of the green—as the ball slows.

In the illustration, I use arrows on the map to correspond to where I place levels on different parts of the green. The arrows always point down the fall line, that is, from the high point—the bubble—to the low point—the center of the level. One arrow represents a mild, gentle slope; two arrows would mean a more moderate slope; and three arrows would represent a severe slope.

A mild slope is where the bubble's center is not outside the inner circle on the green-reading level. This generally means the break would be minimal, maybe a half a cup to a cup. An uphill putt would tend to break less, so you may aim at the right edge, or if it is a slick downhill putt, you may need to play the break for a cup or so outside the hole. This is also based on your speed preference. If you are using the Exelys Breakmaster green-reading digital device, a mild slope would register below a 1.0 on the digital reading.

A moderate slope would be when the bubble's center would be between the first and second ring. The Exelys would register between a 1.0 and a 1.5. This would be a two-arrow representation as seen in the illustration. Three arrows represent a severe slope and would be indicated when the bubble's center is at or beyond the second ring.

This could relate to a break that could be a foot or more from a shorter distance and a flagstick from a longer distance from the hole. Science and art meet here, depending on your speed desired and if the putt is level, or has an uphill or downhill slope to factor in.

Now, you should start to appreciate what a Tour player is looking at when he pulls his yardage book from his pocket as he approaches the green. He is looking at what he has marked for the green's tendencies in the area of the hole's location.

In all the years of my clinics, only one person has raised a hand to the question, "Do you map the greens?" She was a player at Tartan Fields in Dublin, Ohio. Arlene stated she not only mapped the greens of the two courses she belonged to, but she mapped the greens of every course on which she played a tournament. By the way, at the time, Arlene had won thirty-eight international senior amateur tournaments in a row and was still counting. Arlene has also won one hundred tournaments internationally.

Bob Estes on the PGA Tour draws hash lines to represent the ball's roll as well as making notations as to the amount of break in his yardage book. Bob would show the amount of break by designations such as 2" (inches) or 1½' (feet), 2c (cups), 1b (one ball), and so on at the end of the ball's roll. Ideally, map the green when the conditions—the green speed—are more representative of the conditions of the tourney.

I believe mapping your greens is far better than attempting to remember detail, especially when you are under pressure. I am sure you can recollect staring down a putt in the club championship and wondering why you could not remember ever having this putt before. Stress can make you go *blind*, so to speak.

The AimChart.

This approach can help instill confidence to commit to your read. Of course, you will still rely on subjectivity in the long run because of several variables, including green speed, your ideal ball speed, and the putt you are facing is not exactly like the putt you mapped. Now you are bringing in art with the science.

Mark Sweeny has created the AimChart. He is also the inventor of the Aimpoint Line used by the Golf Channel for their telecasts of Tour events. This chart will help you fine-tune your reads (see Appendix B).

After you have introduced science to detecting the slope, you must now incorporate the art of green reading. This becomes the art of interpreting the speed and the line from the scientific measurements.

As an example, your ball lands above and to the right of the cup. Your green map shows that the green breaks from right to left in that area. You think maybe aiming at the right edge is in order. But since it is downhill and the greens are definitely faster than they were on the day you drew the map, you decide to borrow more. You imagine how hard the ball needs to be hit so that you do not leave yourself too long a comeback putt. The final aim becomes a hole out to the right. You picture the ball's entire roll in your mind's eye, and now you hit your putt with that picture in mind.

Charting Your Putts

Many players need to better learn from their experiences. To me, it appears that many players are cavalier when it comes to making their experience a true learning process. When I ask players how many missed putts were from under-reads in their last round, it is as if I have asked them to explain Einstein's Theory of Relativity. Blank stares abound.

For the most part, you know the basics. You are aware that downhill putts tend to break more than uphill putts and slow greens break less than fast greens. Applying the basics may be another story. Is this relevant to you? In the following diagnostic test, recall the last round you played. If this is difficult, then pay attention to the next round and jot down your results as you walk from each green to the next tee.

If you have been under-reading downhill putts, are you making adjustments the next day? Are your misses more from not appreciating and applying local knowledge? If you are truly learning from your experience, you are making intelligent adjustments daily during each round. This is what self-coaching is all about.

Annika Sörenstam, after each round, charts her putts on her computer. She wants to know what she did wrong that day, and how to alter

Start with the first green. Was your putt over-read or under-read, or was it a good read? Also note if it was uphill, downhill, or level. Repeat this for the second green, and so on. Recall how many putts you missed on the high side—over-reads—and how many you missed on the low side. Go ahead, jot down how many putts were under- and over-read. Also note whether they were uphill or downhill. Now, look at the results. Is there a pattern? Are you over-reading uphill, under-reading downhill, and so on? If you are over-reading your downhill putts, I would surmise that you are playing too much break, forcing you to die your ball in the hole with perfect speed. Good luck hitting putts with perfect speed under pressure! This topic will be discussed in detail in the next section.

it through practice or better thinking the next day. Below is an example of what she typically places on her computer, with a little extra added for even more help in maximizing your experience.

18-2 // L-R // U // OR // F // BS

The notation "18-2" connotes the length of the putt and that it was a two-putt. A "3" would mean a three-putt, and just an "18" would mean a one-putt. An "18-0" would be a chip-in. "L-R" is the break, meaning a left-to-right break, "R-L" would be the opposite, and an "L" would mean the putt was fairly level.

"U" is an uphill putt. A level putt is an "L," a downhill putt a "D." "OR" connotes over-read, which means the putt broke less than expected. "UR" means the putt was under-read and it broke more than expected.

"F" means the putt was faster than expected—a mis-read. The slope was more downhill than you surmised. An "S" relates to the opposite occurrence, where the green was slower than you expected and the ball didn't make it to the hole because you misread it.

"BS" is a bad stroke, meaning you either did not hit it as you desired, either on the toe or heel, or the ball exploded off the putter or came off weakly—possibly due to tension. This is important to note so you can focus on this in practice, especially if it is a specific situation such as a left-to-right, downhill putt.

If you use these notes, I want you to categorize this information into a percentage of putts you make in the 4- to 6-foot range, the 7- to 10-foot range, and the 11- to 15-foot range. Another category to keep track of is the number of over- and under-reads and if they are uphill or downhill. Similarly, do you mis-hit putts that are more left-to-right, or longer putts, and so on? Whatever way you prefer to categorize the putts, it is important that you do two things.

First, spend time off the course seeing yourself make the putts, in your mind's eye, that you know you should have made. See yourself make the correct decision, commit to the read, and execute the stroke properly. It is important to see the ball go in the hole.

Second, make notes for the next day on what you need to focus on in order to change your results to a positive outcome. If you are guilty of under-reading downhill putts, certainly adding to your amount of read for these putts for the next round would be in order. Reference your notes often out on the course.

Your Most Important Piece of Equipment

I conducted a study for *Golf Digest* a few years ago regarding the use of sunglasses for protection and comfort. The study was to determine any differences in the player's ability to see or read greens with sunglasses, for either better or worse. The report was revealing for both the eye doctor community and for golfers.

After all, the most important part of your equipment to play the game is your eyes. Despite this fact, unfortunately, most golfers do not wear eye protection against the harmful ultraviolet (UV) rays from the sun. A recent survey of PGA Tour players showed that a majority do not wear eye protection. Yet they are in the sun most days for long periods of time. Some of the stated reasons for not wearing sunglasses were what I would label as excuses accompanied by a lack of investigating the latest in technology. You can bet they don't overlook technology when it comes to their clubs!

The *Golf Digest* study revealed that certain tints, gray in particular, and darker tints were counterproductive to play and especially to reading the subtleties of the greens. This was in stark contrast to what eye professionals have recommended to our patients. We all have recommended darker lenses to relax the eyes. And gray has been the color of choice, as the colors in the environment remain the same through gray-tinted lenses.

Many players who owned gray lenses kept them in their golf bag or had them sitting on their cap. A majority of the players noted that the darker gray lenses tended to flatten the terrain. They would often say that they could not hit shots or putt with the glasses on. The reasons ranged from not being able to see as clearly, the ground appeared to curve, or they just didn't like having them on, as they never wore glasses before. They all were aware that they needed to protect their eyes, but they still kept their glasses off for golf. Most, if not all, of these complaints can now be overcome with the latest in technology.

Several years ago, I was introduced to "PEAKS performance eyewear" by the inventor, Paul Moore. I was immediately able to see a remarkable difference compared to the sunglasses I was wearing, and PeakVision eyewear has been on my face for every round since.

The Dual-Zone patented technology proved to meet the demands of the players in the *Golf Digest* study. The study showed that most players had to take standard gray lenses off to hit shots, as they did not see clearly through the gray lens when they looked toward the ground. The vast majority of players in this study and in my clinics preferred a lighter, yellow or amber-like color to help them better differentiate the subtleties of the slopes. But an all-amber lens does nothing to manage the sun's glare; in fact, it accentuates the bright sun. So PeakVision made the upper zone of their lens gray to effectively manage the glare from the sun and the lower half of their lens amber-tinted to transmit more visual information into the eyes when looking toward the turf.

Not only does the bottom amber portion of the PeakVision lens allow more light into the eyes as desired, but the color actually brings out the subtleties of the slopes on the green. Hence the label: "performance eyewear."

Because of the Dual-Zone lens design, the eyes fatigue much less than with a dark, solid-tint lens or no sunglasses at all! This is because the pupils of the eyes do not have to constantly adjust to different lighting conditions when focusing on the ground, then looking up into the sky. The PeakVision lenses do that for you!

If you are wondering if the lighter lens offers the same UV protection, the answer is a resounding *yes*! Since a 100-percent UV coating can even be clear, UV protection has nothing to do with the darkness of the lens, nor do the lenses have to be polarized to be UV protective.

Another plus is the quality of the optics. These lenses have the least amount of distortion of any plastic lens on the market, and because they are plastic, they are more protected against breaking. Also, PeakVision has the lightest-weight lenses on the market, yet they are *shatterproof*!

Take a peek at more on this fabulous product in Appendix B. Get up to speed with eye technology instead of just club and ball technology.

Note: In regard to reading the subtle slopes of the green, I should point out that a number of students come to me with soft contact lenses, which did not correct for their astigmatism. This left them with less than crisp vision in order to read the subtle breaks. If you are one of these people, make sure your optometrist fits you with soft, toric contact lenses. Technology has bridged the gap, which is good news for golfers.

The Putt Doctor's DIAGNOSTIC TEST

Take the "taste test," as I like to call it. Take any other sunglasses off the shelf of your pro shop, along with a pair of PeakVision sunglasses, and compare them as you stand next to the practice green. Note the differences in the terrain on the green, or even hit golf balls while wearing one, then the other type of sunglasses. You should see a distinctive difference, especially if the other brand is polarized, which is counterproductive to golf.

PRESCRIPTION NO. 9

Plumb-Bobbing Is Not a Scientific Method

Clinic attendees by the droves ask me why the plumb-bob technique of green reading does not work for them. Folks, this is not a scientific technique! Quite simply, the "plumb" has the player close his nondominant eye and hold the putter at arm's length in front of his dominant eye. The putter shaft becomes a measuring tool, as seen in the illustration on page 161. A true plumb would always show the hole and the ball being on the same line. If the player's head is moved slightly to the left or the right—which I believe the player does subconsciously to make the appearance the putt breaks—the hole will appear away from the putter shaft as seen in the diagram. This would depict the ball breaking from the puttershaft to the hole.

I am sure some of you are thinking that I am not doing the plumb-bob correctly. I have tried all the methods provided by colleagues and players and I still come to the same conclusion: it isn't scientific. After all, if it is such a great technique, then why isn't everybody using it and not even bothering with any other technique? The answer: it isn't what it is cracked up to be.

If you are not keen toward plumb-bobbing, be aware of how well you use your eyes to gather necessary information when on the course. When approaching a green from the fairway, look with meaning. Look for the subtleties that may have escaped you before. Turn on your eyes instead of turning them off. Reading greens with the aid of an expert green reader such as your PGA instructor can help you with the nuances of where to look, how to look, and what to look for. Do not go blind out there; use your eyes.

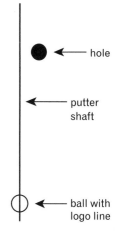

A view of the plumb from the player's perspective where the ball would break from the shaft toward the hole.

The Putt Doctor's
DIAGNOSTIC TEST

Take a look back at your last round of golf. For many greens did you appraise the terrain from off the green? Specifically, did you see if your putt was uphill, downhill, or level? Or did you mark the ball, and only read the putt when it was your turn? In essence, were you using your eyes to gather information at the correct time?

If the answer was not affirmative for many of the greens, make a note to remind yourself to look at each green as you walk up to it during your next round of golf. Look from a good position off the green to see if you notice whether the ball or the hole is higher, or if it is a level putt. If you approach the green directly in line with the hole and ball, what do you see with the terrain near the hole?

See if you can do this for all eighteen greens. I promise, if you fail to write down a reminder for reference, it will not take long before you reach your golf ball without much of a look, maybe while you're chatting with your buddies or are lost in thought. How many of the eighteen greens did you analyze from off the green? Score it. Do the test the next time you play as well.

A Basic Guide and Review

Green-Reading Basics

- Uphill putts generally break less than level or downhill putts.
- Downhill putts tend to break more than level or uphill putts.
- Slow greens are like uphill putts—they break less than fast greens.
- The last 3 to 6 feet of the putt are the most important—this is the *critical zone.*
- On a downhill putt, the last half of the putt or more can be important.
- Your last read should be a combination of factors: the putt's right or left break; if it is uphill, level, or downhill; and if the green is slow or fast.
- Chart your putts to know your tendencies.

Mapping the Green

- Draw a rough map of the outline of the green.
- Be specific concerning the location of sprinkler heads, green-side bunkers, and so on.
- Place a green-reading level on key areas where the pin may be placed; or
- Place the level on the subtle, hard-to-see slopes; or
- Draw arrows on your map showing the high point to the low point, representing the slopes on different areas of the green, or roll a ball and let the ball "read" the slope for you.
- Draw an arrow on your map that points toward the low point, and be specific about where it points in relation to outside reference points (sprinkler heads, etc.).
- Use one arrow for a mild, two for a moderate, and three for a severe slope.

Determining Your Best Read Position

- Place a ball down 5 to 15 feet from a hole.

- Look from beside the ball and hole to determine if it is a level, uphill, or downhill putt.

- Look from behind the ball, then from behind the hole, and make a note of what you see.

- Place the level down 3 or 4 feet from the hole—in the critical zone, and note the actual slope.

- Note where you best see the break. You may be farther back from the ball or hole, or in a squat versus an upright position. Repeat the above procedure for several putts around the practice green. See if there is a position that gives you at least 70 to 80 percent good reads.

- Some players have found that they read best from the low side— from a point looking up the slope.

SPEED CONTROL

Almost All Putts Must Factor This Element into the Equation

Speed is the predominant factor in determining your target line. Having the right speed translates to making more putts. Your practice sessions should be filled with speed drills. In fact, this section should be the primary focus of all golfers, regardless of their skill level.

Dr. Clyne Soley, a research chemist from Canada, compiled statistics from several amateur and professional venues in the 1970s. He discovered that for most players, the percentage of making putts longer than 11 feet was negligent, but that almost everybody made a high percentage of putts at 3 feet and less. He concluded that practice for most players should only be in the 4- to 11-foot range, with one exception.

Dr. Soley also said that practice should include techniques for long putts that will get the ball as close to the hole as possible. He found that the higher-handicap players, compared to the pros, were not getting the ball close enough on longer putts.

These stats are true for today's players, as ShotLink is now confirming. But speed control is not all about long putts. With almost every putt, whether you refer to it as touch, feel, speed, or energy, you must hit the ball with enough momentum from the putterface to get it to the hole without going significantly past it or leaving it short. That is the basic idea of speed control.

Problems often start with misperceptions of the actual distance. There are a number of students I refer to as "nonathletes in space." They look but they do not see. A putt could measure 30 feet but the player perceives it as 20 feet. I have heard a best guesstimate of "25 yards." Now, that is not even in the same zip code! To properly judge distances you must input accurate distances into your brain before you putt. In other words, walk off your putts to experience the distance and the terrain.

This section will discuss why the die-it-in-the-hole mentality is more of a myth today. It is often the thought process of those who distrust their aiming or their green-reading ability. This section will also help you develop a sound plan. Remember, good putters have a methodology to master the challenge of speed.

The player's visual system relays information such as grain, slope, and distance to the brain so it can calculate the energy the motor system must produce. Good athletes master this process quickly. With experience, almost any player can eventually acquire a reservoir of skill to meet the challenge of producing the necessary energy for any putting distance.

If you are constantly coming up short on your putts, you may want to change to a harder ball or a harder-surfaced putter, such as a Scotty Cameron Newport. Likewise, if you are hitting your putts too aggressively beyond the hole, a softer insert, such as the white insert on many Odyssey putters, can make a difference. Additionally, you may misperceive the distance as shorter than it actually is.

You have three primary choices for directing the speed of the putter into the ball:

1. A longer stroke length, back and through typical of the tempo of a stroker; or

2. A faster turn through the impact areas by the arms and body—more of a hit; or

3. A combination of altering both the turn and the speed of the turn.

The prescriptions in this section are labeled as to skill levels: beginner (B); intermediate (I), and advanced (A). These categories are based on a rating scale I have developed from years of teaching.

I've found that the chief faults of players not having good speed control for longer distances are related to technique. They include:

- Too short a backstroke (and too long a follow-through) for the distance
- Too much hands involvement, causing a breakdown at impact
- Too fast a transition, the result of the previous two faults
- An inefficient setup that includes poor balance
- A poor picture or assessment of the terrain for the stroke
- No overall plan to combat the challenge

The first two prescriptions are designed to help you determine your speed-control skill level. The third through the seventh prescriptions deal primarily with techniques to combat the above faults. (Be sure to reread the discussion on the wristy stroke in Section Five.) The remaining prescriptions are more advanced in nature, and when you believe you are ready for them, by all means jump in. Find the prescriptions that apply to your skill level and work to master the challenges they present. Remember, most of your time on the putting green should be spent with speed drills.

Prescriptions for Better Putting

1. Determining your skill level
2. Assessing your skill level with the 30–40–50–60 drill
3. Consistency of hit: developing feel
4. "This looks like a three-putt to me"
5. A technique to control the transition
6. More techniques for improving speed control
7. Eyes on the prize
8. The three-speed and cola-can drills
9. Making more putts
10. Visualization for speed control
11. Are you a good visualizer?

Determining Your Skill Level [B, I]

The following is a good barometer to test your skill with speed control. It is my favorite starting drill, and also is a favorite among a number of more skilled players who need to make more putts. This drill will make you aware that distance control relates to more than long putts. It is all about speed.

The Putt Doctor's

DIAGNOSTIC TEST

You will need three coins or markers, several tees, and three balls. Find a level surface for your putts. Place a tee down on the putting green as your starting point. Pace off 6 feet—two paces—from the tee. Place a coin on the green. Now place two more coins 18 inches (about two shoe lengths) behind the first coin, one to the left and one to the right of the first coin. The coins form an equilateral triangle, as seen below.

Putt each ball with a goal to stop all three of them within the targeted space of the coins. After each successful putt, move the ball outside the triangle of the three coins to signify it was successful.

When three putts in a row stop inside the coins, place another tee a foot back of the first tee (7 feet from the target) and again attempt to stop three balls within the three coins. Be sure to leave the 6-foot tee in place. You may have to return to this spot and start over if you miss any putt from a farther distance. Continue adding a foot, marking your progress with tees until you miss. Note your record and try it again.

Setup for the 6-foot, three-coin speed control drill.

In time, you should be able to be consistent enough to get to the fourth or fifth tee without a miss. When you are successful with this drill on a regular basis, you will find yourself starting to make more of those 6- to 10-footers.

If you have trouble with this drill, putt with your eyes closed a few times. This can help you experience feedback with your stroke's rhythm as well as working toward improving your visualization skills.

What speed control category are you: beginner, intermediate, or advanced? If you are able to progress into the 11- to 12-foot category relatively quickly in fifteen minutes, then you are in the advanced (A) level and you should focus on the "A" drills in this section. If you are able to get to the 9- to 10-foot distance in fifteen minutes, I would place you at the Intermediate (I) level of skill. The "I" drills are a good starting point for those who have streaks of greatness but still average a couple of three-putts per round.

If you have difficulty being consistent at the starting distance of 6 feet, and the 8-foot distance is impossible to move beyond in a couple of fifteen-minute sessions, then you are more apt to benefit from the beginning (B) drills in this section. Also, if you have more than three or four three-putts per round, the "B" drills are your starting point. See the next prescription for further clarification of your speed-control skill level.

During the putt, find which focus works the best for you to get a controlled and accurate speed. You may choose to look at the middle of the triangle as the distance reference to focus on during the putt. You may prefer a visualization of the intended speed of the ball into the cup as your focus. You could choose to focus on your stroke length, increasing it slightly if you find the surface is slower or reducing it if the green speed is faster than usual.

You may imagine that you are rolling the ball underhanded, with your dominant hand, to the hole. Feel the energy you would need to do that properly, and then execute the stroke with that picture. Make sure your grip, your arms, and your shoulders are soft and relaxed. Check your setup and implement your routine. (See Section Ten on focus tips and the routine.)

Be sure to write down your daily drills as well as your progress. Note meaningful feedback regarding your thought process and what was your feeling during the putt. Was it different than your typical feeling? To practice smart, you must maximize your experience.

It's best if you work a maximum of fifteen minutes or less per drill. Anything more can easily result in mindless repetition. Make this drill a regular part of your practice if you are in the beginner or intermediate category.

Assessing Your Skill Level with the 30–40–50–60 Drill [B, I, A]

The first prescription provided a speed-control diagnostic test to gauge your ability to obtain a consistent roll at a *shorter* range. Dr. Clyne Soley's study showed that the biggest difference between the higher-handicap player and the Tour professional is the Tour player's ability to get the ball much closer to the hole on *longer* putts.

Do you have problem distances? The following diagnostic test will yield a proficiency rating for another aspect of speed control—longer-length putts—and will potentially uncover problem distances. Determining your skill level with this test can help you choose which drills to practice.

The Putt Doctor's DIAGNOSTIC TEST Place a tee or a marker on the ground to represent the start point. Walk off a distance of 30 feet (ten paces) from the marker and position a green-repair tool or another easily identifiable marker as the target point. Walk off 10 more feet (three paces and a foot) and place another marker as the 40-foot target. Repeat for distances of 50 and 60 feet, placing a target for each distance. These targets should not be in line with each other.

Putt from the start point to the targets, starting with the 30-foot target and ending with the 60-foot target. Your objective is to have the ball stop at a point no more than 3 feet, or about a putter length, from your target (most putters are 32 to 35 inches long). If you are successful in stopping the ball within 3 feet of the target on the first putt, you have scored a *par*. If not, you must putt until you stop the ball within the desired 3-foot distance. Record the number of times it takes you to accomplish this. Repeat this for all the targets: the 40-, then the 50-, and finally the 60-foot target.

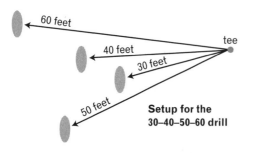

Setup for the
30–40–50–60 drill

Record your total score. Par for this test is four, meaning that every putt finished within 3 feet of its marker. The categories go like this: a score of 4 to 5 is advanced; 6 to 7 is good, an intermediate skill level. Higher scores qualify you as having a beginner skill level. If your score is above 12, see Prescription No. 3 that follows, and also see the recommendations to stop a wristy stroke in Section Five.

This test can also tell you what distances you need to work on in your practice. If you did not score a par on a particular distance, then it would behoove you to practice this distance until you become comfortable with it. When out on the course, always walk off the distance of the putt. Then reference and apply what you discovered through practice that produced a stroke to get the ball close to the hole at this range.

When you achieve the advanced category, mix up the distances. For example, reverse the order to 60–50–40–30 feet. Then on the next session, go 30–50–40–60. Record your score for the day. Repeat this drill often to gain better speed control. Work to lower your score until you are consistently below a score of 6. Then proceed to the intermediate drills. Make sure to revisit this drill often.

Another variation of this drill is to putt three balls to each target. Record your score. Par is three for every distance. This variation helps you eliminate the problem distances as well as improve your consistency of hit. A par on the entire course—all four targets—would be a twelve.

Controlled practice is a necessity to extract useful information that you can apply successfully on the course. For example, be aware of what works best for you—stroke length, tempo, and so on. Is it best to picture the target's distance in your mind's eye, or to picture the stroke length? There are a number of different techniques in this section to assist you. You may want to repeat this test using them.

One more item: Register how far a 30-, 40-, 50-, and 60-foot putt appears to you. Heighten your visual perception of each of these distances.

PRESCRIPTION NO. 3

Consistency of Hit: Developing Feel [B, I]

For developing better speed control, the most popular technique with my students and other players I have interacted with is to increase their stroke length for increasingly longer putts.

The following is another test of your speed-control skills that also serves as a drill. A consistent stroke yields great benefits day in and day out. Let's test your stroke consistency. You will need three golf balls and ten tees.

DIAGNOSTIC TEST

Find a level putting surface and place a coin on the ground to mark the starting spot. Next place a tee in the ground 4 inches behind the coin—a little short of putterface length (as most putterfaces are approximately 4½ inches long).

Next, place another tee 4 inches behind the first tee. Continue to do this until you have five tees, all in a row, one behind the other. The last tee will be 20 inches from the coin. Repeat for the forward side of the coin. (Or you can use the Scoring Line tape shown below—see Appendix B.)

Without hitting a ball, practice a stroke length that goes from the first tee on both sides of the coin. This will be a 4-inch backstroke and 4-inch forward stroke—equal back and through. Now putt the first ball, attempting to duplicate the stroke length you just practiced—4 inches back and 4 inches beyond the start point. After the ball stops, move it off the target line, but keep it at the same distance from the start point. Now stroke the second ball, and move it off the target line. Then stroke the third ball. Record how many feet each ball rolled from the start point.

You may repeat a putt if your backstroke was beyond 4 inches.

The Scoring Line tape can help build hitting consistency.

Your goal is to putt the balls to the same area with the same stroke length over and over. Soon you will be making more putts and rolling the ball closer to the hole on longer putts. Of course, there are plenty of gaps between these distances. So in time, you can refine your guide by using 4-, 6-, 8-, 10-, 12-, 14-, 16-, 18-, 20-, 22-, and 24-inch stroke lengths. This will help you with the distances you face on the course.

Now, let's put this into a practical situation. On the course, you (should always) walk off the distance of your putt. The putt is 40 feet. You then consult your stroke length guide from the above drill. Your stroke length for this putt needs to be 20 inches back and through. You practice the stroke length, recalling your previous practices. Ideally, include a positive visualization of the ball's roll as part of your pre-putt routine.

You address the ball, take one or two looks at your target, then putt using the stroke length you just practiced as a mind's-eye focus during your stroke.

Do not place too much emphasis on the follow-through at first, even though ideally, equal back and through is a goal, especially for the chaser stroke.

How far did the balls roll? Walk off the distances. Add up the distances and divide by three. That gives you the average distance. Ideally the three balls should have rolled approximately 3 feet, or one pace each.

If the balls rolled much more than 4 feet, or if the three balls are a foot or more away from one another, more than likely your hands are too involved in the stroke. If the balls rolled just a foot or two, your stroke probably is decelerating into the ball.

Your goal is to stop the three balls within 4 inches of one another. Keep at it until three in a row stop within 4 inches of one another and they all roll approximately 3 feet. Now you are efficient with your stroke.

Repeat with the other backstroke lengths: 8 inches, 12 inches, 16 inches, and 20 inches. Record your results. In each situation the three balls should stop within the backstroke distance from one another. With a 12-inch backstroke, for example, the three balls should stop within 12 inches of one another. Keep at each stroke length until you are consistent. By using your big muscles for the stroke, you will be able to more quickly obtain consistency in your hits.

Be sure to write down your stroke lengths for different distances. Your notes should look close to like this: 4" = 3.5 (feet); 8" = 11 (feet); 12" = 20 (feet); 16" = 32 (feet); 20" = 41 (feet.) This will become your guide when you are on the golf course.

Some situations require a little adjustment to your preparation. For instance, you walk off the distance and find it is an uphill putt of 20 feet. You may want to add to the overall length of the actual distance to compensate for the slope, and this would require a slightly longer stroke length than you would take for a level 20-footer.

A long-standing recommendation is to increase the width of your stance as the length of the putt increases, using your feet as a visual guide. For instance, the middle of your back foot would be farther from the ball for an 18-inch backstroke than it would be for a 12-inch backstroke.

If you experience problems with this drill after a few sessions, focus on the six keys to a consistent stroke: correct equipment, proper aim, proper setup, efficient mechanics, center impact, and consistent energy into the ball.

As will be discussed in this section, a consistent hit includes the ability to make center contact on the ball with the center of the putter-face. If you feel you hit a lot of putts off the toe or the heel, a change in ball position or putter length or lie may help. It can also be helpful to fine-tune your visual focus during the putt. (See Section Ten for more on focus.)

PRESCRIPTION NO. 4

"This Looks Like a Three-Putt to Me!" [B, I]

In clinics, I ask players, at what length of putt do they start to get a negative thought concerning their ability to get down in two? Face it: There is a distance where players start to worry about three-putting. Whether it is a long distance or any sort of elevation from the ball to the hole, anxiety can set in.

If speed control is your problem, where you often have two or more three-putts a round, then you may find your mind racing when you face a long putt, instead of starting with a plan of action. Do you have a proper plan of action for when you are faced with a difficult putt?

Confidence in your distance putting comes from success, and success starts with a good plan. The following discussion will either serve to confirm that you have a correct plan, or hopefully will start you off in the right direction toward mastering speed at any distance.

You need to adopt what I call a visual-mental plan of action (VPA).

The VPA in this section began with the first prescription drill. You categorized the skill level of your speed control. Was it beginner, advanced, or intermediate? Seek out the correct drills for your skill level.

The next step in your VPA is to experience the speed of the ball's roll with different situations. Practice 40-, 50-, and 60-footers. You may not need a new technique for longer distances, just some experience with them.

Is there a green on your course where you always have difficulty avoiding a three-putt? You should take

The Putt Doctor's

DIAGNOSTIC TEST

Now I'm asking you, what is the distance or the slope of the putt that starts to make you a little anxious about a possible three-putt? Is it anything beyond 30 feet—about ten paces? Maybe it is more like 50 feet? Is it a slick, downhill putt or a dreaded upslope near the hole? Maybe there is a green on your course that drives you nuts.

the time to go out early or late in the day and practice specific difficult putts on that green. Place a tee down to represent different hole locations. Walk off the distance of various putts from different positions. You will become more comfortable by doing purposeful practice. Using the tips and techniques in this section will help you replace fear with a better comfort level. It should be a part of your VPA!

I sometimes observe players *eyeballing* the target—just looking at the hole while standing behind or beside the ball. They subconsciously use the size of the cup to assess the distance. I believe this does not give the brain enough information. Eyeballing the target allows misperceptions of the true distance to take over. By this I mean that if you are like the majority of golfers, you perceive the distance as shorter than it really is. To see if you fit into this category, try this exercise. Hold a string up against your nose and tie the other end to a doorknob or leg of a chair. It is best if the string is approximately 12 to 15 feet long.

When you look down at the far point of attachment of the string, you will see two strings, as they represent the visual axis of your right and left eyes. This is what you should perceive. If the strings cross in front of where it is attached by a few feet, or the strings cross at or near the halfway point, your tendency is to see distance targets as shorter than they are in reality. This is quite common. The crossing of the strings shows you where you are actually pointing your eyes. Now, instead of eyeballing the far point, start at your nose and slowly "walk" your eyes down the string. You should see the strings crossing where you are looking, and when you arrive at the far end, do not be surprised if the strings now cross much nearer the end instead of halfway to the end.

Especially if you misperceive targets as closer than they really are (as seen from the above test or from your experience), another part of your VPA should be to have your eyes "walk" the distance down the target line from the ball to the hole. This is opposed to only eyeballing the target. Also imagine the ball's roll with your mind's eye. To do this well, you must make an accurate assessment of the slope, the grain, and so on and call on the experience you gained through practice and play for feedback.

If picturing putts is foreign to you, it would help to stand off to the side of the putting green when other players putt and focus on the ball's roll. Here, you can take in the entire roll until the ball stops. This is an excellent visualization position, so use it often.

Another part of your VPA is to make note of what you are doing. This incorporates both your pre-putt strategy as well as what technique you are implementing. Try to be mindful of what you were thinking during the putts that yielded successful results. As you read other prescriptions in this section, you will no doubt be able to add to your pre-putt plan of action.

PRESCRIPTION NO. 5

A Technique to Control the Transition [B, I, A]

I often see players adjust to longer distances by speeding up the transition from the backstroke to the forward stroke. It is next to impossible to avoid being handsy with a fast transition, and the same can be seen with too short a backstroke.

You must be in control of your putter and avoid flipping it during the transition from the backstroke to the forward stroke. Ideally, the stroke incorporates a back motion, a slight pause, and then a motion forward. Here is a good check of your transitional control—and it's a favorite drill of Peter Kostis. Try it.

The Putt Doctor's DIAGNOSTIC TEST

Place a nickel on the back flange of your putter. If you have a mallet design, try to borrow a putter with a back flange. The Rossie 2 is an ideal putter for this drill.

Now, make a stroke as if putting to a target approximately 10 to 15 feet away. During the stroke, if the coin stays on your putter through the impact zone or falls off just before impact, you have a controlled transition. If it falls off on your backstroke or at the start of your forward stroke, you are too handsy with your stroke. This test can be performed at home or on the practice green.

Another way to assess your stroke's transition is with a simple question. When faced with a long putt, do you take a backstroke length similar in length to a shorter-distance putt? If so, you no doubt rush the transition, releasing your wrists, hands, and arms to gain the necessary power.

The transition drill can be done with a coin on a putter or (as shown here) with a ball on the **GAIM** putter.

Too often, especially under pressure, a fast transition results in the player's hands starting the forward stroke before the shoulders are ready. This often results in the back hand closing the putterface or at least a breakdown in the wrist angles. If the transition is a challenge for you, the following is a popular technique with many of my students.

A Pause for a Cause [B, I]

Place a ball approximately 20 feet from a hole. Take the putter back with a stroke length that you believe necessary for the distance for the putt. When the putter blade reaches the farthest point, instead of going forward immediately, hold this position and pause—you could say to yourself, "Pause now"—before starting the forward stroke.

This pause, for a second or two, is an extreme drill. It allows you to "reorganize," as I call it, before starting the forward stroke. The pause can enhance your awareness of the power source for your forward stroke. If you are not sure what powers the forward stroke, repeat this technique a few times, or close your eyes, as this can heighten your awareness. Ideally your upper arms and shoulders—with the focus on your back shoulder—are the power source. This moves the emphasis to your larger muscles, which can execute the transition with more fluidity than your hands, especially under pressure.

With most students, this pause in the backstroke not only encourages a focus on the big muscles, but also brings the putterhead back a little farther than on their typical backstroke. In other words, their stroke length is more like it should be for the distance of the putt, reducing the chance for the hands to be involved. Additionally, students often report that they impact the ball with the center of their putterface, which delivers more energy to the ball.

On the course, the pause will only be for a fraction of a second. If your big muscles are in control of the stroke, the tempo and the transition are automatically controlled. When you take a slight pause during the transition, the benefit is both in distance and direction: not only in starting the ball on line but also in being able to stop the ball consistently nearer the hole. If it applies, practice this drill daily as a start to longer-distance putting drills.

PRESCRIPTION NO. 6

More Techniques for Improving Speed Control [B]

This prescription will introduce you to more techniques to improve your skills for the longer distances. One technique does not fit all, and it is beneficial to have more than one way to tackle the challenges of distance control. If practice has not improved your scores when stroking putts to 30, 40, 50 and 60 feet, per Prescription No. 2, it may be time to try something different.

The Putt Doctor's DIAGNOSTIC TEST

Execute a few practice strokes before putting this method to the test. This technique, if executed properly, should have your putterhead finishing closer to the ground than is typical. Now repeat the 30–40–50–60 test with the above technique and see if your scores improve. If so, take it to the course.

One such technique entails your back arm extending on the forward stroke. Your back arm lengthens when you straighten your back elbow. Your back forearm and elbow rise slightly as your arm extends across your chest, while the chest stops a few degrees beyond impact.

On the forward stroke, as your back arm extends forward, your front arm is then pushed to the side by your back arm until the front upper and lower arm is vertical, aligned to your front side, and your elbow is pushed backward near the middle of your front side. (This is opposed to my earlier recommendation of keeping the elbows at the same angle from address throughout the stroke, as discussed in Section Three, which I still recommend for short- to mid-range putting distances.)

This technique of straightening the back arm I label "secondary release." This secondary release technique is for uphill and longer putts and is not applicable for shorter or fast downhill putts.

I remind you of the Gary Player tap drill (see Section Five) for those with a tendency toward a longer follow-through with the chase stroke. By using more of your front side for resistance (see Section Three), you should enhance the speed off of your putter. The more the left side resists, the more connected your stroke becomes, and the more efficient and consistent you will be in getting the ball to your target area.

I find the left-side resistance technique quite useful, especially for those who cannot overcome a short backstroke length. I mention left-side resistance for those who need more speed and are often using the front side for leading the forward stroke. I want increased speed with the forward stroke from hitting into a firmer front side as a crack-the-towel type of action, using the drill of hitting into your front foot as described in Prescription No. 5 in Section Three. Try this through a slight tightening of the front side as it is pushed into a vertical position by the back side during the forward stroke. You must keep your front side connected throughout the forward stroke. You may discover that this technique causes a slight recoil of your putter blade at the end of the forward stroke.

Another technique for especially long putts, which I label the load and release technique, is characterized by a shorter overall stroke length. This technique is more for the advanced, motor-skilled player. This method entails a slight loading—hinging of the wrists—during the backstroke on the longer putts. During the forward stroke, you release your wrists back to their original neutral position at impact. Importantly, do not flip your wrists beyond their original angles at address. Just unhinge them back to where they started at address.

This technique allows for more power or energy to the ball with overall less stroke length. It also can produce a more consistent center contact with the ball on the putterface, and results in a putt that heads straight where the putterface was aimed at address. I personally prefer this technique for putts over 60 feet as opposed to a longer backstroke. Try this technique for several putts. You may initially over-release the wrists or flip them through impact, but keep working to perfect the proper release.

The Tour average of makes over 25 feet is 5 percent. And we are talking good to elite putters here. That means your chance of making these putts is less than the pros, meaning less than one out of twenty!

So, the focus for longer distances needs to be on the correct speed and not on making the putt.

To help with this focus, putt to tees or ball mark repair tools as targets. Importantly, I prefer most techniques to be initially performed without a ball and hole whenever possible. This way your focus is entirely on the technique and not on the result. There are a number of drills that could be undertaken to fine-tune the technique you are working on, whether it is stroke length, the pause, the secondary release of the back arm, or the hinging of the wrists. One of these is putting to the fringe from distances that start at 30 feet and then increasing the putting distance by 3 feet with each putt. Your goal is to barely reach the fringe with the ball's roll.

PRESCRIPTION NO. 7

Eyes on the Prize [I, A]

Because the ball is stationary in golf, players have choices on where their eyes are fixated when they putt. A number of golfers, including Tour players, have mentioned that they look at the hole when they putt during practice rounds, and they like the results. Most have said that they are just too uneasy to try it in a tournament.

The Putt Doctor's DIAGNOSTIC TEST Stroke a few putts to different holes from distances of 5 to 10 feet. You may use the logo for aim. Note your typical speed as the ball approaches or enters the hole.

Now, switch to looking at the hole during your stroke. Before the stroke, look back at the ball for a quick moment as a kind of mental assurance of where the ball is located.

Next, look at the entry point of the hole you chose, and at that moment, start your stroke as you continue looking at your entry point. You may find it comforting to use your peripheral vision to see the ball while looking at the hole during the stroke.

Question: Did your speed to the hole improve compared to your usual speed? Was it faster or slower? I often observe the ball going to the hole with much better speed with this technique. This is especially true for players who typically leave their putts short of the hole. If this wasn't the case for you, it may be because you are tentative with the technique. If so, stroke a few more putts looking at the hole.

If you did like the speed from using this technique, after a few practice putts or sessions you may put it to the test when out on the course playing a casual round. When on the course, use a pre-putt visualization to track your eyes to the hole at the speed you desire. Then, take a quick look back at the ball before looking at the cup's entry point to start the stroke. For downhill putts, you may prefer to look in front of the hole instead of at the hole and vice versa on uphill putts. This helps the brain tell the motor system to adjust to the different slope's effect on the ball's roll.

In a short time, you will find looking at the hole quite unique and comforting. Overall, you may find it effective up to 15 to 20 feet from the hole. If so, but this approach is too radical for on the course, I suggest you take a final look at the cup, then when looking at the ball, stroke the putt while imagining you are looking at the hole. This would entail more of a soft focus on the ball with your eyes.

The Three-Speed and Cola Can Drills [I, A]

Hitting the ball with just enough speed to creep into the hole has been a recommendation of instructors for years. "I just hate those three-foot comebacks," I often hear. You may be part of the vast majority that professes to this mentality. To me, it is another myth.

In my experience, if the read is accurate, players make more putts with good speed compared to the die-it-in-the-front-edge speed. Invariably, those Tour players who complain of the need to make more putts are those with a die-it-in-the-hole approach.

What speed do you prefer? Are you avoiding, at least subconsciously, using greater speed? Are you aware that conditions can necessitate a change in speed? Spike marks, trampled greens, the "doughnut" and "volcano" effect from traffic around the cup, as well as green surfaces like Poa annua, can necessitate a need for more speed. How flexible is your speed control? Get ready for the three-speed test and drill.

This test enhances awareness of your tendencies. You may be well aware of your tendencies but may not realize how embedded your habits are. As you went through the five cycles, it may have become clear how hard it was to change your speed. So if you prefer a die-in-the-hole putt, hitting the back of the hole is as much fun as hitting your shin with your sand wedge—it hurts.

As you gain more confidence in getting the ball on line, I recommend using the drill below to get your eyes and your brain more comfortable with accepting a faster ball speed off your putterface.

The Putt Doctor's DIAGNOSTIC TEST

For this test, stroke all putts at a 5-foot distance from the hole on a surface that has a slight sidehill slope to it. Go through the following three-putt cycle five times.

The first putt is to fall into the hole at a speed that just drops it over the front edge. The next putt is to be hit with enough speed to drop it into the center of the cup. The third putt should have enough speed to hit the back edge of the hole and drop in. Repeat the three types of putts until you have completed five cycles. In case your speed did not match the intended speed, you are not allowed to repeat that speed. Keep going through the cycle, but make note of your actual speed for each putt.

After each cycle, jot down which putts were hit as desired and which were not. For instance, place a check mark if the putt had a desired speed on the first putt, the front-edge attempt. If the middle-of-the-cup putt was not successful, you could place a (-) if it died in or a (+) if it hit the back of the hole. Also note if the putts were made or not.

After the five cycles—fifteen putts—you will be able to note how flexible or inflexible you are with your speed control. Ideally you will adapt within a few cycles. If you find, for example, that it was much easier to die the ball in the hole than to hit the back of the cup, you no doubt are used to a slower speed of the ball into the hole. It also shows that you could use a little more practice on different speeds for better flexibility.

A Tour player came back for a second session with me. It had been three months since our last visit. He reported that he'd had a number of putts burn the edges every tournament. "I know I am closer to what you want," he said.

On several putts he lacked the speed to get the ball to the hole. "That is my miss, an inch or two short," he said. I then had him practice with the three-speed drill. He went through six cycles at 5 feet. He did not miss one of the putts that hit the back of the hole, or any putts that dropped in the middle of the hole. But he missed three of the six when attempting to die it in the front of the hole. So we progressed to the following drill.

When I place a cola can in the hole with the instruction to "hit the can," players make more putts in the 6- to 10-foot range than without the can. Try this drill for yourself. You will make more putts. When on the course, visualize hitting the can.

You must be able to trust your aim and your ability to get the ball on line initially. Soon you will feel comfortable hitting the can!

I believe a putt with more speed has a better chance of avoiding the rub of the green, time after time. Additionally, when faced with that 4- or 5-footer with a little uncertainty of the break, your ability to have your ball rattle the back edge of the cup can help take away that uncertainty. Pay attention to the next prescription as well.

If you are a die-in-the-hole player and need more speed, work on more speed with slightly longer putts, up to 6 or 7 feet. See how far you can go and mentally accept a roll with a little more speed transferred to the ball. Increasing the speed will allow you to make more putts, day in and day out. That is one way to lower your scores immediately! Be patient, your bain and motor system will adjust.

Be patient with this concept. For distances of 10 to 15 feet, work on attempting to hit the putt with the idea that the best speed has the ball dropping into the middle of the hole instead of dropping over the front edge or hitting the back of the cup.

A key for more speed is to use your mind's eye to see the ball hitting the hole with the intended speed as part of your pre-putt routine. Using a pre-putt visualization of the desired speed goes a long way toward the brain's accepting this speed and the transfer of this speed to the body to obey the brain's command—the eye-mind-body loop of performance.

Making More Putts [I, A]

What are your tendencies as you play? I believe the following test can assist even the advanced player.

The Putt Doctor's DIAGNOSTIC TEST

Review the putts from your last two or three rounds of golf. What did you do on the first hole? Was your putt short or long of where you intended it to stop? If you made the putt, was it hit with good speed or did it barely drop in the hole? Analyze your putts on the second hole and so on to the best of your recollection. If this is impossible, then tabulate your next couple of rounds.

Categorize your putts as short, long, exact, or mis-hit. A mis-hit putt was when you knew that your speed was off from the moment you felt the ball leave the putterface.

After you tabulate, see if there is a pattern. You might tend to leave your putts short or too long beyond the hole. You may be split among too long, too short, and exact, due to inconsistent putterhead control. If you made a number of putts, then you are already adept at speed control.

You must be aware of your tendencies, including, was your backstroke too long or too short? Was there too much hit with your hands? Did you decelerate the putter through impact, or tighten your grip, or commit other errors? There could be several problem areas if you took a dozen or so strokes into account. When you know why you fail, you can work through it in practice.

If your speed was consistently off, I offer you the following ideas.

- Dedicate time in each practice session on the techniques discussed in this section by applying them to drills such as the 30–40–50–60.

- Find a favorite technique or, better yet, work to master more than one technique. Be sure to visualize the ball's roll.

- Get comfortable with putts of 4 to 5 feet by stroking putts with a goal to see how many you can make in a row or how many can you make out of twenty-five or fifty. See the N–S–E–W drill in Section Twelve for a good drill. Also, shorten your stroke length!

- If you tend to miss on the low side, move the ball back in your stance for right-to-left putts and up in your stance for left-to-right putts.

- Practice the three-speed and cola can drills in Prescription No. 8 for flexibility to handle situations such as bumpy conditions, or just to take the break out.

- Work on breaking putts and the best speed for you from 4 to 12 feet with drills in this section and Section Twelve.

- Good players miss more putts from misreads than any other reason. Review Section Eight on green reading. Work on 100 percent commitment to your reads.

A Straight Line or the "Adjusted Center" Approach

There are a variety of methods to get the ball in the hole. Some players see every putt as a straight line and use the logo to aim to a point at or beside the hole. For example, if they read a break of two holes—8 inches—they aim to the left of the hole by two cups and hit the putt toward that spot at the speed they believe will make the ball stop slightly beyond the hole. This has been labeled the "linear approach."

Some players, including Tiger Woods, imagine a gate or a window they want the ball to travel through—what I call the apex of the putt's curved path. I like my players to imagine they are going to propel the ball through the gate by 12 to 18 inches. Other players prefer to imagine aiming their logo to a point just above the gate, as this tends to be the "true" apex of the break for moderate to severe breaks. This helps them visualize speed.

Some players have commented that they are "feel putters." "I don't use a line, I just see sort of a path to the hole," one player told me, drawing a curved path in the air with his hand. It was these feel putters who got me thinking about my teacher and his visual approach to breaking putts and speed control.

That teacher was the famed Paul Runyan, and I first heard of this approach years ago when playing many rounds with

A gate to putt through.

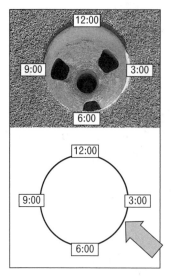

Adjusted center approach.

him. He would constantly ask me, "What o'clock is this putt going to enter the hole?" This was because I was just looking at the front of the hole, not visually referencing the necessary entry point for putts with any degree of break.

He imagined the hole as a clock, with twelve o'clock at the top of the cup and six o'clock at the bottom. He would say, "I see the ball entering the hole at four o'clock." A four o'clock putt would be a right-to-left putt, as depicted at left. The right side of the terrain the ball would travel over would be higher than the left side, tilting the roll to the left due to gravity.

If the terrain's high side near the hole is on the left, then the ball must enter somewhere between six o'clock and nine o'clock on the hole—a left-to-right putt. With this "adjusted center" concept, the player can imagine the ball coming into the hole at an angle and will avoid looking at the front of the hole as the final fixation point.

I recommend using an image of the last 4 to 6 feet of roll into the entry point—the adjusted center—as your pre-putt picture. Start your stroke with that picture in your mind's eye. During practice, it may help to place a coin at the entry point to help your visual fine-tuning. After a couple of putts, you may need to move the coin for more or less break for the situation. See if this approach allows you to make more putts.

I have found that this parallels what I hear and see with good players who often complain of "over-reading" their putts. In reality, they hit the putts with enough speed to carry the ball a couple of feet beyond the hole, but choose too much break for the speed they roll the ball. I tell them to maintain the speed and adjust the read, instead of changing the speed to match their read.

Your visual plan of action (VPA) to make more putts can be enhanced using the adjusted center, the gate, or the straight-line approach. With a good plan, you will make more putts, like the Tour players do. Paul Runyan did.

Visualization for Speed Control [I, A]

Not enough players go the extra mile in regard to the process of visualization. Visualization is the most common part left out of players' pre-shot routine. One reason is that it is very difficult to master.

More players use it negatively than positively. Too often the mind's-eye picture is predicated on a past negative image. When I hear a player say, "I knew I was going to miss that," I know that meant he had a bad picture in his mind before the putt. It is common to hear that same player say that a pre-putt positive mind's-eye picture is hard to have. So a bad picture appears easier than a good picture for this player.

Visualization is too powerful a skill to ignore. Visualization represents the mind in a thinking mode. It is either regenerating a past experience or generating a preview of what a player should do before

The Putt Doctor's
DIAGNOSTIC TEST

Place a ball on the practice green approximately five or so steps from the hole. Survey the slope from a position midway between the ball and the hole. This is the best position to get a mind's-eye picture of the ball's roll from start to finish.

Whether visualizing the ball's roll from the side, behind, or over the ball at address, the act of visualization is a vital putting tool. For now, picture the ball's entire roll from start to finish. Eventually, you may end up preferring to imagine only the last few feet of the ball's roll.

After you complete your address, picture the ball's roll once more. Now, close your eyes and stroke the ball to the hole with the speed that you pictured. You may feel more comfortable closing your eyes immediately after impact instead of before the stroke.

After impact, imagine the ball's roll to the hole. Your eyes should follow the ball's (imagined) progress, even though they are closed. When your mind's eye tells you the ball has reached the hole, call out "now" and quickly open your eyes and assess where the ball really is at that moment.

How was the accuracy of your visualization? If you were correct the first time, attempt the same test but with a different distance. You can choose a putt that gives you trouble, such as a slick downhill putt, and repeat the drill.

each putt. There are many ways to enhance this skill in a positive way, including seeing a sports vision optometrist.

So, how well do you visualize?

I have found that a number of golfers cannot visualize well enough to see the ball's roll with their mind's eye. That is why I came up with the term "in-vision-ing" in my first book. This asks you to run your eyes over the green's surface at the speed you believe is necessary by dividing the roll into three phases: (1) the initial acceleration; (2) the neutral phase, when the ball starts to glide along after it stops its skid; and (3) the last phase, when the ball appears to lose the most momentum as it approaches the cup.

Do not be surprised if you are way off with your assessment of the ball's position. A majority of players picture the ball traveling much farther than it actually has. When they open their eyes, the ball is often several feet short of the hole. If you are off on your visualization, repeat this drill to improve your visualization. Keep practicing and you will improve.

The act of imagining that the eyes are "pushing" the ball through these phases can transfer this effort from the brain's motor cortex to the body's motor system. The body feels this energy and then impacts the ball with the energy to mimic the in-vision-ing.

If you were accurate with the above test, by all means make sure to integrate visualization into your pre-putt routine all the time. If you were inaccurate, practice to improve your visualization accuracy. Work on downhill and uphill putts, incorporating visualization as part of your pre-putt routine. Then, putt the ball with that picture. Improving your visualization accuracy will translate into putts starting to be hit with the proper speed.

If speed continues to be a problem, observe the speed of other players' putts. Appreciate the ball's speed as it rolls from start to finish. As discussed in the previous section, players with good speed control always spend time observing the terrain from the sides, between the ball and the hole.

Remember, great athletes precede great performances with a clear, accurate picture of what they want to do before they do it. If you want to see great visualization in action, just watch Tiger's eyes as they transverse his intended line. Visualization is too powerful a tool to ignore, so do not omit the pre-putt visualization of the putt's roll into the hole. The more accurate you are in projecting the target in space, the more you can depend upon visualization as a tool to improve your performance.

Are You a Good Visualizer? (A+)

How about another chance to rate your visualization skills? Take the following test.

For an uphill putt you must hit the putt with more energy so it rolls up the hill faster than the level putt. As it rolls near the hole, the slope will slow it quicker than the level putt. Overall, the putt will take less time by a second or so. Simple when you think of it in these terms, isn't it?

The downhill putt is like a fast green. The putt will need to be hit with less energy than the level putt because the slope—gravity—helps propel it down the hill. The downhill putt can take a couple of seconds more than the uphill putt of the same distance because the deceleration phase takes up a greater portion of the total roll.

I call this approach "real time." I chose to label putts in time, which translates to space or distance. This encourages your eyes to travel over the terrain at the speed the putt must travel in order to finish as close to the cup as possible. A number of Tour players have told me the concept was a "life-saver" when they faced different green speeds from week to week on the mini-tours and the Asian Tours.

If you are faced with an uphill slope that is near the hole, your real time will need to be less than if the slope was a gradual rise from the ball to the hole. This is because the slope will have more affect on the speed, as the ball tends to slow in its last few feet of roll, so the ball will need to be hit with more energy. Work to perfect this technique and you will improve your speed control.

The Putt Doctor's

DIAGNOSTIC TEST

Picture a 25-foot level putt taking 3.5 seconds to travel from the start to the finish. Now, let's test your visualization skills.

How long would it take if the putt was again 25 feet, but the slope was a mild to moderate uphill? Would it take a longer time, a shorter time, or the same time as the level putt?

Likewise, for a downhill 25-foot putt: would it take more time, less time, or the same time as the level putt?

SECTION TEN

ATTITUDE, CONFIDENCE, AND THE ROUTINE

Putting has produced moments of anxiety in all of us. It can get frustrating when your drive goes 260 yards down the middle of the fairway, yet you miss 5- to 8-footers all day long.

Many players are already "whupped," as Muhammad Ali would say, when they step on the putting green. They don't exude the same confidence as they do with their tee shots or other aspects of their game. Some players simply don't emphasize putting in their practice routine. You know who you are. You are more likely to be found pounding drives on the practice tee than stroking putts on the practice green. But—no surprise—a 3-foot putt counts the same as a 325-yard drive.

Do you look forward to that birdie putt? Are you so excited that you cannot wait to make it happen? Or, are you in the camp of those who despise the act of putting, often dreading the putt you know you should make? You would rather face a 15-footer than a 6- or 8-footer.

If so, it is time for you to make an attitude adjustment.

Your attitude is directly linked to making the putts you should make. The right attitude is based on creating a positive picture in your mind's eye. Those with better results have positive pictures imbedded in their gray matter. When addressing that 6-footer, they are convinced they can make it because they see it happening before they stroke the putt.

Elite putters look at what speed is necessary and where their ball is going to enter the hole. They do not think about anything except, "This putt is going down!" It is no wonder their putts hit the cup with enough speed that the ball seems to smack the back of the hole. They erase any pictures of past failures and execute their putts only when good pictures are dancing in their head.

Compare this attitude with yours when you faced makeable putts during your last couple of rounds. When you think about it, did you replace any negative pictures in your mind before stroking putts you should have made? If not, you shouldn't be surprised that your performance was less than stellar. Why should you have good pictures, you may be thinking? After all, your mind is focused on rolling your putts over a green that's far from perfect, that is fraught with bumps, grain, footprints, even "volcano" and "doughnut" impressions that mar the surface! If that is your mentality, it is time to turn your thinking around.

Do you believe in yourself, or do you perceive yourself as having too many negative attributes to succeed? It is important to realize that you can change your thinking, and this can alter your beliefs. A belief is more than a thought. It is a thought that possesses you.

Cybernetic studies indicate that our body is composed of an automatic guidance system that can be programmed for either success or failure. Do you set yourself up to expect failure or to expect success? Remember, it is your choice.

A start to changing your attitude could be as easy as surrounding yourself with successful people. This can mean playing with golfers with lower handicaps than yours.

A good mind-set can translate into the belief that there is seldom a putt you cannot make at one time or the other. Elite putters have confidence to make the putts they should make and then some more, in every round they play.

Despite all you have read to this point about improving the technical aspects of your putting, there may be nothing more important than your ability to turn misfortunes on the greens into a chance to build confidence. Confidence, in this case, translates to trust in your ability to make putts you know you should make.

So, let's focus on ideas to help you regain confidence even after you have missed a series of putts. This includes establishing a solid address position and pre-shot routine, adopting whatever variations fit your personality. Overall, just like in mastering speed control, you need a plan. Putting these ideas into action will help restore your lost confidence, or give you confidence you never had.

Successful players exude excitement, conviction, desire, confidence, and commitment, as well as positive energy. To acquire these qualities, start by raising your expectations. Just be realistic about your chances. To make a point, I quote Mark Frost, in his compelling book, *The Match*: "None of us are here forever; we're not even here for long."

Remember, even though our individual lives do not register as even a speck on the eternal universe of life, all of us should measure ourselves in two ways: First, how much have we touched and positively affected at least one other person's life? Second, when all is said and done and we look in the rearview mirror, did we come as close as possible to being the best we could be?

It is up to you.

Prescription for Better Putting

1. Using putting statistics to be realistic
2. The Faxon approach
3. I want to putt like a kid
4. Adopt the Gary Player attitude
5. Confidence
6. Preparing to go
7. Is this the routine you are familiar with?
8. A routine for you

PRESCRIPTION NO. 1

Using Putting Statistics to Be Realistic

You need to be realistic about how much you can improve your putting and how long it will take before you see concrete results. Let me share with you some interesting statistics.

Through ShotLink, the PGA Tour has produced meaningful statistics about Tour players and, more recently, amateur golfers. While this is a step in the right direction, golf analyst Peter Kostis has recommended gathering better statistics for putting in the form of the "total footage of the putts made in a round." I believe categories of distances should also be used in everyday statistics.

Some of the statistics revealed below are from Dr. Soley's 1970s study, primarily on amateurs. Despite this being some thirty years ago, they still apply, since the amateurs' handicaps haven't changed in four decades. This means the changes in equipment and green surfaces have not produced resounding changes in handicaps.

Changes in scoring have come more from the Tour players, who are setting records in every category, as almost all scoring records at most tournaments have been eclipsed in the last couple of years, despite the toughening of the courses and hole locations.

Improved scoring has come from better opportunities for birdies from approach shots that land closer to the pin after monster drives. And, the professionals are making a greater share of putts they didn't used to make.

Compile your stats with the test shown here.

Looking at statistics compiled by Dr. Soley and the PGA Tour can lead to some conclusions about your results.

Amateurs with low handicaps, including women with 6 to 13 handicaps, make 82 percent of their 3-foot putts, while high handicappers make between 53 percent (women) and 67 percent (men.) Tour players make 98 percent of their 3-footers.

Scratch players' percentages of makes of 6-footers were the same as the high-handicaps' percentage of holed 3-footers. Overall, amateurs made more putts in the 6-foot range when there was no slope; and the worst percentage of makes was on straight downhill putts by the 23 to 29 handicappers.

Dr. Soley's statistics revealed that players were considerably more likely to three-putt on downhill putts. In the 4- to 15-foot range, downhill putts were sunk only about 80 to 90 percent as often as uphill putts.

The Putt Doctor's
DIAGNOSTIC TEST

Review your last few rounds of golf or take notes of your next few rounds. Keep track of the number of putts you attempted and made from each of the following distances: inside 6 feet, 7 to 9 feet, 10 to 15 feet, and over 25 feet. Also, note when an initial putt was followed by two more putts. In other words, did you three-putt, say, from 45 feet? If you walk off your putts, you will have a pretty good measurement to use as your guide.

At the U.S. Open at Pebble Beach in 1972, Tour players three-putted three times as often on downhill putts from 15 feet compared to uphill putts. In an LPGA event, the women made a higher percentage of uphill putts compared to downhill putts from all distances up to 20 feet.

ShotLink has produced these statistics for the 2008 PGA Tour on putts hit in greens in regulation (GIR):

- 81 percent of the putts are made from 4 to 5 feet.
- 70 percent are made from 5 to 6 feet.
- 60 percent are made from 6 to 7 feet.
- 52 percent are made from 7 to 8 feet.
- 45 percent are made from 8 to 9 feet.
- 40 percent are made from 9 to 10 feet.
- 28 percent are made from 10 to 15 feet.
- 17 percent are made from 15 to 20 feet.
- Tour players make 5 percent of putts from 25 feet and beyond.
- The Tour player averages 29.35 putts per round and 6.5 one-putts per round.

Higher-handicap players take approximately 30 percent more putts per round than Tour players. This amounts to a total difference of eight strokes from putting alone. The higher handicaps are prone to three-putting six times more than the Tour pros. In other words, they don't get the ball as close with their first putt.

Dr. Soley summarized his statistics quite simply. He felt that the chance of making putts over 11 feet was minimal compared to putts inside that distance. He felt that short-range putts of 3 feet and less were of little consequence for most players. Tour players have improved upon their accuracy, and it is understandable that the 11-foot range he discussed in the 1970s could be extended to a 15-foot range today.

He also stated that the key to making more putts and reducing the chances of three-putts was to get your longer putts closer to the hole and to practice putts from 4 to 11 feet. Your practice time should include downhill and sidehill putts in the 4- to 11-foot range.

The value of these statistics is threefold. First, are your expectations realistic for putts beyond 10 feet? Second, if your putts made are not on par with Dr. Soley's research, then shouldn't you include practice time on the 4- to 11-foot range, with emphasis on breaking putts? Third, if you are unsuccessful with the results of your practice sessions, shouldn't you apply the various techniques in this book for stroke and speed control?

PRESCRIPTION NO. 2

The Faxon Approach

Compare yourself to the game's greatest putters. Remember, there are just a few things under your control out on the course. For example, you cannot control the weather, your playing group in tournaments, hole locations, and so on. But one important thing you can control is your attitude.

I have Tour players fill out a questionnaire before their putting session with me. It gives me a chance to see how the players rate themselves in certain categories. It also yields insight into what they are doing, and cognitively, what they are thinking during their pre-putt routine as well as the act of stroking the putt.

There is no disagreement among Tour players that Brad Faxon is an elite putter. His questionnaire responses can give you insight about how a top performer views his putting skills. Brad has the correct attitude. The questions and Brad's answers follow.

Q. What are your strengths?
A. The consistency of my speed.

Q. What are your weaknesses?
A. Starting left-to-right putts enough left.

Q. Describe your pre-round preparation.
A. Working on green speed and mentally going through game strategy. I need to let my subconscious take over the read of the green and the speed of the putt. I want to avoid overthinking the situation.

Q. What would your fellow players say about your putting expertise?
A. They would like my confidence and tempo. They would also notice my transition between back and through.

Q. What are your thoughts when over the ball?

A. I trust my stroke and use my instincts as much as possible. I look and shoot. I don't evaluate my stroke after a missed putt.

Q. What did you learn from your last round concerning your putting?

A. You can put a good stroke on it and you can roll the ball well, but all putts don't go in!

How is that for a great attitude?

Brad doesn't look at each putt as a life-or-death situation. He certainly doesn't overanalyze before or after the putt. Brad has excellent visual skills, so I believe his instincts are derived in part from an ability to trust his eyes and commit to his read.

Brad understands his focus during the stroke. He doesn't get confused and mix up his goals with his job. While his goal is to make the putt, he is quite aware that this cannot be his job.

I tell students that they need to think of a job or a focus over the ball as something they can do close to 100 percent of the time. As you are getting ready to "pull the trigger," I prefer that you don't think it's your job to "make the putt." So, what can you focus on as your job?

Here are a few areas you could choose as your focus. It is your job to:

- Attempt to start the ball on the line you choose at the speed you believe is appropriate

- Attempt to execute a good stroke

- Attempt to hit the putt with a smooth tempo

- Attempt to make the stroke feel just like the practice stroke

The key word here: "attempt." You can always attempt something, and this is much more likely to be accomplished than is executing a perfect stroke. Keep your job in mind, and your goals will be met.

Realize that most missed putts for Brad, and for other elite putters, are caused by inaccurate green reading and the "rub of the green," and not from the stroke itself.

Also, realize that all players, including the average Tour player, can improve upon their attitude. As an example, the Tour player makes, on

The Putt Doctor's DIAGNOSTIC TEST

Take the same test as Brad by answering the above questions. How do you stack up with your answers? Are you as positive as Brad on your approach to putting?

average, 96 percent of the putts from inside 5 feet in "overall putting" statistics. But when the putts are counted only when they hit the green in regulation (GIR), their percentage dropped to 81 percent. This means that they made putts inside of 5 feet less when faced with a birdie putt rather than a par putt from the same distance.

PRESCRIPTION NO. 3

I Want to Putt Like a Kid

I was standing on the clubhouse porch waiting for my host, Kevin Kwak, the golf professional at the Davenport Country Club in Davenport, Iowa. The sun was setting and the course was radiant. I caught myself thinking about the sheer beauty and setting for golf and nature.

My attention turned to a youngster on the putting green. He was nine or ten years old and was wearing golf shoes, a glove, and a golf hat—just like an adult. Countless players have told me how fearless they felt when they were young, and how they "made everything" as they put it. Of course, they wished they could get back to that same mental state of "putting like when I was a kid."

Here was a chance to witness that quality firsthand, so I watched him putt for several minutes. Now in truth, no one makes everything, especially a kid. Did you make more putts when you were younger? I would say that you probably were more fearless. You probably stroked putts with a little more speed without trying to guide them. While you may not have made more putts as a kid, you no doubt remember more of the good ones that went into the cup. After all, kids are excited just to get the chance to putt. My, how things can change when we become adults!

After watching this youngster putt, I realized what the players were trying to tell me. The meaning of "putting like a kid" finally hit me.

I watched this youngster make maybe one out of ten putts. He would place his ball beyond 10 feet from the hole, take no time at all to size it up, walk right up to the ball, and fire away. What caught my attention was how he dealt with his misses. He would walk up to the ball after missing the putt and tap it to the other side of the hole, where he fired away again from beyond 10 feet. There was no show of emotion with the missed putts.

Also interesting was that all of his misses were pulls, or he aimed with a closed face. But that didn't prompt him to change anything. This young golfer just wanted another opportunity to stroke the putt. He wasn't worrying about the misses, where he missed, and what he could he do to change anything.

For some reason, he also liked to putt the same distance every time. It appeared this distance made it more fun to him. It wasn't a distance that many players would count on as a "make" most of the time.

Can you practice like a kid? By that I mean, can you stroke a putt with the mentality that you are excited about getting another opportunity without worrying about any missed putts?

The goal here is not to get used to missing as much as it is to just enjoy stroking the ball. It should not take long to start enjoying the act of putting without the result getting in the way.

Fight through times when you try to make putts. Instead, adopt a "second childhood" attitude when it comes to putting. Shift away from making putts to just stroking putts. It's okay to focus on attempting a smooth tempo or a good transition. Just do not get caught up in the results.

If the act of putting is difficult, be sure to reserve a portion of all your practice sessions to focus on just the opportunity to stroke a few putts. You may discover that this is an easier task if initially you putt without a hole as your target. (Also see "Putt to Nowhere" in Section Twelve.)

The Putt Doctor's DIAGNOSTIC TEST

The next time you are on the practice green, schedule five minutes of just stroking a few 10- to 15-footers with no attempt to make them. Do not aim them. Do not adjust—at least consciously. Just have some fun feeling the ball come off the blade and enjoy watching the ball roll. Try to make this a peaceful, fun time. It may be more beneficial to just putt to a tee.

How may putts does it take for you to appreciate and adopt the mentality of putting like a kid? How many sessions does it take to be able to play an actual round and putt with the purpose of just giving yourself another opportunity to roll the ball toward a desired destination with no fear of missing? It may happen sooner than you think!

PRESCRIPTION NO. 4

Adopt the Gary Player Attitude

Gary Player was paired in a practice round with a Tour rookie during a Champion's Tour event. After the round, Player asked the rookie to join him for lunch. The rookie seized the chance to ask Player a number of questions, including how he liked the greens. The rookie said that he felt they were a little slow for him. Player responded that he "loved the greens."

A few tournaments later, the rookie was at a restaurant waiting to be seated when Player spotted him and asked the rookie to join him. The rookie couldn't wait to get Player's assessment of the greens, since in practice they were much faster than the earlier course where Player had "loved" the slow greens.

"How did you like the speed on the greens today?" asked the rookie.

"I loved the greens," Player replied.

The rookie was exasperated and blurted out, "But Mr. Player, weeks ago the greens were noticeably slower and you said you loved those greens!"

"Son, I love every green I putt on," Player was quick to say.

Every golfer must make the best of every situation. The type or speed of greens is no different for anyone in the tournament. Every player putts on the same eighteen greens for each tournament round.

When you look back on adversity, how did you handle it? Was it with excuses, or did you accept the situation and deal with it the best you could?

Too many times I hear a student say that he missed putts because, "You know how the greens are there!" "Well," I say, "some players must have made putts. In fact, a whole lot of competitors were under par." Then, with a smile, I tell them the Gary Player story. They get the point. And, it's a painless way to help them stop making excuses.

To pass this test every time, establish a daily diary. Start with positives. This may mean writing something like "Nice golf cart" or "Nice clubhouse" if you had a less-than-sterling day on the course. A little humor could go a long way to establishing a positive mental attitude.

Write down as many positive things about your day on the links as possible. Do not dwell on negative aspects of the round. Avoid statements like, "I couldn't get the speed all day" or "Those greens were too slow for my stroke!"

After noting the positives of your practice and play,

instead of writing "My three-putts were nothing short of embarrassing" in your diary, jot down that you are going to work on reviewing putts in the previous round during your time off the course. This should be a time every morning or evening. Picture a good outcome, seeing yourself in your mind's eye executing those missed putts correctly.

Also, note what you need to work on for your next practice session. This should always include your setup and alignment checkpoints and a drill or two. Eventually, you'll be on the road to having a great mental attitude.

Please resist making negative comments or dwelling on negative thoughts. Your task is to find a way to make the best of everything! For example, this could mean changing the putter weight or loft. It could mean getting professional assistance to correct a putting fault. Plus, it means mentally replaying certain putts after each round, seeing them drop into the cup or rolling close to the hole on longer putts.

During your replay, it could mean making a change in your thoughts over the ball or moving the target closer or farther in your mind's eye if you did not adapt well to the speed of the greens during your round.

Create positive pictures on the course as well as off the course. This is a powerful attitude adjustment that can turn a negative period of play into a positive one. The player who makes the quickest adjustments, including her attitude, is the one who often wins the tournament while several other competitors are in the background still complaining about the slow greens.

If needed, make a pact with yourself to start an attitude adjustment. Talk positively and write down positive things about yourself, your golf game, and especially your putting. Review any negative situations. Replay them by seeing a mind's-eye picture of a positive outcome. Do this as soon as possible, and especially before your next round. Do the same on the course.

Confidence

I want you to focus on elevating your confidence level, despite your failures. "Wait a minute," you may be thinking. "Do what?"

Nothing boosts confidence like success. Success and confidence appear to go hand-in-hand. Without success, confidence can be diminished very quickly. Yet golf, with its many challenges, can really zap your confidence. Golf appears to challenge our ability to maintain confidence seemingly by setting us up for failure at every turn: uneven lies, slick downhill putts, bumpy putting surfaces, and so on.

The Putt Doctor's

DIAGNOSTIC TEST

Take a self-confidence test. How do you perceive yourself?

- Do you fall off the confidence ladder after only one bad putt or mistake?

- Do you lack control of your emotions in pressure times?

- Are you unsure of your skills to make critical decisions under pressure?

- Do you doubt your ability to concentrate, especially under pressure?

- Just before a tournament, are there too many self-doubts of your abilities, such as negative pictures of pitching or putting?

- Is your discussion concerning your play composed more of negative than of positive comments?

If you answered two or more of the above questions with a yes, then it is time for an attitude adjustment.

If you are playing a game that is going to make you fail, how you handle failure is a key. Remember, it isn't the experience that is as important as what you do with that experience.

Accepting that you will never master the game completely should not stop you from trying to improve as much as possible. This should include lessons with your golf professional as well as practice with a purpose and focus on your mental game.

Confidence can be placed in a "can do" category. You may not yet be able to trust that you can make each and every putt you face, but at the very least, you can prepare for each putt with a good picture in your mind.

Still, gaining confidence takes a plan and discipline. You add "a plan and discipline" by properly preparing for every tournament round.

Self-confidence relates to a belief in your abilities. Confident athletes often walk, talk, and think differently than those with low self-confidence. They believe they can succeed. Make it your plan to believe in yourself and act, talk, and in every way become a confident player.

The biggest obstacle may lie with how you perceive yourself. If you believe you are a poor putter, you will no doubt find a way to make that your reality. Self-evaluation can be of immense help. Take an occasional peek into a mirror. Talk out loud to yourself about how you view yourself. It is time for hardcore honesty.

Commit to making only positive statements to others. Stop your self-bashing talk. Promise yourself to answer questions with a more positive tone. You place yourself in a deep rut when you start to perceive yourself as a poor putter. You also validate this image with your talk to others. Review your conversations with others. Listen to what comes out of your mouth. It may surprise you to realize how many negative statements you make. A good way to change is to review your conversations mentally, and edit what you said by turning them into positive statements. Spend some quiet time seeing yourself performing successfully.

Use your imagination to change your thinking. Through visualization, create game-day situations during off-course mental sessions. Do the following as a drill:

- Imagine difficult putts and see a positive result.
- Imagine anxious moments on the course. See yourself apply stress-reducers such as deep breaths, then sinking the putt.
- Mentally role-play being down after a poor shot and see yourself refocusing and playing winning golf.
- Create practice games you can score, like putting challenges on the practice green. Challenge a buddy to a putting game.
- If putting has been difficult, visualize hitting putts or replaying poor putts from a recent event and see yourself performing well.
- On the practice green, imagine a putt or a situation that gives you fits on the course. See yourself performing successfully. Work through any anxieties!

If you have lost your self-confidence in putting, I recommend that you do the following each time you approach the green:

- Create a good mind's-eye picture of your putt going into the hole at the correct speed. Repeat this picture two more times from different viewpoints on the green. Include positive pictures as part of your pre-putt routine—always!
- Execute a good routine over the ball—spend less time rather than more.
- Commit to your read and never question your read once you are ready to "pull the trigger."
- Make sure your cognitive thinking is out of the way as you execute the stroke.
- Use quiet time off the course to replay putts going in the hole that did not but should have.

Your mind-set can be your biggest advantage or your biggest disadvantage. It is your choice. Change your image, not yourself. Think good thoughts more often and replace any negative ones when you catch yourself beating yourself up mentally. Positive self-talk and thoughts translate into positive energy that will produce a positive result.

Preparing to Go

As you approach the ball, are you mentally ready to go? Or do you have more of a get-it-over-with mind-set? If you are mentally and physically ready to "pull the trigger," you will make more putts. Most elite putters have an inner sense that helps them know when they are ready to stroke the putt.

When you are not ready, your heart rate goes up and you are somewhat anxious, jumping over the steps of your pre-putt routine or speeding up your routine. You may not even recall your mental focus during your stroke.

Contrast this to when you are truly ready. You are calm and focused as you approach the ball. You have a mental picture of a good setup and you complete your address with that picture. You have that look that says, "This is going in!" Your time over the ball is short, and your mind has a good picture of the ball going into the hole before and during the stroke.

Are you in the category of being ready to putt, or could you be more ready to putt? Take a look at the two scenarios below. Tabulate how many points apply from each of them to see which portrays your last round or two of putting.

If you have more checks in the first than in the second scenario, you are not ready to putt. This awareness signals the next step for your plan: to focus on the areas that get you ready to improve. During off-course mental sessions, see yourself applying them as you visualize a round.

Note in your diary the areas that make you ready to putt. Refer to them before and during your practice as well as before you play. Your goal is to eventually have your pre-putt and your focus during the putt mimic most of the points of the second scenario. Then, you are ready to putt!

The Putt Doctor's

DIAGNOSTIC TEST

Scenario 1: When you are not ready to putt (check the ones that typically apply).

☐ My setup doesn't feel just right but I putt anyway.
☐ The lines on my putter and on the golf ball don't appear to match up to the target.
☐ I don't have a clear, positive focus when executing the stroke.
☐ I am not sure of my read when I "pull the trigger."
☐ I am fearful of missing it left or right.
☐ I get too tied up in my stroke mechanics.
☐ I get line conscious and don't have a good picture of the ball's speed.

Scenario 2: When you are physically and mentally ready to putt (check those that apply).

☐ When I walk into my setup I am committed to my line and speed.
☐ I stare down the entry point of the hole for a couple of seconds at address.
☐ I get into the setup with a mental picture and a feeling that I have practiced.
☐ When my target line looks a little off, I adjust my setup or my logo aim.
☐ I focus on seeing the ball roll over the last 4 feet and fall into the hole.
☐ I focus on the speed and feel the energy needed as I stroke the putt.
☐ I look at a spot on the ball or in front of the ball as my target during my stroke.

I find that confidence can come from simply applying what you do well in the game to areas where you don't do as well. For instance, take a look at a part of your game that is reliable and positive. What is it mentally that you do well before you attempt a shot? You may realize that your ability to drive the ball well is preceded by a positive visualization of the target and the ball landing "miles" down the fairway. Importantly, rehash your round and check the areas where you did well. Mentally replace the negative images with a positive outcome.

Some instructors suggest that players "just move on" after a negative event. I believe you will get a greater mental benefit by replacing the negative with a positive picture. Since the brain does not recognize the difference between imagined and real events, imagining the putt hit well is a chance to leave the scene with a positive thought before the next putt occurs. That way, you are less likely to follow a three-putt with another one!

Additionally, are you using past successes to your benefit? We all have had good moments on the green as well as good putting rounds. When things are not quite going as planned, you must have the discipline to reach back in your memory bank to the good rounds, the good practice sessions, and the good strokes that felt wonderful.

For some, this entails replaying the moments over and over again: what worked and why; what were you thinking, seeing, perceiving, and so on. The answers are there. You cannot do this enough! Stick with it. It is a process. Be sure you are ready to go!

Is This the Routine You Are Familiar With?

One of the easiest ways to establish confidence is with a pre-shot routine. A systematic routine can keep your internal cadence and external physical movements consistent. A pre-shot routine becomes an important means to get mentally and physically ready to stroke the putt.

It is crucial to make each shot like all others, a one-shot-at-a-time mentality. The routine is made up of a series of visual checkpoints properly sequenced that help you get into the *now*—the present time. To properly focus on each task, you must ask, "What is my job at this moment?"

The four words—"what," "is," "my," and "job"—carry a lot of meaning and are extremely powerful. They should be said with the understanding that this is how you start getting ready to stroke the putt—with a mental and physical *purpose*. I recommend that you say these four words to yourself before each and every shot and putt.

A *purpose* is not to hit a 300-yard drive down the middle or to make every putt. Instead, purpose should signal you to make a decision as to what sensory system you are going to use as your focus during the stroke.

Choosing a focus simplifies and defines your task when you stroke your putt. You can focus on a multitude of sensory items. You could focus on the back of the ball or on a positive picture of the ball rolling into the hole. This would be a visual system focus.

You can attempt to make the stroke feel like your practice stroke, which would signal the kinesthetic—muscle/joint—system to be the focus during the putt. If you are going to focus on the mechanics of the stroke, I prefer you do it with a picture of what you want the putter or your body to do at a certain moment in the stroke.

If you are humming a tune for stroke tempo, you would be signaling the auditory—hearing—system. Grip pressure would be a tactile sensory system. Identifying the sensory system before the putt provides clarity to your brain during the stroke, instead of letting it run helter-skelter along, especially allowing a negative thought to occur such as: "Don't three-putt."

The Putt Doctor's DIAGNOSTIC TEST

What steps constitute your routine? Write down the steps you typically use in your routine. Do this for your full swing, then your short game shots, and then your putting.

Look at the following routine and note what areas are included in every aspect of your pre-shot and pre-putt routine. What area or areas are not included in all aspects? Ask yourself, why are they omitted?

Analyze

The analyzing step is the cognitive aspect of the routine. Being a good observer of the terrain, for example, starts the here-and-now process. Could you be even more attentive in this phase? You could consult your green map to help remove any doubts and allow yourself to totally commit to your read.

During this step you will be analyzing the slopes and their positioning, and you may need to factor adjustments such as green speed. These factors lead to an accurate visualization of the speed.

Visualize

In my research, visualization is the most common step left out of the pre-shot routine. Why? Because it is the pinnacle of visually related skills and the hardest to implement.

Visualization is the chief visual guidance system for the mind. Your actions are actually responses to pictures you create in your mind. A good picture of the ball rolling into the hole is a great way to calm your mind and body. Always self-direct the mental with a positive picture, relating to a "finest hour" occurrence or another positive visualization. Imagination always trumps will.

(continued)

(continued)

Visualize the ball's roll after assessing the slope factors from the side, between the ball and the hole. This picture of the ball's speed is a response to the characteristics of the slope you see and what you have realized concerning the texture of the surface. Focus on the entire roll of the ball from the start to the hole. Burn the line into the green with your mind's-eye

Visualization can also take place as you complete your address position. With your mind's eye, see the speed you believe to be necessary over the final few feet of roll with the ball entering the cup. If you like, go to a point 4 to 6 feet from the hole and imagine the speed necessary if you stroked the putt from there. Use that visualization as you "pull the trigger."

Some instructors advise you take a deep, calm breath just before executing the stroke. I prefer the deep breath to come just before you visualize the putt's roll. I believe the calmer you have your mind and body, the better you benefit from visualization.

Target

Golf is a game of specifics, not generalities. If possible, keep your target narrow. Your target is not the cup but, instead, a spot in front of the hole if the putt is on a downhill slope or the opposite for an uphill putt. It could be a spot in front of the ball you want the ball to go over. This spot can also serve to keep your eyes and head still during the stroke.

Visualization gives you a target to putt to. It could be left, right, behind, or in front of the hole. It could be the adjusted center point where the ball will enter the hole. Your target could be the apex—high point—of the putt. The target is finalized after you visualize on a straight or a breaking putt.

If it makes you anxious to have a small point for a target, then you have the option to think of the right side of the hole, for example, on a right-to-left putt, or a soft focus on a 3-inch-wide path to the hole instead of a line. The target also becomes an energy source based on distance. In addition, having a good picture of the target during your putt can help to control any subconscious negatives.

Align

Monitoring your aim can help avoid misdirection, which results in unnecessary stroke compensations. The visual system can be too malleable to leave on its own. Use the enhanced logo, a spot, the leading edge of the putterface, or other alignment aids. Always work to trust your aim. Check it often.

Remember to aim the logo line only after you have made your decision on the speed necessary—speed determines the line.

Your practice strokes need to be purposeful and mimic the actual stroke of the putt. During your practice strokes, look at the hole, the entrance point, or the adjusted center as your focus, instead of looking at the putterhead. Looking at the putterhead during your practice strokes shifts your focus to stroke mechanics.

Make sure to give yourself a "trigger point" to signal your brain and body that you are ready to address the ball. This could be a smile as you stand behind the ball, picturing the ball's roll into the hole. By the way, a smile is a great way to decrease tension during your putt—a relaxed face can transfer to a relaxed mind. It could be touching your cap or bumping the ground with your putterhead. You are now in the *go* mode. No more thinking—just *go*!

Execution: The Moment of Truth

Lock on to your job—your focus—here. Your job is never to make the putt—that is a goal. Your job should be more like attempting to hit the ball at your target with the speed you believe to be necessary. This is your last chance to control concentration. This moment of truth requires trust in the visual steps that preceded this task.

Your focus during the stroke can be a picture of the stroke path you desire, the putter speed, the ball's imagined roll into the hole, a point to roll the ball over, and so on. When you were warming up on the practice green, you decided on the focus you would apply when putting on the course. Now execute!

Replay

The mind can't separate fact from fiction. Replay represents an important chance to store a positive picture in your mind. It is important to acquire the mental discipline to see poor putts and shots hit well, preferably as quickly as possible after you have struck a poor putt. In short, counter the negative with a positive.

To their credit, I have seen players make a good practice stroke or two following a poor putt. I believe you can go even farther in your mental replay. After your practice stroke feels good, I challenge you to add a good picture of the ball's roll and see the ball go into the hole with the correct speed. That is the best form of *replay*.

As I tell my students, "It is important to leave the scene of a crime with a good picture." Give your mind something positive to chew on before the next putt or shot. Now, you are mentally ready for the next attempt. Injecting a positive picture helps in a number of ways. I find that players can avoid following a bogey with another one when they replace the bad image with a picture of the desired outcome. This should occur immediately after they take a practice swing or two that feels like it should have felt for the actual shot.

I challenge you to implement this kind of replay as one of the purposes you write down before you play the next few rounds. Seize the opportunity and make it a part of your everyday post-shot routine. When you practice the sequence of your routine, be sure to first go through it mentally in your quiet-time sessions off the course. Quiet time is a great time to accentuate the positive. No matter the previous outcome, see yourself performing successfully—as it should have happened during your last round.

A Routine for You

When I give a lesson, it isn't long before I see a talented student make a crossover to my suggestions regarding an aspect of his putting skills, whether it is the stroke, distance control, or setup. He just sort of takes charge of the suggestions and makes them his. This is especially true of the elite players.

While making my suggestions "their own" appeared at first to diminish my value as an instructor, I soon realized that players need to mold my ideas into what works for them. They need to experience what it feels like and how to apply it in their terms.

An instructor can give you options, but you should own your routine. Your routine options can include: where to take practice strokes—beside or behind the ball—if at all, your thoughts before and during address, the use of targets, and when to use visualization. You must develop your own specific routine to fit your skills and personality.

The analyzing phase is necessary in order to come to some sort of conclusion on the speed and the read. Hopefully, you start this phase before you even step on the green. But it is also important so you can commit to the read once you are set to fire. If you do not do this completely, and trust your analysis, good luck applying a confident stroke.

After analyzing the terrain, see a picture of the ball's roll. During the visualization phase, I recommend that you stand away from the target line.

If you are alignment-challenged, you should try making practice strokes behind the ball, facing down the target line, instead of beside the ball, as this gives you a better perspective of the target line. This is your typical binocular view when looking at a target.

If you need to emphasize your mechanics, do this only during your practice strokes. This could even involve exaggerating what you want to do, such as taking a longer pause at the end of the backstroke, because you tend to rush your transition.

I recommend you look at the hole, or at the distance you are planning to use as your target, and execute a stroke similar to what you will use for the actual putt. Practice strokes can physically free you up as well as serve as a rehearsal for the real action to follow. If you need to reduce your hands in the stroke, you can benefit by doing the Trunk Rotation drill at waist height, then knee height, to accent the big muscles of the arms and shoulders (see Section Three).

After placing the putter behind the ball, stare down your intended entry point for at least a couple of seconds. This is called "looking with intent." You can now switch to a good mind's-eye picture of the correct setup posture as you complete your address. Settle in for a second or two and gain a comfortable mental and physical feeling about your chance to attempt a good stroke.

The next task should be to get a good mind's-eye picture of the ball's roll. Recall the speed that you mimicked when at 4 feet, imagining the speed and direction your putt will take over these last few feet. Nothing harmonizes mind and body more than a good picture of success.

The time you spend over the ball should be minimal. You know your focus for the putt and the necessary speed. For a putt of over 5 feet, you may want to focus on a spot in front of or on the back of ball, depending upon what has been working the best for you. You may recall the speed you have pictured, and feel that energy during the stroke. This would be the same stroke length and energy you used for your practice strokes.

Once you complete your address position, your time over the ball should not exceed four to five seconds. You have to love Aaron Baddeley's approach. When he completes his address, he looks at the hole for a brief second, looks back at the ball, and fires. It is a no-time-to-think, just-time-to-act routine. It is a look, then fire.

The options you choose for your routine should be based on your eye dominance, your visualization expertise, and other skill levels. As you go into your practice sessions, experiment with what works for you, understanding that all the cognitive thinking is to be done before address, with the emphasis on mental pictures versus words and less overall thought throughout the routine.

When you next practice, dedicate a portion of your time to establishing your routine. Be mindful to use time off the course to imagine yourself implementing that routine. Now, you can own your routine.

THE YIPS

Something is going on in the world of golf—flinching is becoming commonplace when it comes to putting! In three different groups I watched finish a round in succession one day, two players had long putters, one used a belly putter with the claw grip, two others used the claw with a regular-length putter, one player putted left-handed but swung right-handed, and one player had a long putter for short putts and a conventional length for longer putts. He used a claw-type grip for both putters.

I have seen a number of players almost, if not totally, unable to control their hand action during the putting stroke. Near impact, their hands appear to spasm, and the ball can go off line from the shortest of distances. To some casual observers, it looks comical. For those with the yips, it is more than embarrassing. And, for those of us who teach, it is quite painful to watch.

These flinches, commonly called the "yips," must be from drinking too little water. There is too much of this going on to believe it comes from much else!

Seriously, the Mayo Clinic has been conducting research on golfers who have developed the yips. The research has found that brain activity is different in those with the yips compared to those without this affliction. Mayo Clinic researcher and Arizona State professor Dr. Debbie Crews has labeled it "focal dystonia."

Those with the yips report that their brain tends to "go off" like a lightning bolt near impact with the ball. But this is the effect, not the cause! One reason appears to be that the neurological wiring is "frayed" in the player's dominant back arm and hand. Constant repetition, coupled with poor results, along with an endless mental replay of negative results in one's brain, are no doubt contributing factors.

My experience tells me that there are three primary causes for the yips: using the old handsy stroke with minimal use of the big muscles, approaching putts with the same result-oriented mentality from everyday life, and being unable to trust aiming the putter.

The old all-hands-and-wrists stroke, which was common in the era of Billy Casper and Arnold Palmer, led to many players acquiring the yips. This is not to say that all handsy players of that era got the yips, but plenty did. Their yips started when the greens took on the speed and appearance of putting on a downhill concrete driveway—or it must have looked like it to them. Advances in agronomy as well as maintenance equipment since then have produced incredibly smooth, fast putting surfaces that are light-years apart from yesteryear's.

The result-oriented thinker can develop the yips. He is usually a genius with on-course strategy. But this can also translate into thinking too much when "pulling the trigger." In other words, a strength can be a weakness.

Bernhard Langer would top this list. He went through several episodes of the yips, but to his credit, he always found a way to master the situation—starting with a grab-the-wrist technique and then on to using the long putter coupled with the claw grip.

I consider the most predominant cause of the yips to be mistrust. By this I mean both in the reads of the green and in the ability to aim the putter at the target. As discussed previously, misreads are by far the biggest reason for missed putts even with the more accomplished players.

Likewise, a big challenge confronting players of all levels is that of being able to trust where they are aimed. There is good reason for this mistrust. Barely one of ten good players aligns consistently at the target at a distance of 10 feet, and hardly one of twenty average-handicap players is able to align inside the cup twice in a row at a 10-foot distance.

Personally, I am all too familiar with this problem. When I was playing for club championships in my early thirties, I would stand over a relatively easy short putt and have no idea where my putter was pointing.

When the putter came forward to impact the ball, my legs would shake like I was doing a shimmy on the dance floor. I can recall feeling a kind of explosion in my brain near impact. I know my visual system shut down, because I rarely recollected seeing impact. Everything appeared to happen so fast. This affliction went away when I came up with ideas to improve my alignment. It also helped to realize that this game does not require perfection.

The Mayo Clinic and Dr. Crews have offered some suggestions for players with the yips, including trying different-style putters, some of radical design, that I believe give the player a fresh look as much as anything else. Instead of going through the process of testing at the Mayo Clinic, you can use a very good indicator for the yips that I have come up with, thanks to one of my students. And most of all, there are options to counter this affliction.

Prescriptions for Better Putting

1. The Infamous Yip Stroke
2. Quieting your mind with your eyes

PRESCRIPTION NO. 1

The Infamous Yip Stroke

"Doc, you are going to earn your money with this lesson," a student commented to me a few years ago, after setting up an appointment for his wife. Soon into her lesson I could see what he was talking about. She was having a horrible time making short putts, often missing the hole from just a few feet away.

I told her that putting could be simply thought of as rolling the ball with her hand, and I picked up a ball and rolled it—underhanded—to the hole. "It is as simple as that," I said enthusiastically.

"I can't do that," she said. I prodded her into trying to roll the ball. When she did, I wasn't ready for what I was about to see. Instead of rolling the ball, she flipped it directly to the right, with her thumb and forefinger acting as if she was shooting a marble. I was standing at a right angle to the path to the hole, and the ball hit me in the shin.

"See!? Did I hurt you?" she yelled.

After some more prodding, I got her to repeat her unique roll as I stood off to the other side. Again the ball spun off to the right.

My student then showed me the solution to her problem: "I can roll it like this." She then turned her hand so that the palm was facing down instead of up. She spun the ball out of her hand, keeping the palm facing down during the toss. It was a smooth, soft roll, similar to what any good athlete would do.

An underhand ball roll.   **A palm-down ball roll.**

I have since seen a number of students in my clinics roll the ball with hands that trembled or spasmed at the moment of release. It has led me to believe that this drill of rolling the ball is a good way to determine if a player has the yips.

The following test can be quite interesting even if you do not have the yips. Give it a try. All you need is a golf ball.

The Putt Doctor's DIAGNOSTIC TEST

Position yourself about 5 feet from the hole or a target on the floor such as a cup or glass. Bend over (or crouch down) so the hand that will be rolling the ball is near the surface. Now, roll the ball underhanded, with your palm facing up, to the hole. Repeat this a few times, attempting to roll the ball into the hole each time. Be aware of your arm and hand tension.

From the same position, roll the ball with the palm down, again attempting to roll the ball into the hole. Now, which technique of roll is more accurate and physically feels freer?

A player with the yips—true focal dystonia—will not be able to roll the ball smoothly. In clinics, I have students roll the ball underhanded back and forth to each other on the green. The players are not even rolling it to the hole, yet you can still spot those with a nervous twitch. I then ask all the players to roll the ball with their palms facing down. I have even seen really accomplished players show quite different results when they roll the ball the two ways.

I was a guest instructor at the Jane Frost Golf School. A student of Jane's attending the clinic became frustrated when she couldn't comfortably roll the ball underhanded. Her hand looked like it went into a mini-spasm. She commented, "For crying out loud, I was a softball pitcher in college and I can't even roll the ball a few feet underhanded!"

When she was asked to use the palm-down roll, her motion was perfectly smooth. "I feel much freer when I roll it that way," this astonished student was happy to report.

"Freer" is how many players describe their feeling when they use the palm-down position versus the traditional underhand roll. What is the reason for this? It must go back to what the Mayo Clinic surmised: that missing too many putts with the hand in the traditional grip has frayed the nerves.

As my earlier student soon discovered, that difference can be quickly transferred to putting as well. Her successful demonstration of the palm-down roll prompted me to devise a similar position for her back hand on the putter handle. I took her back hand and placed it on the grip, in a position similar to that seen in the top left picture on page 218, so her palm was facing more toward the ground than down the target line.

"We are going to have you putt with the claw," I explained.

Her next few putts mimicked a good putter's stroke: smooth and with a good roll. While not all her putts fell immediately into the hole, most had a chance, even at 6 to 8 feet. That student is still using the claw years later.

Changing to a claw grip is by far the best counter to the yips. The claw grip physiologically changes the muscle action that causes the yips. The claw, by the way, is not new. The late Paul Runyan, a great player and teacher of the game, showed me a modified version that he deemed the claw for my wedge practice around the greens. He had me hold my

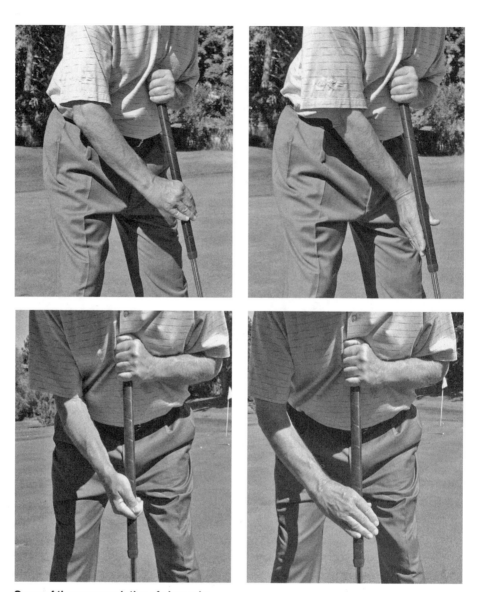

Some of the many varieties of claw grip.

wedge between the second and third fingers of my back hand because I had "too much back hand in my pitches." This was in the 1970s!

A Wisconsin judge, John Pfannerstill, is said to have come up with the modern-day claw grip that stopped his putting woes. He called it the "pencil grip." He later showed it to PGA Tour player Skip Kendall.

When Chris DiMarco discussed his problem with the yips, Skip remembered the grip Judge John had shown him. Chris switched to it and became a much more confident putter.

You do not need to be afflicted with the yips to adopt the claw. I have seen a number of good collegiate players, men and women alike, use the claw grip. Stewart Cink, PGA Tour player, always known as a good putter, uses a belly putter and the claw grip, as he feels that both aid his ability to get the ball on line consistently. These players are not afraid to put it to use, and neither should you be.

The claw is useful for overcoming another common problem. I have many players practice with the claw to help lock in their back hand to prevent them from flipping their wrists.

Too much back hand can cause a number of problems. If you feel you are too strong with your back hand, with some wrist breakdown or at least a case of the pulls, I suggest you stroke a few putts with the claw as part of your practice sessions.

When doing a clinic at the famed Prairie Dunes Golf Club in Hutchinson, Kansas, head golf professional John Lanham suggested that I have every player in our afternoon group adopt the claw for a while. "Doc, when you had a couple of players who were yipping in the morning group switch to the claw, I saw such an improvement. I am curious to see how many others would find it helpful."

The second group had less skill, with a few players somewhat new to the game, so John felt they were more likely to give it a good go. At the session's end, all eight players said the claw improved their ability to get the ball started on line and they would definitely give it a try on the course.

Practice with the claw. You may be aware that your back wrist is more able to stay solid throughout the stroke. After a few putts with the claw, switch back to your conventional grip but attempt to mimic the solid-wrist feeling you had with the claw throughout your stroke, especially through impact.

Even if you tried the diagnostic test and rolled the ball as well with the traditional underhand position, you may benefit from the claw by starting the ball more consistently on your target line.

On the other hand, I have switched a number of players away from the claw and cured the yips through a renewed focus on the big muscle turn. This foregoes any hands involvement in the stroke. When conducting private putting lessons at Denver Country Club, I had as a student a retired surgeon who had adopted the claw as a way to improve his stroke. He had switched to the claw a few months earlier.

I showed him the five key points of the Putt Doctor's Stroke. We worked on his setup for a while, focusing on his upper arm's connection to his body. We then spent a good deal of time on his back shoulder as the power source, stroking some 40-footers to the far end of the green. I noticed that he switched back to a conventional grip during these strokes.

After he had a good sensation of the motion of the back shoulder as the power source, I asked him to stroke a few short putts. Again, he stroked the putts using a conventional grip. After he had sunk several putts with a smooth stroke, I pointed out to the doctor that he was doing this with a conventional grip. "I guess I am, I did not notice that," he responded.

The late Jamie Thompson—face-on putting.

Later that day, he stopped by the putting green and was shaking his head in disbelief. "I would never have guessed my putting would straighten out from that back shoulder power source," he said. "I was not perfect on the short putts, but I was very encouraged using your method and the conventional grip," he explained.

"Good for you," I responded, "but do not hesitate to go back to the claw if you need to."

There are many other good ways to counter the yips:

- Use the belly or mid-length putter.
- Use the long putter.
- Use the cross-handed grip.
- Putt facing the hole, as seen here by one of The Palms' club champions, the late Jamie Thompson.

The "croquet style" or "face-on" style of putting has gained some disciples in the last few years. It was first brought on the Tour by Bob Duden and later made more visible by Sam Snead. Those who use it believe they can better see the target line.

It certainly is a viable option for someone with the yips. Many use a regular-style long putter, bent to around 78 degrees of lie.

You cannot straddle the target line, so the stroke must be initiated with the ball on your side and not in front of your body. The handle is placed near the body's center or under your shoulder with the ball placed approximately two putterhead lengths from the outside foot. The ball is positioned slightly in front or at the tip of the feet. If all else fails, face-on putting can be worth a visit.

PRESCRIPTION NO. 2

Quieting Your Mind with Your Eyes

"So you think you have the yips?" I asked a student during her phone call telling me she felt she was yipping some short putts down the stretch on her way to her first tournament win on the Futures Tour. "You are only eighteen years old, for crying out loud," I said. "You haven't been playing long enough to develop frayed nerves causing the yips." I then talked to her about attitude and confidence—the same points you read about in Section Ten. I haven't heard of or seen any flinching by her since that conversation.

Now, if you feel you are fighting the yips or have a "flinchy" stroke, but you did not fail the Ball Roll diagnostic test, you can try something else. George Archer once told me he had had some great stretches of putting when he watched his hands during the stroke. It has been proven to combat the yips. Tom Watson also discussed his use of this technique in an article in a leading golf magazine. And, Johnny Miller has said that watching his putter handle produced a quieting feeling. Let me tell you why it worked for these pros and why it can work for you.

For some very anxious players, the technique of watching the hands during the stroke can be very quieting to the brain. The brain tends to be less active when the eyes are occupied with the movement of the hands. This physiological concept has been proven. Give watching the putter handle during your stroke a try if you are prone to anxiousness over the shorter putts.

Find a 4- to 5-foot putt, with or without a little break to it. Go through your pre-putt analysis, then step up to the ball, take a look at the entry point to the hole, then look back to the ball, then to the putter handle just before you start your stroke.

As you follow the handle with your eyes, you will be aware of the ball in your peripheral vision. While this can be comforting for some, others may get distracted by the ball and lose focus. A split focus can be disruptive. If so, be sure to make the handle your primary focus of your eyes during the stroke. Also, keep your head still. Just let your eyes move with the handle.

If you feel freer during the stroke, you could next give it a go on the course. You may well unlock your brain and your body and enjoy the act of putting those tricky short-range putts.

As always, first attempt it on the practice green before trying it on the course.

See, even if you have the yips, there are solutions to keep you in the game!

SECTION TWELVE

DRILLS AND PRACTICE WITH A PURPOSE

I f you wish to separate yourself from the pack and leap to the forefront, take a look at upgrading your practice regimen. Too many players at almost every club go through mindless practice, hour after hour, day after day.

They do the same old thing, practice after practice. Hit a few balls with their wedge and then move up the ladder of the clubs. They do it with little change in their regimen from one day to the next. And on the putting green, they demonstrate even less of a regimen.

I see few players using teaching aids to give them feedback. It appears their only feedback is whether the ball goes in the hole or not. I believe using training aids is quite important to point out areas that need attention, as well as to check your progress.

Many players, immediately after learning a new technique, are in too much of a rush to put a ball in play without doing any practice. After a few putts go astray I ask them, "Are you really ready to stroke a ball, let alone hit it to the hole?"

Of course, the question is rhetorical. Despite my hints, it isn't long before the player grabs a ball and fires away. First and foremost, techniques need to be done initially without a ball and a hole so you can focus on the technique and not on the results. It is all about the process. Being patient is but one point. Here are some others:

- There is no magic dust to sprinkle on you to get better—you must pay your dues.
- You must set conditions for learning through the use of training aids and a set practice routine. You cannot be helter-skelter with your practice.
- You should use a notebook for jotting down what you have learned or you *will* forget!
- You must implement new ideas by practicing them first—then go *play*!

For years, I have stood in front of clinic attendees expounding on the virtues of making notes on what they have learned. I advise using two primary categories. They should note what they did, physically and mechanically. This includes how their bodies felt during a successful stroke. And, they should note what they were thinking before and during their action. (Performance is based on what you do and how you think.)

Maybe the late, incomparable Byron Nelson can help here. Accompanying the announcement of his death in 2007, there was mention of his 1935 season and his first Tour victory. At that time, he started to carry around his "Little Black Book," keeping track of his scores and making notes on ways to improve his game.

In 1944, after he won eight times, he declared in a New Year's resolution that he desired to reduce careless shots and improve his chipping. "Lord" Byron was not going to rest on a great season of eight wins and coast from there. He not only came up with a plan to improve upon his play, he wrote it down!

What followed was a year for the ages. In 1945, Byron won eighteen times, eleven in a row, and set a scoring average that lasted for fifty-five years: 68.33! He also finished second seven times and shot under 70 nineteen times in a row! With the equipment he had!

So, what notes need to be written down in your Learning Diary? Done properly, these will help you get to the next level—guaranteed! It is imperative that you write down:

- The areas to mentally work on during off-course quiet-time sessions
- The drills you want to do each day
- The time you want to spend on each drill (fifteen minutes maximum, please!)
- Each drill's purpose (what you are working on—mechanics, routine, focus, etc.)
- Your goal—results or score
- What you learned or felt that was different, and what you were thinking

This section will add to the drills you have already been introduced to in previous sections. Be mindful that drills are not magical all by themselves. When you have specific drills to practice, you must have a purpose—what you desire to accomplish—and note what you learned from the drill—write it down.

Practice can make for great rewards or it can be more of the same old thing. Too many players are guilty of just throwing three balls down on the putting green and firing away. A few players have a somewhat regimented routine of ten to twenty minutes just before going to the first tee. They start with short putts and end with longer putts, or vice versa.

If you are a streaky putter or are fighting to get down to around thirty putts per round, you no doubt need more structure in your practice routine, and this includes pre-round practice.

The first drill in this section will give you immense benefits in your practice. It requires construction of a simple training aid. It will help you identify any problem areas that need to be addressed, as well as indicate your areas of strength.

As in Section Nine on speed, the drills here are categorized as beginner (B), intermediate (I), and advanced (A) to help you zero in on the more appropriate drills for your skill level.

For your practice sessions, include drills from previous sections that you know will help you improve your putting. Stick with them until you believe you have mastered the skill and are comfortable with it. Continue to challenge yourself with ever-increasing difficulty of drills. Be confident, but work to make yourself better and better. And one more time—make notes!

Prescriptions for Better Putting

1. Setting conditions for learning
2. North–South–East–West
3. Tiger's tee drill
4. Reducing anxiety, part one: putt to nowhere
5. Reducing anxiety, part two: soft or fine focus
6. Stopping the slice stroke
7. Visually speaking, seeing it correctly
8. "8 + 4 + 2 + 1"
9. Keeping your flexibility of adaptability
10. The Putt Doctor's real-world drill

PRESCRIPTION NO. 1

Setting Conditions for Learning [B, I, A]

I saw three students in a row who told me they were struggling with makeable putts inside of 10 feet. I had observed them time after time with no structure to their putting practice except organized chaos. They seldom if ever used the aids I recommended. They stroked three balls, going to one hole, then another and another on the putting green.

All three players' problems stemmed from one thing: poor alignment. After a few putts during the start of their lessons, I had them try the training aid discussed here. They all had been given this aid, but were not using it. Within moments they went from consistently missing to making over 80 percent of their putts from 8 feet.

Controlled learning maximizes your practice time by providing the feedback you need to be a consistently good putter. Feedback—the breakfast of champions, as my good friend "Coach" John Mackovic likes to say.

The Aim Aid, using needles and a string, is three or four drills in one. I give it to all my students. I believe it can help you identify your strengths and weaknesses. Here are some benefits of this simple training aid:

- It gives you accurate aim every time.

- It assesses if you are starting your putts on line.
- It enhances your visualization skills.
- It controls learning and maximizes your time on the putting green.
- It restores your confidence by helping you make putts consistently.

Use the Aim Aid to control your practice.

To make this aid, visit your local fabric or department store and obtain two 4.5 or 5.0 mm crochet needles and a "Stretchrite" round elastic cord, marked "five yards." I prefer to cut the elastic cord to approximately 3½ feet in length before tying the string to the needles. This allows for the string to be stretched to 12 to 15 feet. Of course, you could use a regular string and cut it to a 15-foot length.

Purchase some beads at an arts and craft store that can be threaded onto your elastic cord or string. These beads have several purposes. They can:

- Mark the placement of the ball when it is under the string
- Help with stroke length control and consistency
- Mark where you perceive the ball needs to break away from the string on a breaking putt as a visualization mechanism

Next, find a relatively straight putt of about 10 feet in length. Stroke a few putts to determine the break. If it is a straight putt, then run the string directly over the center of the hole. The string is your aiming device and your target line. Push one needle into the ground a few feet behind the ball, and the other needle directly behind the hole. Push the needles' pointed ends at least three inches into the ground. Lower the string on the needles to approximately 3 inches above the green's surface. That gives the ball enough room to run under the string while producing a better chance to place the center of the ball exactly under the string. Now go to the diagnostic test on page 228.

For now, use the needles and string for a straight putt, so there is no break and minimal speed decisions to factor in. If you have lines on your putter, make them match—be parallel to—the string. If there are no lines on your putter, align your putterface perpendicular to the string. You have now taken aim out of the equation.

Now you are ready to test your stroke mechanics. Stroke a few putts. If the ball rolls under the string and into the hole at least seven or eight out of ten times, you have a consistent stroke and you can trust your stroke. You can eliminate your focus on the stroke and work on other problems that may be causing you to miss putts. For example, you may need to work on trusting your aim, or on improving and committing to your green reading. Attempt to make ten putts in a row in each session before replacing this drill with others. Ten in a row does wonders for your confidence.

If getting the ball started on line is difficult, first evaluate your setup and then look at the key points of your mechanics. This could mean being better connected or, during the stroke, staying more in control with your arms and shoulders instead of your hands. (Also reread Sections One and Three.) When you can roll the ball consistently under the string for straight putts, note what you have changed and what you feel that is different and file it in your mind as well. This goes for all improvement you have seen when doing the drills.

Use the string on straight and breaking putts as well. If the green breaks slightly—as can be determined by stroking a few putts—the string would be placed to the right or left of the hole.

The beads on the string can be used to assist your stroke length, as discussed in Prescription No. 3 in Section Nine.

I prefer this to be a good starting drill for most of my putting sessions. I will find a straight putt, then put the strings and needles in place and putt three or four putts from 4 feet and then 6 feet, working back 2 feet or so at a time. I desire to keep my stroke mechanics solid for each length. The last few putts I will stroke under the string are from approximately 10 feet.

PRESCRIPTION NO. 2

North–South–East–West [I, A]

You can take a lot of pressure off the rest of your game when you are confident that you can make the 4- and 5-footers. Here is a drill that can help you with your confidence.

Start with four golf balls, each placed 4 feet from the hole in a "north, south, east, and west" pattern. Mark the four spots with markers. Stroke each of the four putts. Replace each ball at its respective marker after you stroke the putt and go to the next ball. Continue until you miss, then start over. Record your score as the number of putts made in a row. This is your baseline.

Your eventual goal is to make twenty in a row—five cycles of four. When this is accomplished, raise the level of the challenge by increasing the distance to 6 feet and then to 8 feet.

Record the number of makes in a row for each distance. Also record what it was that you were thinking and feeling that allowed you to make the putts. These are things you can easily forget unless you write them down and refer to them from time to time.

If this proves to be outside your present abilities, see how many out of twenty putts you make from each distance instead of how many you make in a row. If making 80 to 90 percent of the 4-footers is difficult, start at 3 feet.

Repeat this drill several times a week for two to three weeks to improve your confidence. For each putt, go through your pre-putt routine. This should include reading the break for your initial putts. Be consistent with your setup, your grip, your stroke, your mechanics, and your routine. A reminder: Spend no more than 15 minutes on this drill unless you are on a roll to making forty in a row.

A variation of this drill is to attempt to make three putts in a row from 4 feet. After making all three, move a foot farther back and make three in a row at 5 feet, before moving to 6 feet, and so on. Each cycle of three allows you to move the putts a foot farther away from the hole. If you miss, start again at the 4-foot spot. Record how far you got before missing a putt, such as "6-2," which means you got to the third putt at 6 feet before a miss.

The N–S–E–W drill.

Tiger's Tee Drill [A]: A Great Drill to Improve Your Putter Path and Impact Point

The following test and drill, described in the September issue of *Golf Digest*, is Tiger Woods's favorite drill.

The Putt Doctor's DIAGNOSTIC TEST

You will need two tees along with a golf ball and your putter. Find a straight putt of approximately 4 to 5 feet. Place a ball down at that spot. Place two tees in the ground, one on each side of the ball, above and below the intended target line, as seen below. The tees are spread apart by slightly more than the length of your putterhead and perpendicular to the target line. Tiger says it forms a "gate."

Stroke a putt. If your putterhead misses the tees at impact, you successfully returned your putter to the address position. More than likely the ball will go in the hole. Attempt to make five in a row without hitting the tees. Eventually work up to ten in a row. Then you can move on to other drills as part of your practice routine.

If the heel of the putterhead hits the bottom tee, you have changed your path by shortening the radius of the path. This is often due to a shortening of the muscles from tension in the hands, shoulders, or arms. It could also be from you shifting your weight toward your heels, or from executing an out-to-in stroke path. It also could signal a change in your ball position by moving it slightly farther from your feet, a change in your lie angle, or the length of your putter, as discussed in Appendix A.

If the toe of your putter hits the top tee, you have increased the radius of your stroke. This occurs when you disconnect your upper arms from your body, or you straighten your elbow. It could also be from an in-to-out stroke path, or a need to bring the ball position a little closer to your feet. It could signal that you should change your equipment.

If this drill is difficult, make a stroke in slow motion without a ball in place. This is a great way to work on your stroke and path to effectively return the putter to impact. You can do this drill at home. Just turn the tees so the top of the tee is on the floor. Your goal is to return the putter back to the ball on the same path it was taken back on. Try to make ten strokes in a

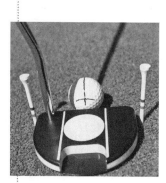

Tiger's tee drill.

row without hitting the tees. A good key here is to use the tees as a visual guide to help square your putterface at impact. This is a great picture to use on the course as well.

I have seen this drill improve the stroke of a number of players. In the computer analyses below, the top one shows a student's typical stroke. The bottom image shows her first stroke using the tees as a gate. Quite an improvement. And it was all based on a visual guidance technique.

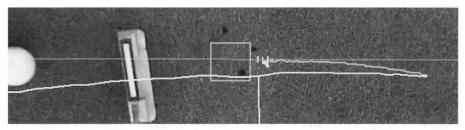

Slice stroke path of a good amateur player.

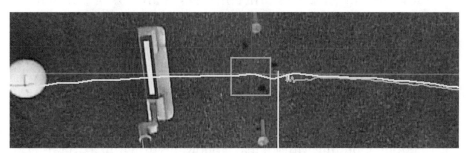

Same player's stroke path after two practice strokes with Tiger's tee drill—what an improvement.

By the way, Tiger says he alternates between hitting twelve putts with his right hand only, then six putts with both hands on the putter, until he makes fifty or a hundred in a row. Now, that is some serious practice time!

Just a note on the above wording: Performing this drill with your back hand only on the putter handle still involves your back upper arm staying connected to your back side during the stroke. The back arm should not be the only part of your body that is moving. The back, shoulder, and arm should move as one.

Reducing Anxiety, Part One:
Putt to Nowhere [B, I, A]

A number of players have talked with me about suffering from a case of the nerves, especially when over a short-range putt. Whether it is because of past negative experiences, the fear of missing, or trying too hard to make the putt, short putts can cause plenty of anxiety.

Missed putts can cause your brain to start producing a flight-or-fight response such as an increase in heart rate, sweaty palms, or outright panic before you even complete your address. This lack of control, when your brain is on a whirl, can result in your eyes jumping around, not being able to focus on anything. You sort of go *blind*.

It may be time to discover how much tension is part of your putting, and time to establish a tension-free moment. I introduced the following test and drill in my first book, and it remains an important one for many students. This drill enhances awareness of your tension control or lack of it, as well as a means to achieve the ideal tension level when you putt.

The drill has you putting without a hole—to nowhere. Stroking without any worry of missing is a tension-free endeavor. You may discover a distinct difference in tension between putting to a hole and putting to nowhere.

Repeat this drill every practice session for two weeks. Give your mind the freedom of putting without fear. Follow this drill with a drill you can score, such as the number of putts in a row from 5 feet.

Eventually you can take this to the course and elicit the same mindset you had on the practice green. Precede each round of golf for a few weeks with a few putts to nowhere. Feel free to repeat this drill at any time in order to capture the tension level necessary for putting.

On the course, include in your routine a deep breath to calm yourself, followed by seeing the ball going in the hole in your mind's eye. Just after completing your address, close your eyes and recall the situations of tensionless putting to nowhere. You could do this with your practice strokes. Next, open your eyes, complete your address, and just process the here and now—the distance and fine-tuning on the target—while your body is still experiencing a tension-free moment.

The Putt Doctor's

DIAGNOSTIC TEST

Begin by putting to a hole 5 feet away. Imagine that this putt will win you the club championship. After the stroke, close your eyes and recall your tension level during the putt.

Next, stroke another short putt. But this time the area you putt to must not have any borders—no hole. In other words, stroke the ball to nowhere. Again, after the putt, close your eyes and recall your tension level during the putt to nowhere. Compare your tension level in this putt to the last putt.

You should notice that when you putt to nowhere, your tension level is quite low. It is the same as if you were tossing a wad of paper into a wastebasket a foot or so away. You don't have any fear of missing. You just do it!

Again, putt to a hole 5 feet away. Immediately after the putt, compare the tension level to the putt to nowhere. Did you have the same low tension level? Or did you take a little more time over the ball—could the stroke have been performed with less tension?

If your tension level approximated the tension level you exhibited without a target, you are ahead of the pack. If you noticed a distinctive rise in tension when putting to the hole, repeat the putt to nowhere at least five times. Each time, close your eyes after the putt and appreciate the tension-free moment. Now, again putt to the hole. After the putt, close your eyes and compare the tension level to the times you stroked a putt to nowhere. Hopefully the tension level is close to the same for both. Repeat this cycle three times.

When you make progress in controlling your tension when putting to the hole—and you will—reduce the number of times you putt to nowhere before putting to a target. Your goal is one-to-one—eliciting the same tensionless stroke for a putt to a target as with a putt to nowhere.

PRESCRIPTION NO. 5

Reducing Anxiety, Part Two: Soft or Fine Focus [B, I]

The first portion of the drill has you stroking a putt to a tee that you place in the ground as a target. The objective of putting to a tee is to practice fine-tuning your eyes to a smaller spot, providing your brain with a more specific motor response.

When I worked with hockey players, I found that the poorer passers tended to pass to a visually wider area. The better passers fired to a spot,

Instead of hitting a ball to a tee, place two tees approximately 3 inches apart—use the width of two golf balls as a measurement. Attempt to putt the ball between the two tees without hitting the tees. Even though this is a narrower visual focus—as you often look at the entire hole—it can free you up mentally to let the stroke work with a minimum of stress.

Alternate hitting three or so putts to one tee, then to two tees, and see which produces the best results.

either to a part of their teammate's stick, or if they were moving, to a specific spot in front of their teammate.

Better golfers tend to get the ball started on line with a smaller target. Try this when you putt to a tee at a distance of 3 feet, then 6 feet. If you hit the tee or get very close to it you may benefit by fine-tuning your aim when putting to a target, at least at the shorter distances.

For some players, putting along a line or to a small target produces anxiety. "I feel as if I have to hit the putt perfectly," I often hear players say. It may reduce your stress to realize you have at least a 3-inch path that the ball can travel along and still fall in the hole, as the hole is 4½ inches in diameter. See the diagnostic test on the left.

A student came to me the day before his club championship stating that he hadn't made a 3-foot putt all day. We eventually got to the problem. He believed he had to hit the ball perfectly down the target line in order to make the putt. We laid out a 3-inch-wide path to the hole using two clubs on each side of the target line—and he felt a great relief. Jamie Thompson went on to win the club championship by nine shots!

Whichever focus produces the best results should be what you use when you execute the stroke. If your putting goes awry, revisit this drill to see if a change of focus is warranted.

PRESCRIPTION NO. 6

Stopping the Slice Stroke [B, I]

For a number of players, the shape of their putting path mirrors their full swing path. They tend to slice or cut across the ball. The putter finishes to the left of their front foot. The problem with this slice stroke is that the path tends to open the putterface before impact.

A prime reason for this slice stroke is a poor setup, with open shoulders to the target line and the back forearm dominating the front forearm at address. Unless a player's setup is efficient, it becomes nearly impossible to correct this slice stroke.

Another key reason for the slice stroke is the player's desire to execute a straight-back, straight-through stroke path. When this occurs, I feel the player subconsciously finds a way to arc the stroke, often an exaggerated amount, near or soon after impact.

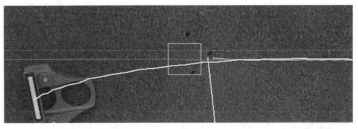

The cut or slice stroke path.

Adding to the problem of an open blade at impact is that the contact point occurs on the toe of the putterface. In the picture above, the bright line represents the putter's center as it moves on the forward path. As the bright line is distinctly below the horizontal target line, this forward path causes the ball to impact the putterface more toward the toe. This adds to the tendency to miss to the right.

A sliced toe hit seldom feels like a solid, square hit. With high-speed photography, the ball can be seen to have side spin when it stops its skid portion and starts rolling.

The Putt Doctor's

DIAGNOSTIC TEST If you are prone to a slice stroke, first check your shoulder line, which may be open, or your eye line, which may not be square to the target line. Go back to the recommendations in Section One on Setup and check to see if one or both apply to you.

After you are square with your eyes and shoulders, you may still need to work on your stroke path. If so, you can use a simple aid—a golf tee—as seen on page 236, to help you visually perceive the inside-to-inside path I recommend.

Simply, place a tee in the ground 4 to 5 inches behind the putter's toe of your putter when addressing the ball. The tee should be slightly inside the toe edge, so that it will force you to turn and stay connected in your backstroke. The tee visually helps direct your putter more to an inside path on the backstroke. This creates more symmetry in your forward stroke path.

Attempt to miss the tee ten times in a row with your backstroke—and forward stroke—as your putter takes more of an inside path than you are accustomed to take. Be sure to avoid the hands making the turn and keep the focus on your upper arms and shoulders turning around your center. You can do this drill at home by turning a tee upside down and placing it behind the putter's toe.

Stop-the-cut drill. Having the tee 4 to 5 inches behind the putter and near the toe will help produce a visual image of the desired inside path on the backstroke.

This inside path on the backstroke also aids your ability to release your putter, something that is difficult to do with a cut stroke. The intent is to maintain a connection of your shoulders, arms, and back as a unit to control the action, as well as to execute a turn instead of a shoulder rock. Practice this drill several times a week.

When out on the course, before you start your stroke, picture a tee in the ground as if you were practicing. Take your putter back accordingly. It will not be long before your stroke path improves.

One student saw his slice path stroke on my computer. Soon after, through self-discovery, he went to a cross-handed grip, and this produced a path that was much improved. He promptly won his club championship. He said that once he changed his grip, everything just fell into place, stroke-wise.

You might remember from previous discussions in this book that there are additional ways to stop the cut stroke:

- Stand farther from the ball or move the ball further back in your stance.
- Stand more upright.
- Use a putter with a flatter lie.
- Combine this drill with the Tiger tee drill above.
- Keep your elbow angles the same throughout the stroke. Do not lengthen your arms on the backstroke and shorten them on the forward stroke as I often see with players trying to perform the straight-back, straight-through stroke.

PRESCRIPTION NO. 7

Visually Speaking, Seeing It Correctly [A]

This drill has multiple facets. It is designed to help you better perceive the target line, execute a controlled stroke, and use sectioning to control the speed and to gain confidence. You will need your Aim Aid string and needles.

Find a 10- to 12-foot putt by stroking a few putts. Set up the string and needles of the Aim Aid as described in the first drill in this section. Putt under the string a few times to find a straight putt. Once a straight putt has been established, lower the string on the needles until it is an inch or two off the ground. The string must perfectly bisect the middle of the hole. Place two tees, one on each side of the string, and approximately 4 feet from the start point. They should be slightly more than a ball's width apart.

Next, place a colored dot or a small ball marker directly under the middle of the string and about 2 feet in front of the hole. Repeat this with another dot or marker 2 feet in front of the first dot. Repeat a couple of feet farther down the string.

Place two dots on either side of the ball to mark the starting position. The dots should be 10 to 12 feet from the hole. Now remove the string and needles.

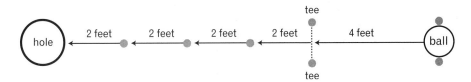

The Seeing It Correctly drill.

Get into your address position. Rotate your head so you are looking down the target line to the hole. When this is done correctly, you should perceive the dots and the hole to be in a straight line. If they are not, your eyes are not parallel to the target line at address and/or not parallel to the target line as you look at the hole. It is imperative that your eyes be parallel to the target line for you to perceive the correct target line.

Ideally, both eyes should be on the target line or slightly inside the target line. As your head rotates to the hole, if the dots and hole do not appear in-line, work to get your eyes and head to rotate properly so the dots and hole appear in line. (See Section One on Setup.)

Once you have learned to position and rotate your eyes correctly, look through the opening of the tees, then move your eyes to the first dot, then the next dot, then the next dot, and then the hole. I call this "sectioning." Sectioning helps your eyes better appreciate the distance and assists your ability to control your speed. If you tend to be short with your putts, this is a good technique to carry to the course. Look back to the ball and fire away.

Your goals are to see the dots in a line to the hole, appreciate the distance by using sectioning, and then get the ball started on line at the correct speed. Soon, you will be sinking eight of ten putts consistently from 10 to 12 feet. That is a good percentage to shoot for or exceed!

Remember, a good picture and a good attitude are essential components as well. Keep a record of the number of successful putts you make in a row or how many you sink out of ten.

8 + 4 + 2 + 1 [I, A]

This drill is used by several players on the PGA Tour. It will raise your confidence level as well as your ability to handle pressure.

The Putt Doctor's DIAGNOSTIC TEST

Start with a relatively straight putt. Take your driver and lay it on the ground on the intended target line with one end at the hole. Place a tee in the ground next to the other end of your driver.

From the tee, measure another driver's length away from the hole. Place another tee down at that distance. Repeat this two more times. This will leave four tees on the ground, at one driver's length, two drivers' lengths, three drivers' lengths, and four drivers' lengths from the hole.

Using one ball, putt from the first tee. Repeat this eight times. Note how many of these you make initially— "4/8," for example, would indicate you made four of the eight. The purpose of using just one ball is to give you time between each putt to capture in your mind the good things you did when you made the putt, as well as to replay a positive picture in your mind's eye if you miss. This is a good habit to get into to maximize your experience.

Now, go to the second tee and putt four times. Note how many of these you make. Now, go to the third tee and putt two times, and note how many of these you make. Finally, go to the last tee and note if you make this putt or not with a "1" or a "0." These results are your start point. You will strive to better this every time you perform this drill.

Feel free to repeat the drill several times during your putting sessions. When you believe you are ready, increase the challenge level. See how far you go before missing a putt. If you are perfect throughout this drill, your note will read "8 + 4 + 2 + 1." You may record this as 8 (first tee) + 3 (second tee) or 8 + 4 + 1, for example.

Your long-term goal is to make all eight putts from the first tee, all four from the second tee, both putts from the third tee, and the last putt from the fourth tee. This would be fifteen putts in a row. You will improve your focus when you are one putt away from an all-time personal record. Fifteen in a row may appear impossible, but a student playing recently on the mini-tours did it the first time he attempted the drill.

It is important to reflect as soon as possible on your thoughts as well as what you felt when you were successful with your putt. This will allow you to repeat your success more often. This is a great drill to do every practice session.

Keeping Your Flexibility of Adaptability [B, I, A]

Henry David Thoreau once said, "The true measure of your intelligence is the flexibility of your adaptability." The more flexible you are to adapt, the better you can handle even the most unexpected situations.

Let's face it, course conditions, especially the speed on the greens, can change from day to day as well as course to course. The one who adapts the quickest on the greens will have zero or less three-putts than those who do not adapt quickly or at all.

Greens at your course can change, based on if they are cut that day or, for instance, the day of your club championship, you walk on the putting green and notice they are faster than you can remember. For the championship, the grounds crew has been instructed to roll the greens and double-cut them, making the challenge on the greens the next couple of days a different one than you have been used to.

How can you be more flexible? One way is to adapt as quickly as possible by putting more downhill putts on the practice green to adjust your stroke tempo and length to the speed. Another way is at right.

The Putt Doctor's
DIAGNOSTIC TEST

You are at a new course and you note the greens are quite slow compared to the greens at your club. Choose a location on the green that is sloped as much as possible but not too severely. Place a tee in the ground, then walk directly uphill and place another tee in the ground 20 feet from the first one. Then place another tee 10 feet further uphill, and repeat with a tee in the ground another 10 feet further uphill. This gives you a 20-, 30-, and 40-foot target to putt back and forth to.

Start with an uphill putt to the first tee (20 feet), then putt the same ball back to the starting tee. Repeat the drill two more times. You will do six putts, or three cycles, at each distance. Your objective for each putt is to stop your ball within 2 to 3 feet (the length of your putter) of the target tee. Record this as a par. Repeat this for the 30- and 40-footers. All along, you are working to control your speed for each distance and each slope.

This drill should be done regularly, even without a change in conditions. After this drill, make note of the distances where your putts were not successful and practice these distances. Also, recall what you were thinking during the putts when you were successful and when you were not.

Implement different strategies and techniques you have learned from other sections to see which produce better results. Through self-discovery, find what works best for you most of the time. Keep records of your results and what worked. For most players, the pause drill (see Section Nine) is a good technique to practice for longer distance control drills.

The Putt Doctor's Real-World Drill [I, A]

Let's face it, there is not much you can do on the practice green to approximate the on-course scenario of eighteen holes comprising different putts, green after green. Exercises such as the Aim Aid string drill are good for helping you discover what mechanics and thoughts assist you in starting the ball on line consistently. You cannot help but gain confidence when you begin to see putts drop with regularity on the practice green.

Obviously, putting ten putts under a string to the same hole as a drill is a far cry from being on the course. So the question becomes: what kind of drill could best transfer your practice to the course? Take a look at the following.

I call it the "Putt Doctor's Real-World drill," and it goes like this: You are to stroke eighteen different putts on the practice green. If your green is flat and unimaginable in design, it may behoove you to go to another facility. You could do this on the course, perhaps in the early morning or late in the day.

If your reads and speed are off, it is imperative to discover your best read position, as discussed in Section Eight. Repeat this drill often. It will reward you.

On a sheet of paper, mark down the numbers "1" to "18," each on a separate line. You will note your results for each putt on the appropriate line. Here are the rules:

No putts are to be the same—each must be different in distance and there should be a mixture of left-to-right, straight, and right-to-left putts as well as level, uphill, and downhill putts.

Vary your distances—hit three putts from 6 to 8 feet, four putts from 9 to 11 feet, four putts from 12 to 15 feet, four putts from 15 to 25 feet, and one putt each from 30, 40, and 50 feet.

As an example, place a ball in the 9- to 11-foot range from one of the holes on the practice green. Read the putt as you would on the course. On the first line, jot down the distance, and your read. For example: 11' L-R / UH. This would indicate that you stepped off the putt and it was 11 feet. You saw a left-to-right break that appeared to slope uphill.

Go through your routine and then stroke the putt. If your read was correct, you would add a (1) for the one-putt, "GR" for good read. Putt and record your results as a make (1) or a miss (2 or 3.) If you miss, putt out. If it was a poor read, mark down the correct read. Also, did you get the ball on line or was it a bad stroke (BS > pull)? If the speed was off, was it long (+) or short (–)?

Continue this for all eighteen putts. Record your results. Note what appears to be the number-one reason for your misses. It could be read, speed, pull, or something else.

Your goal is to improve your percentage of makes by identifying deficient areas, such as your reads, your ability to start the ball on the intended line, your commitment to your reads, or your ability to control the ball speed off your putterface.

The chart below is a way you can organize your practice sessions into a purposeful practice session. The drills include some from several sections in this book. You can mix and match the drills as you see fit and change them once they are mastered to the best of your ability. Be sure to reread the positive comments you make on occasion to refresh your memory of the positives you discovered and found were from your diligent practice.

DRILL	DESCRIPTION	PURPOSE	GOAL	RESULTS
Mirror work on setup	Have a picture in mind of good setup and then mimic in a mirror	To get into the desired setup using a mental picture of the setup without talking myself into the setup	A good setup address position five times in a row	Good setup with all but still fighting knee flex—legs too straight.
Tiger tee drill	A 5- to 10-minute drill using regular and slow-motion strokes if necessary for practice	Make my stroke path consistent and be consistent as well with center contact on the putterface	Work to miss the tees ten times in a row	I kept hitting the heel of the putter on the tees until I got my big muscles in charge of the stroke. It helped to do the trunk rotation drill at waist height a couple of times before each stroke.
Putt to Nowhere	Six putts to no target to one to the hole, then reduce to three to one—a 5-minute drill	To get used to putting with less physical and mental tension when you do putt to a target	To reduce anxiety over a putt and putt like a kid— an opportunity.	Was easy at first, but every time I tried to picture a putt for the club championship, anxiety was high—need more "role play."
String and needles/ Aim Aid drill	15 putts × 2 (Two cycles)	Five in a row from 4 feet Five in a row from 5 feet Five in a row from 8 feet Repeat	Improve upon 20 of 30 by better focus on routine	Made 28 of 30/missed @ 8 feet/Good focus of a steady routine over the ball. The two misses were from not being mentally ready to putt and thinking of stroke before and during the stroke.
30–40–50–60 drill	Go thru five or more cycles—15 minutes	Work on what mental and physical thoughts and methods work best for me	To get below 6 as my score on two of the cycles	Initially trouble with 30 feet and beyond/all over the place with long AND short but mainly short. Discovered if I thought about speed as if I was watching it from halfway to hole and tried to duplicate it, I was better. Got to 8, then 7.
Three-speed drill	Three cycles of six	To be comfortable with hitting the hole with more speed	Make all the putts	Made all but two that hit the back of the hole—better when I saw the speed of the ball go in the hole with my mind's eye.
North-South-East-West drill	How many made out of twenty from 3, 4, then 5 feet	To get more confident with these distances so when on the course I am more comfortable putting these distances	To establish my baseline with first cycle/also to go thru my routine on each putt	I found myself switching routines without thinking/too often went into stroke thoughts and not a good picture of the ball going in the hole. Made 15 of 20 from 3 feet, 13 of 20 from 4 feet, and 11 of 20 from 5 feet.
Closed eyes drill	Feel tempo of stroke 5 minutes	To have a tempo that is not rushed	To lengthen my backstroke length and slow down transition area	Have to focus on picture of where putter needs to go on backstroke as my tendency is to go too short then rush transition using my hands/more work!!!!

PUTTER FITTINGS

With the Ralph Maltbie/Todd Sones of Coutour Golf fitting notes

There are several putter-fitting systems. A good fit to a putter sure can shortcut the process of having an efficient, consistent stroke. Below are several points that can assist you in seeking a better fit.

If the toe is up in the air at address (a typical scenario I see with my players)

- the putter is too long
- the lie is too upright
- promotes heel hits at impact
- the player is too far from the ball
- the aim will tend to be more left

If the putter's toe is down and the heel is up at address

- the putter is too short
- the player is too close to the ball
- the lie is too flat

- promotes toe hits at impact
- the aim will tend to be more right

A putter that is too long
- will cause the player to be too far from the ball
- will cause the player to have her arms too far to the sides and elbows excessively bent
- will cause more weight to be placed on the player's heels at address
- will result in the player choking way down on the handle
- could result in the handle getting caught on the player's clothes during the stroke
- could result in heel hits
- will cause a player to aim more right of his target

A putter that is too short
- will cause the player to be too close to the ball
- will cause the player to have his arms too straight
- will decrease the swing weight of the putter
- will result in more toe hits
- will cause a player to have too much weight on her toes at address
- will cause a player to aim more to the left

Closed face at address
- stems from poor assessment of square face or target location or both
- can be corrected by using the dominant eye (*only*) to check the face and line or spot
- is helped by a shaft with more offset
- can be resolved with a center-shafted putter
- can be improved with longer putter length (belly or long putter)
- use better putter lines/design or line or lines on ball

- face aim or use two points or lines on the putter
- flatten the lie angle if the toe of the putter is in the air at address

Open face at address
- either poor assessment of square face or target location or both
- dominant eye (*only*) check of face and line or spot
- use of less offset
- center-shafted putter
- longer putter length (belly or long putter)
- use of more or less putter lines or no lines
- face aim/two points or lines on putter

Closed face at impact
- putter toe-heavy
- putter too long a length
- putter too flat

Open face at impact
- putter too heel-heavy
- putter too short a length
- putter too upright a lie

TRAINING AIDS THAT ARE A MUST

Aim Aid
www.puttdoctor.com

AimChart
www.aimpointgolf.com

CheckerBalls (putting stroke
    trainer)
www.checkerballs.com
303-933-3026

Eyeline Putting Mirror/Green
    Reading Level/Golf
    Metronome Pro
www.EyeLineGolf.com
800-969-3764

GAIM Putters
www.gaimgolf.com
1-865-776-2237

The KURE
www.kureputting.com
888-952-PUTT

PeakVision Performance
    Eyewear
www.peakvisionsports.com
888-856-3419

The Putting Template
www.puttdoctor.com

Scoring Line
www.Puttdoctor.com
See & Score Golf Schools

Spot Liner (ball marker)
Golf around the World
800-824-4279

AimChart

Aimpoint Technology has proven that putting is highly predictable, and this chart will teach you how much break to expect for any putt inside of 20 feet. If you have mapped your greens already, then understanding expected breaks will give you a tremendous amount of confidence.

CheckerBalls

This simple aid is a big hit in my clinics. It is composed of two golf balls, cut down and fused together. Checker-Balls provides great feedback in the effort to establish a square putterface at impact. If your putterhead is square at impact, the ball will roll with the stripe going end over end. If your putterface is open or closed at impact, the ball will wobble like an egg. You will be able to work on your stroke at home with this aid. Since you are not putting to a target, you can focus totally on stroke improvements. You will find this training aid is hard to quit using—it is addictive!

Eyeline Putting Mirror

This device provides important feedback as to your head and body position at address. A consistent setup is critical, yet difficult to attain time after time. Controlled practice with a device like the Eyeline putting mirror is critical.

You will see where your eyes are positioned, and if your shoulders are parallel to the target line. It also provides an alignment help when you are putting to a target.

GAIM Putters

GAIM Golf was founded with the purpose of creating an innovative and technologically superior putter compared to anything previously seen in the golf industry.

GolfTest USA, an independent golf equipment testing facility, rated GAIM as the number-one putter in golf after testing hundreds of different putters for features such as distance, accuracy, appearance, and feel. In addition to the putter's superior technology and fine quality, it also has a unique and innovative design feature that allows the golfer to retrieve the ball from the hole without bending over. Now, that is truly unique!

GAIM Golf has two more putters in the prototype stage that will soon be released. With a focus on unique designs and key optical alignment systems, GAIM Golf is making its mark on the world of putter manufacturing.

The KURE

This is a high-tech device with a module that attaches to your putter and is aimed at a modular target. Lasers provide immediate feedback for three key components of putting: alignment, square face at impact, and stroke tempo.

When the module shows that you are correctly aligned, your eyes will start to recognize and appreciate what part of the putter appears to be aligned correctly. For example, your eyes might see the middle line on your putter as pointing to the left, yet the module says the putter is correctly aligned. Now, you can attempt to discover what other aspect of the putterhead yields a correct perspective to your eyes.

I often find that a player perceives correct alignment more with the leading edge of the putter, or with a back line, or even with the two back lines, than with the center line. But the key here is what part of the putter your eyes can focus upon to trust the alignment.

The KURE also provides valuable feedback for squaring the putter blade to the target at impact. If you have squared the putter blade, the module produces a green light. If not, the light shows amber. You can start at a short putting distance and experiment with what you must do with your stroke to produce a green light consistently.

This device can be used indoors and outdoors, and really fine-tunes your aim and putting stroke.

PeakVision

As an optometrist, I must warn you of the perils of excessive UV damage—including cataracts and possible macular degeneration. It is just smart to protect your eyes as well as the rest of your body.

For years, eye doctors have recommended tints to keep the eyes from squinting from the bright sunlight. Squinting diminishes the eyes' blink rate, resulting in dry eyes and/or dry contact lenses. Comfortable eyes can translate into a comfortable body, and this can transfer into comfortable swings. The reverse also applies.

UPPER ZONE
Manages Bright Sun & Glare

LOWER ZONE
Enhances Contrast Sensitivity for Improved Green Reading

If you have experienced problems with sunglasses in the past, it may be partly from the lenses being so dark that they interrupt your eyes' ability to perceive subtle depth clues, especially if you are of a more mature age. This is because the crystalline lens inside the eye turns yellow and diminishes the light reaching our retinas.

The tint that used to be recommended was often a dark gray. The gray lens was originally called "true color," as the colors viewed through the lens remained the same. For light-colored, light-sensitive eyes, a dark tint makes sense most of the time.

I have used my clinics to "test-drive" sunglasses tints. Some interesting findings have surfaced about the once-popular dark gray lenses for the majority of golfers. I have found that the lighter tints are more beneficial for most golfers.

Eventually, I found a unique brand of sunglasses for the majority of golfers: PeakVision sunglasses. Players have told me that the lens helps them see more sharply when they are standing next to the green. Others have said they can see more detail and slopes with this tint.

These lenses not only are the lightest weight—yet shatterproof—but also have the best optics from the center to the periphery of any lens I have tested. Their "dual-zone" technology gives good depth for distance viewing and a lighter lower portion of the lens allows for hitting shots without having to take off the glasses. For those of you with prescription glasses, yes, they make lenses for distance prescriptions. By the way, 100 percent UV protection is in all of their lenses. You do not need polarized or dark lenses to be completely protected from UV radiation.

The Putting Template

This is my favorite training aid for the putting stroke. The Putting Template provides a path and putterface feedback for your stroke. It is designed to be for the curved stroke path. After a few minutes of daily

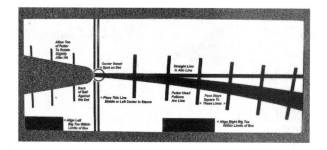

sessions at home and on the putting green with this device, you will feel like you cannot ever miss a putt again.

A number of students have told me they feel like they are cheating when they use it. They seldom miss putts when using the template, and neither will you. What a confidence builder!

Scoring Line

The colored boxes of the Scoring Line become a visual guide for your stroke length. *Golf Magazine*'s panel voted it one of the best aids they had seen and gave it 4½ stars (out of 5!) And here is why.

The colored boxes are designed to improve your feel for putts of any length through a guide to the proper stroke length—for you. With a

controlled practice regime, you can establish a consistent hit as well as a plan to handle the putts that give you trouble. In short, it can give you great confidence in your ability to reduce and potentially eliminate three-putts from your rounds.

INDEX